The Battle against Isolation

Courtesy of the "New York Times"

Fight for Freedom, Inc., was right. War came less than two months after this advertisement appeared.

The
Battle against
Isolation

By Walter Johnson

University of Chicago Press ∗ Chicago

Drawing for title-page by Clarence Pontius
Jacket design by Clarence Pontius

University of Chicago Press · Chicago 37
Agent: Cambridge University Press · London

To

TINK

Preface

THE UNITED STATES HAS BEEN A GREAT WORLD POWER SINCE the last decade of the nineteenth century. The American people, nevertheless, have been slow to recognize America's position in the world. The epoch-making changes that took place in the world from September, 1939, to December 7, 1941, however, made many Americans aware that the affairs of the United States are inevitably tied up with world events. This awareness on the part of the American public, which slowly grew from the German invasion of Poland to the attack on Pearl Harbor, is the history of a great upsurgence of the American spirit in a movement to protect its way of life from the menace of naziism, fascism, and Nipponism. This book is a study of America from 1939 to Pearl Harbor; it is the story of "the Battle of America."

The origin of the book dates back to January 2, 1941, when I arrived in Emporia, Kansas. I had been working on a biography of William Allen White for some time, and I went to Emporia on this particular visit to absorb local color and to read all of Mr. White's letters—a privilege which no other researcher or writer has had. Mr. White was kind enough to permit me free access to all his materials. The story that I found there is the foundation of this book. As I read the wealth of material written in recent years, I determined to write a book which would endeavor to explain something of the disturbed times that America has faced since the outbreak of war in 1939. Ordinarily, the unpublished letter material on which this book is based would not be opened to writers for many years to come, but William Allen White realized its immediate value to the American people and thus encouraged my efforts to untangle the troubled story of the years leading up to Pearl Harbor.

In addition to the White manuscripts, through the kindness of Clark Eichelberger, executive director of the Committee To Defend America by Aiding the Allies, I was permitted to use the materials of the Committee at the national headquarters at 8 West Fortieth Street, New York City. I am also indebted to John A. Morrison and Albert Parry, formerly in charge of the middle western regional office of the Committee in Chicago, for access to the files of this branch of the Committee. Courtenay Barber, Jr., director, turned over to me the files of the Chicago Fight for Freedom Committee, and a large number of people have aided me in reading and criticizing the manuscript. Joseph A. Brandt and John Scoon of the University of Chicago Press have been most helpful in this regard.

I am indebted to Avery O. Craven, professor of history at the University of Chicago, for advice and inspiration throughout my work; to Quincy Wright, professor of international law at the University of Chicago, for reading the manuscript and offering suggestions as to additional material; to Ernest Martin Hopkins, president of Dartmouth College, for reading my material on the Century Club group with a critical eye; to Courtenay Barber, Jr., and Stuart Haydon for their constant interest; to Frederic R. Coudert for reading the manuscript; to Francis P. Miller and Robert E. Sherwood for reading certain sections of the manuscript; and to Robert Redfield and Louis Wirth of the Social Science Research Council for their interest in the book. The staff of the *Emporia Gazette*, particularly Frank C. Clough, managing editor, and Paul Chandler, telegraph editor, who microfilmed the White letters for me, were very helpful during the six months that I was in Emporia.

Above all, William Allen White was willing to offer his help at all times. In addition to interviews with Mr. White, Mr. and Mrs. Clark Eichelberger spent many hours with me talking about the history of the White committees, and Mr. John Morrison gave interviews and read the manuscript in the light of his work in the middle western office. I am also indebted to many people—particularly President Roosevelt, Cordell Hull, and the late Frank Knox—who permitted me to use their letters, which are incorporated either in the text or in the notes. I am, furthermore, grateful to the authors and their publishers who permitted me to quote from their material in this book.

I hope that this book will aid the American people to gain a clearer perspective on the problems of those confused days from the outbreak of war in Europe to our own entrance into the conflict. It is primarily a study of the thinking of a cross-section of the American public. William Allen White, who was the spark of the internationalist movement during these years, became something of a folk hero to America. The great middle class looked upon him as a sane, mellow philosopher who could lead them; and generally his views reflected the attitudes of middle-class America. The isolationist opposition is woven into this book, but I have not attempted to deal exhaustively with this particular phenomenon, since two published works— *Sabotage* and *Undercover*—present this material in detail to the reading public.

The struggle against the isolationists was carried on with

immense ardor by the members of the Committee To Defend America by Aiding the Allies and by the Fight for Freedom Committee. This book is an attempt to recapture that fervor in order that future Americans may have a record of the way in which the public magnificently rose to meet the challenge during those grim days when the fate of Western civilization was hanging in the balance.

Mrs. Johnson has aided me in the research and in the countless revisions of this manuscript. For any errors in the text I alone am responsible.

WALTER JOHNSON

CHICAGO
August 1944

Table of Contents

. . xi . .

I

Is It Our War?

AMERICA SLEPT UNEASILY WHILE ENGLAND EVACUATED DUN-
kirk. Isolationists insisted frantically: "This is not our war!
America has nothing to fear from a Hitler-dominated Europe.
We quit European power-politics in 1918. Why can't we stay
quit? . . . ."

Germany, too, had once ignored Adolf Hitler as an in-
significant upstart; Italy had welcomed the clean streets and
the efficient trains that ran on time. France and Britain had
once closed their eyes to an Italian rape of Ethiopia, to a Franco "New Order" in Spain, to a "putsch" of Austria, to the dis-
memberment of Czechoslovakia. The world's democracies
had frankly not believed in a "March on Rome" or in *Mein
Kampf*. While they had slept in the self-centered smugness of
the early thirties, the leaders of fascism had gone about their
grim business of building up the most powerful military machine that the modern world had yet seen.

Then Munich failed—war came—Poland fell. After more
than a year's fighting, the German mechanized legions
marched across Denmark and the Netherlands; and now a
Belgian king surrendered; and the British people, groping for
every available means, were desperately working to salvage

their trapped army. In those nights of late May, 1940, America watched anxiously as each fateful day waned—but, while we somehow sensed that with the fate and destiny of those British soldiers lay the future of America and the democratic world, we nevertheless closed our eyes to any responsibility on our part.

On June 8, while France was tottering, the *Chicago Tribune*, oblivious of the menace of fascism, observed: "Inflamed by commercial radio commentators, the east has fallen into a complete state of hysteria. . . . . The mental confusion could hardly be worse if the enemy were in Long Island again."

Even after France fell in June, 1940, and England was left alone facing the Fascists, the voices of confusion in America still refused to recognize reality. Senator Nye sneered that through demands for aid to Britain "a campaign of fear is pushing the country into 'Europe's war,' " a war which "is nothing more than a continuation of the old European conflict of power politics, a fight to save an empire."

In arousing opposition to the Selective Service Bill, Senator Wheeler declaimed: "If this bill passes, it will accord to Hitler his greatest and cheapest victory. On the headstone of American democracy he will inscribe—'Here lies the foremost victim of the war of nerves.' " On June 12 the *Chicago Tribune* decided that "the proposed bill for universal military training is premature. Its principal effect will be to disrupt our industries without adding to our military strength. The only effect that can come from it at this time is the highly undesirable one of spreading thruout the nation the war hysteria that already has New York and Washington in its grip."

The isolationist spokesman, Charles A. Lindbergh, declared as late as August 4, 1940: "In the future, we may have to deal with a Europe dominated by Germany. . . . . An agreement between us could maintain peace and civilization throughout the world as far into the future as we can see."

In spite of such cries, the American public had begun to awaken from its twenty years of fateful sleep. Some of our leaders had known for a long time that the cause for which the Allies were fighting on foreign battlefields was our cause, that the menace to those abroad was also a menace to American security. As soon as war had broken out in Europe, in the fall of 1939, we as a people had begun to stir uneasily. By the time France fell, men were declaring in public that the nation's fate was bound up in the Allies' fight for life; powerful pressure groups were arising who demanded all possible aid to the enemies of totalitarianism. And as America gradually awakened, its government reflected this feeling by ever advancing steps toward maintaining the democracies on the fighting line.

The country as a whole was slow to realize the acuteness of the Axis threat to the democratic way of life, but others had also been slow to see the full import of Hitler's war—actually, it had been only after the defeat of France that the people of Great Britain, Denmark, Norway, the Low Countries, and France learned what naziism really was and what the war was really about. As Carl Becker puts it:

"Then it was that the British people learned that they were fighting, not merely for redressing the balance of power against a too strong Germany, but for the complete destruction of the Nazi state as totally incompatible with any sort of political independence or freedom in Europe or in the world at large. The Russian people learned all this as soon as their country was invaded by the Nazi armies; the people of Ethiopia, Spain, and China had already learned it before the European war began. . . . ."

The United States did not really see the peril or become

fully aroused until the attack on Pearl Harbor, even though it is now obvious that this assault was only the precipitating event and that, without Pearl Harbor, war would still have been inevitable. America, though isolationists did their best to convince us otherwise, could not live in a world rocked by war and remain permanently at peace.

Thus it was that on December 7, 1941, America became an active belligerent for the second time in twenty-four years. Only then did the American public accept its role in the war against fascism. The tragedy lies not so much in the nation's entry into the war as in the fact that our thinking has met the challenge of its responsibility only after an actual attack and not in the more important years—those of intervening peace— when wars really *can* be prevented.

America became a great world power at the end of the nineteenth century, and as early as 1890 she was ready, commercially and economically, to take her place among the powers in the world. But it was not until the outbreak of the first World War and her final entry into that conflict that America's destiny in world affairs became an actuality to the mass of her citizens. During this first war the American public on the whole realized its inevitable role and responsibility for world leadership. Its part in the war it accepted wholeheartedly and vigorously. But the fiasco of the Versailles Peace Conference, the Senate rejection of the Treaty, and the war of partisan politics turned the United States away from international co-operation. Disillusionment swung us back to "100 per cent Americanism," to the Ku Klux Klan, to the great Palmer Red scare, and into a general intolerance toward all liberal doctrines.

Americans proved that they could win battles on the fighting line, but they refused to fight the war for peace. In fact, most of them at the end of the first World War closed their eyes to the realities and events of the world outside; and so it was that they refused to see the true facts back of the tragedies of Ethiopia, Spain, Austria, Czechoslovakia, Denmark, Norway, Holland, and Belgium. Only a few opened their eyes in the twenties and the thirties.

But during Dunkirk and the fall of France somnolence yielded at last to something resembling awareness, and the United States began, though at first unknowingly, to prepare for war. Winston Churchill, with a keen knowledge of our past, told the English Parliament on the day following the fall of Dunkirk (June 4, 1940) that America would eventually come to rescue the Old World—and by this rescue save itself:

"We shall not flag or fail; we shall go on to the end. We shall fight in France and on the seas and oceans; we shall fight with growing confidence and growing strength in the air. We shall defend our Island whatever the cost may be; we shall fight on beaches, landing grounds, in fields, in streets and on the hills. We shall never surrender and even if, which I do not for the moment believe, this Island or a large part of it were subjugated and starving, then our Empire beyond the seas, armed and guarded by the British fleet, will carry on the struggle until in God's good time the New World with all its power and might, sets forth to the liberation and rescue of the Old."

Why did America sleep through the fateful years between the wars? If a German victory was a threat to American security, why did the American people for so long do nothing to stop it? How did we rise to meet the needs of the first World War? What happened to the Versailles Treaty and the League of Nations? What blinded America in the twenties and early thirties? How did she finally emerge as an active participant in this war? By now the significance of these questions is only too clear.

The American public in entering the first World War—and again when the second came—suddenly became aware that great forces were altering the course of world events, events that were shaping American history as they never had done in this country before. The first war brought a great revolution in American thinking: the concern for purely domestic affairs which was characteristic of the United States of the nineteenth century was supplanted by an awareness of the impact on American life of foreign issues and American participation in those issues.

Short-lived, however, was this acceptance of responsibility, for it was a reality only so long as armed conflict lasted. To America world responsibility was an infant and immature idea, and only the exigencies of war gave it a chance to grow. Like a child playing with fire, the American public, though apparently fascinated for a brief spell with this new idea and horizon-plaything, began to feel its burns and shrank from the flame, fleeing from the equally serious battles of postwar reconstruction. When the shooting war was over, violent reaction set in, and the new plaything was abandoned while we became preoccupied with an exaggerated form of isolationism. One of the tragedies of the modern world is the story of the refusal of its most powerful nation to take part in maintaining the peace that nation had helped to win and in reshaping the world society of which it was such a significant part.

Actually, the Versailles Treaty, in which the League of Nations was incorporated, was never considered in the United States Senate purely upon its merits. The debacle which accompanied its debate was rife with bitterness, partisanship, and hostility. Certain influential senators, such as Henry Cabot Lodge, had a deep personal hatred for Woodrow Wilson; others were personally piqued that none of their body had been included on the Peace Commission; some partisan Republicans did not favor passing, in an election year, a peace treaty drawn up by a Democratic president for fear that it might mean a Democratic victory in 1920.

Interestingly enough, when President Wilson presented the Versailles Treaty to the Senate on July 10, 1919, there was not a clear-cut senatorial split between those who favored the Treaty and those who opposed it. Instead, the Senate split into four groups: (1) a pro-Treaty group, composed of forty-three Democrats and one Republican who were for ratification without reservation; (2) the "mild reservationists," made up of about fifteen Republicans who were warmly for the Treaty but desired some reservations; (3) the "strong reservationists," consisting of about twenty Republicans who favored ratification but with extensive reservations; and (4) the "irreconcilables," twelve Republicans and three Democrats, led by William E. Borah, who opposed ratification under any conditions.

The vast majority of the Senate—eighty out of ninety-six—were for the League either entirely or with reservations, but the opposition never allowed it to be voted upon as a straight issue. This strategy consisted of never letting the League's proponents get into a position where they could unite and agree upon the conditions of ratification and thus vote together. The majority which favored the League and which was backed up by a majority of the American people could not devise the strategy necessary to bring its members together on a vote which was not a conflict over reservations.

When the two votes on ratification occurred (November 19, 1919, and March 19, 1920) the Treaty was defeated, not by its enemies, the irreconcilables, but by its most ardent friends. On both occasions when the Treaty with reservations came to a vote, the reservationists voted for it and the irreconcilables, in combination with the Administration Democrats, voted against it. The Administration Democrats did not want to defeat the Treaty; they only wanted to defeat the Treaty with reservations, in order that a vote could be had under more acceptable conditions. In so doing, they were acting on the advice of President Wilson.

A majority of the senators, then, clearly desired to accept the Treaty and the League, and there is no doubt that they were supported by a majority of the American people. The *Literary Digest* conducted a poll of newspapers in April, 1919, and found that 718 were for ratification, 478 were for ratification with conditions, and only 181 were against ratification. Henry Cabot Lodge, Republican majority leader and chairman of the Senate Committee on Foreign Relations, admitted that the vocal classes—the clergymen, teachers, writers, and editors—as well as the main part of the public were for the League. He publicly claimed to be for the League with reservations; but there is a great deal of evidence to show that he was, in fact, an irreconcilable out to kill the League under any circumstances.

Lodge was a partisan Republican, opposing a treaty drawn up by a Democratic president and one whom he personally hated. His daughter, who claimed to be close to him during the struggle, has stated: "My father hated and feared the Wilson league and his heart was really with the irreconcilables. But it was uncertain whether this league could be beaten straight out in this way, and the object of his reservations was so to emasculate the Wilson pact that if it did pass it would be valueless. . . . ."

The initial plans to attack the League were made in December, 1918, in consultation with Theodore Roosevelt. When the new Congress met in special session in May, 1919, the irreconcilable Republicans had gained a great advantage. The Republicans controlled the Senate by a majority of two, and thus they would have a majority on each committee. In control of the Committee on Foreign Relations they could delay or hasten action on the Treaty. When the composition of this committee was announced, of the ten Republican members six were openly irreconcilable. The other four Republicans were Lodge, the chairman, who was really an irreconcilable; McCumber, the Republican most outspokenly for the League; and two party regulars, Harding and New, who would follow party leadership. Lodge seems deliberately to have packed the Republican membership of the committee with men hostile to the League, thus gaining the power to keep the Treaty in the committee's hands while a campaign was launched to arouse public sentiment against the League. Millionaires H. C. Frick and Andrew Mellon contributed money, and a propaganda campaign of mailings and speaking tours was started.

The Committee on Foreign Relations kept the Treaty for two months. During this time all types of aggrieved parties— German-Americans, Italian-Americans, Irish-Americans— were permitted to denounce the Treaty before the committee. It seems clear now that the committee allowed this delay deliberately; one of the irreconcilables later said that if the rules of the Senate had permitted a quick vote, "the Versailles Treaty would have been ratified without reservation."

When on November 19 the Senate rejected the Treaty with reservations, there was so much dissatisfaction among the senators themselves, as well as among the public, that it was agreed to bring the question up in the next session. When the second voting took place on March 19, 1920, President Wilson again persuaded enough Administration senators to oppose the Treaty with reservations so that it was rejected. Wilson believed that the public wanted the League unhampered by reservations, and he was willing to wait for the approaching presidential election to serve as a popular referendum on the subject.

Unfortunately, the presidential election did not fulfil this purpose, although the majority of seven million for Harding cannot be translated into a majority of seven million against the League. The Republican platform was ambiguous, but it did advocate entrance into an international association of nations. During the campaign Harding interpreted this plank on some occasions to be pro-League and on other occasions to be anti-League. Such outstanding Republicans as former President Taft and Herbert Hoover campaigned for Harding, making it plain that they considered support for Harding equivalent to support of the League of Nations. On October 14, 1920, thirty-one leading Republicans, including Elihu Root, Charles E. Hughes, Henry L. Stimson, and William Allen White, issued a public statement that a vote for Harding was the surest way of indicating that the citizens favored joining the League.

Probably thousands of voters took these men at their word, and many pro-League citizens undoubtedly voted for the Republican candidate. Vice-president-elect Calvin Coolidge himself, in a postelection statement, observed that many pro-League people had voted Republican and that it could not be said that the election was a mandate against the League.

The United States with its immense economic strength and naval power might well have been expected to play a bold and statesmanlike role in international affairs in the post-Versailles world. That it refused to do so can largely be attributed to the tacit agreement among the American people, after the Senate's rejection of the League, to ignore international responsibilities and to return to "normalcy" at home. The Republican party during the interval between the two wars was predominately isolationist. A few notable exceptions, like Secretary of State Stimson, Elihu Root, Nicholas Murray Butler, and William Allen White, were internationalists. (I take the term "internationalist" to mean a man who realizes that the United States must take an active part in world affairs and must work collectively with other nations to secure international peace.) And after the "normalcy" of Harding and Coolidge, Secretary Stimson did permit the country to participate increasingly in the nonpolitical activities of the League. However, the isolationist attitude of such men as William E. Borah dominated the Republican party.

When the Democratic party came back into power in 1933, it was still the party of Wilsonian internationalism. From 1933 to 1939 the United States government followed a policy of attempting to improve international relations and thus prevent the collapse of world peace. This policy, however, was carried on in a world which was being overcome by ruthless aggression. Japan seized Manchuria in 1931. Two years later Germany began to rearm under the dictatorship of Hitler. In 1935 Italy invaded Ethiopia. The following year Hitler tore up the Treaty of Locarno and fortified the demilitarized Rhineland. In 1937 Japan again attacked China. In 1938 Hitler occupied Austria and dismembered Czechoslovakia. During the first six months of 1939 Hitler finished destroying the independence of Czechoslovakia and seized Memel, while Mussolini invaded Albania. On September 1, 1939, Hitler struck at Poland—and the world was again at war.

President Franklin D. Roosevelt and Secretary of State Cordell Hull were avowed internationalists. They attempted to point out to America the danger that Hitler, Mussolini, and the Japanese represented to the democratic way of life. The Japanese and Nazi Germany, both preaching the superiority of their own people over other peoples of the world, were planning world domination. In the highly technological world of the twentieth century, President Roosevelt realized that no nation could escape this threat. No nation could isolate itself; inventions in the field of transportation and communication had reduced the world to a veritable neighborhood. After the United States entered the second World War, the State Department published a volume entitled *Peace and War 1931–1941*, in which the following statement appears:

"During a large part of the period with which this volume deals, much of public opinion in this country did not accept the thesis that a European war could vitally affect the security of the United States or that an attack on the United States by any of the Axis powers was possible. In this respect it differed from the President and the Secretary of State who early became convinced that the aggressive policies of the Axis powers were directed toward an ultimate attack on the United States and that, therefore, our foreign relations should be so conducted as to give all possible support to the nations endeavoring to check the march of Axis aggression.

"Our foreign policy during the decade under consideration necessarily had to move within the framework of a gradual evolution of public opinion in the United States away from the idea of isolation expressed in 'neutrality' legislation and toward realization that the Axis design was a plan of world conquest in which the United States was intended to be a certain, though perhaps ultimate, victim, and that our primary policy therefore must be defense against actual and mounting danger. This was an important factor influencing the conduct of our foreign relations."

As a more forthright policy for world peace, President Roosevelt sought to enlarge upon American co-operation with the nonpolitical activities of the League. The new ad-

HARK! THE LYRE!

We almost fell for it

ministration also was willing to support an embargo upon the trade of aggressor nations which violated the Kellogg Pact. Such a step, however, failed to reckon with the strength of isolationist feeling in this country. The intense nationalism of the dictatorships in Italy and Germany and Japan's belligerent attitude aroused fears that the world might be plunged into a new war, and the American reaction was that the United States should remain aloof.

This fear of a new war came at a time when the country was extremely skeptical of the wisdom of having entered the last conflict. In 1934 a great many books and articles were written describing the intrigues and profits of munitions-manufacturers. In the spring of that year the Senate set up a committee with Gerald Nye as its chairman to investigate the activities of the American munitions industry. The committee showed that excessive profits had been made during the first World War by bankers and armament-makers. The investigation revealed the profits that had been gained by J. P. Morgan and Company as agents for Allied purchases in the United States and showed that American industry was prosperous largely because of orders from the Allies. It also demonstrated that an Allied defeat would have struck a severe blow to American prosperity. The question then arose as to whether the country had gone into the war as a free agent to save democracy or whether it had been shoved into the war by selfish international bankers and munitions-makers.

Senator Clark of Missouri, speaking before the Senate Munitions Investigating Committee on December 11, 1934, said that the American export of munitions to the Allies "ultimately led us into war. . . . . There is no evidence whatever to show we would ever have entered in the war or ever fired a gun except for that course of action." In 1935 Charles Seymour, diplomatic historian at Yale University, published his well-reasoned book, *American Neutrality*, to disprove this thesis; but the Nye committee in its final report declared that selfish industrial and financial interests had built up such a heavy stake in the Allied cause that "it prevented the maintenance of a truly neutral course."

The reading public's attention also was captured in 1935 by an influential book by Walter Millis, *Road to War*, which emphasized the Nye committee's contention and stressed in addition that the pro-Ally bias of Wilson and his advisers was the factor that plunged the country into war. (Incidentally, in *The Faith of an American*, published in 1941, Millis has a far different attitude toward the second World War.) When the *Memoirs* of Robert Lansing, Wilson's secretary of state, appeared in the same year with the statement that he had wanted Germany defeated from the outset, the number of Americans who accepted the Nye-Millis approach increased.

This whole thesis was greatly overemphasized. The United States went into the first World War primarily because American sympathies were with the Allies from the outset. Ties of language, literature, law, and custom bound the United States to England. London was the social, intellectual, and cultural capital of many of our citizens, and it was the center from which most American newspapers received their European news. A majority of American newspapers were pro-Ally from the start of the war. The *New York Times*, on August 2, 1914, saw it as a crusade for "the crushing out of the imperial idea, the end, once for all times, in those three empires [the Central Powers] of absolute rule and the substitution for all powerful sovereigns and their titled advisers of an executive with power to carry out only the will of the people." The political leaders of the nation—Woodrow Wilson, Theodore Roosevelt, William H. Taft, and others—were much closer to

English traditions than they were to German. American relations with France were sentimentally cordial, but also the functioning French democracy was closer to American ideals than to German autocracy.

In addition to all these ties, England and the United States had been growing closer and closer together in world diplomacy. Ever since 1896 the older country had encouraged the expansion of American influence and empire, as can be seen, for example, in her friendliness toward our acquisition of the Philippines and in her encouragement of the doctrine of the Open Door in China. While this tie was developing, the rising empire of Germany appeared to be more and more of a menace to the United States. Germany was considered to have a covetous desire for the Philippines, to be largely responsible for the Venezuela affair of 1902, and to be seeking strategic posts in the Caribbean area.

The suspicion held by Americans that Germany was a militaristic nation made our entrance into the war on her side impossible. In 1914 it was also held inconceivable that the United States would join the Allies, but there can be little doubt of the American desire for an Allied victory.

Although President Wilson had a personal sympathy for the Allies, as president he seems to have worked to prevent this feeling from affecting national policy. In the eyes of Charles Seymour, Wilson was so successful in this that "he was attacked in turn by each belligerent group as being favorable to the other." Wilson felt that his first duty was to maintain peace and his second duty to preserve the neutral rights of the United States. If, however, one of the belligerents attacked the neutral rights of America, these two concepts would be contradictory. In a speech at Milwaukee, January 31, 1916, the President demonstrated his awareness of this fact:

"I know that you are depending upon me to keep this Nation out of the war. So far I have done so and I pledge you my word that, God helping me, I will—if it is possible. But you have laid another duty upon me. You have bidden me to see to it that nothing stains or impairs the honor of the United States, and that is a matter not within my control; that depends upon what others do, not upon what the Government of the United States does. Therefore there may at any moment come a time when I cannot preserve both the honor and the peace of the United States. Do not exact of me an impossible and contradictory thing."

Wilson might have avoided a rupture with Germany by abandoning the right to send American ships and citizens on the high seas. Such a suggestion was made to him, but he felt that no nation should surrender its rights. If a country began to surrender its rights, there might be no end to the process.

Soon after Germany resumed her policy of unrestricted submarine warfare in 1917, the President sent his war message to Congress. He was opposed to this type of warfare, not merely because American property rights were endangered, but because it involved attacks on human lives as well. Wilson envisaged the submarine campaign as a war on humanity. In his note of June 9, 1915, after the sinking of the "Lusitania," he had written:

"The sinking of passenger ships involves principles of humanity which throw into the background any special circumstances of detail that may be thought to affect the cases. . . . . The Government of the United States is contending for something much greater than mere rights of property or privileges of commerce. It is contending for nothing less high and sacred than the rights of humanity, which every Government honors itself in respecting and no Government is justified in resigning on behalf of those under its care and authority."

Although President Wilson based American entrance into the war on Germany's resumption of unrestricted submarine warfare, there were others who saw the whole question in a larger perspective. They saw that the rising power of Germany threatened the European balance of power and that a German victory would be a threat to the security of the United States. In 1913 Lewis Einstein, a minor American diplomat, wrote a remarkable article contending that the United States could no longer be indifferent to political events in Europe. He pointed out that Great Britain had contributed for more than a century to the security of the United States through maintenance of the European balance of power; that the balance was now threatened by the rise of Germany; and that, if Germany were able to defeat England and achieve dominance upon both land and sea, she would become a menace to the United States and to all other nations.

Colonel Edward M. House, confidential adviser to President Wilson, and Secretary of State Lansing also realized that the United States should play a larger role in European politics. Lansing, in particular, believed that the future welfare of the United States depended upon an Allied victory. In his *Memoirs* he wrote that he had advocated American intervention in case it became necessary to prevent a German victory. He disliked Allied infringement on neutral rights, but in spite of this he was firmly convinced that "the German Government, cherishing the . . . . ambition of world power which now possesses it . . . . must not be permitted to win this war or to break even, though to prevent it this country is forced to take an active part." Although his attitude was clear, Lansing seems to have had little influence on Wilson. When he argued that America had a stake in an Allied victory, the President was unmoved.

When isolationists and others who questioned the wisdom of

our having entered the first World War quoted Lansing's *Memoirs*, they disregarded the smallness of his influence on Wilson. Also, confused as they were by the charges of the Nye committee and Walter Millis' book, they failed to see the importance of the European balance of power to America's security. When the public was asked in a poll conducted in April, 1937, "Do you think it was a mistake for the United States to enter the World War?" 71 per cent replied "Yes."

The American people were so confused and forgetful that they showed no realization of the strong probability that the alternative to American entrance would have been a German victory—a victory which would more than likely have been far more punitive to the defeated Allies than the Versailles Treaty was to Germany. Following the Nye committee's investigation and the books and articles attacking America's entrance into the first war, Congress moved to pass legislation designed to keep America neutral in the case of another conflict. President Roosevelt wanted a law which would place an embargo on trade to an aggressor. Such a law would make it possible for the United States to deter aggression or cripple it and at the same time to aid the victim of aggression. The President's request was based on the frank assumption that it was vital to American security to aid the democracies if they were attacked by the dictators.

This power to apply an embargo on the aggressor would have given the President a powerful weapon in world diplomacy. He would have been able, from 1935 on, to warn the dictators against steps of aggression, on the ground that the world's most powerful industrial nation would throw its support to the victim. The President's bill also would have given him the power to forbid American ships to enter the war zone;

prohibit loans to the belligerents; and warn Americans that they traveled on belligerent vessels at their own risk.

Congress, however, would not accept the President's suggestion. Its measure, signed by President Roosevelt on August 31, 1935, prohibited the export of arms, ammunition, or implements of war to *any* belligerent nation, made it unlawful for an American vessel to carry arms for or to any belligerent, and empowered the President to warn Americans that they traveled on belligerent ships at their own risk. But it did not permit the President to discriminate between aggressors and victims; and as a result, it deprived the United States of the chance to play a powerful role in maintaining peace from 1935 to September, 1939. The power of the nation's chief executive was definitely handicapped, and the dictators could feel sure that if they plunged the world into war the United States would refuse to aid their victims. Congress' shortsighted policy, therefore, unintentionally aided them in plotting their aggressions.

One of the underlying assumptions of the congressional bill was that the people of the United States would be willing to close their eyes to it if the other democracies of the world were threatened with extinction by the dictators. A few farsighted people, however, realized in 1935 that this was a false assumption. They knew that some Americans, when they saw these countries being crushed, would demand aid for them. This is exactly what happened after September, 1939. As the mechanized columns of Hitler plowed under one country after another, many Americans rose up and demanded immediate aid to the remaining democracies opposing Hitler. But it was not until after war had broken out that this country as a whole realized how foolish this Neutrality Act was. Then we had to support steps to revise it.

When President Roosevelt signed the bill, it was with the

protest that it might well "drag us into war instead of keeping us out." Former Secretary of State Henry L. Stimson pointed out the futility of a policy of automatic embargoes by saying: "Not only is the President given no power to act in concert with other nations of the world in seeking to prevent a war by putting brakes upon the aggressor who may be starting it, but the action which is provided for may be entirely ineffective in accomplishing its main purpose of keeping us from being embroiled in animosities with other nations."

Charles Seymour, drawing upon his knowledge of the causes of America's entrance into the first World War, warned in November, 1935, that the American people should not accept the false hope that they could stay at peace by declaring a policy of isolation. Peace could not be legislated by Congress, he pointed out, since the question of peace depended upon the willingness of the people to accept injuries to their interests without retaliation. "It is much easier," he said, "to promise to be patient now than it will be to be patient when the national interest begins to suffer at the hands of belligerents. . . . . No nation of importance in all history has escaped its problems by refusing to face them."

The outbreak of the war between Italy and Ethiopia in October, 1935, led the President to apply the Neutrality Act. The embargo did not operate overwhelmingly to the advantage of the aggressor, Italy in this case, since Ethiopia was able to buy arms from the members of the League of Nations. On the other hand, private American interests sold large amounts of oil, copper, trucks, scrap iron, and tractors to Italy, which aided that country greatly in the prosecution of the war. This trade, denounced by the President and Secretary Hull, had some influence in weakening the halfhearted sanctions applied to Italy by the League powers. Our Neutrality Act, in the case of this conflict, probably operated to make British diplomacy cautious in its opposition to Italy. If Britain went to war with Italy, she knew she could not buy equipment from the United States, and Mussolini was aware of this as well. Since there was no real co-operation among the democratic powers against the aggressor, Italy was able to capture Ethiopia by the summer of 1936.

As a peaceful world further disintegrated with the Italo-Ethiopian war, President Roosevelt warned on Armistice Day, 1935, that if the United States wanted peace we could not "build walls around ourselves and hide our heads in the sand" but would have to work with other nations to obtain peace. By this time the League was negligible as a force for peace. The aggressors knew that they could defy it with impunity. In July, 1936, came the next incident in the collapse of collective security: civil war broke out in Spain. What started as a revolt against Republican Spain, launched by General Franco and his Fascist following, before long became much more than an internal conflict. Germany and Italy sent men and equipment to help Franco destroy the democratically elected government, while Russia sent a little material to the government.

The American Neutrality Act did not specifically apply to civil conflict, so Congress amended it on January 8, 1937, to extend its provisions to Spain. While this was taking place, England and France persuaded other governments to sign a pledge not to interfere with the Spanish conflict. Germany and Italy openly broke the agreement and continued to send aid to Franco. The Loyalists, on the other hand, were deprived of any material aid from the United States and the other world democracies. Germany and Italy used the Spanish war as a dress rehearsal for the great conflict to come. The military lessons learned were especially valuable to Germany in the early years of the second World War.

By a shortsighted policy the world's democracies allowed republican Spain to be destroyed by Franco, Germany, and Italy. Liberals in the United States protested the actions of our State Department; but the public was largely indifferent to the struggle, failing to see that the defeat of Spain's republic was another step toward Fascist domination of the world.

The Neutrality Act expired on May 1, 1937, and Congress was again convinced of the need of stringent legislation. The new law signed by the President on May 1, 1937, retained the embargo on arms, munitions, and implements of war to all belligerents. It made travel by Americans on belligerent ships unlawful. It permitted the President to extend the embargo to civil war, and it retained a provision enacted in 1936 which made it illegal to buy or sell belligerent securities after the date of a neutrality proclamation. A new feature was added—the "cash-and-carry provision"—which required that materials like cotton, scrap iron, oil (the President was to make up the list) could not be shipped to belligerents in American bottoms. The belligerents had to carry these goods themselves and pay cash before the goods left the United States. This plan was limited to two years, and it was a surrender of the belief in the freedom of the seas, which had been an important doctrine accepted by the United States since the early days of the Republic.

Isolationists were overjoyed at the passage of this bill. They believed that a way for keeping the United States out of world troubles had been found. It was expected that this law would automatically insulate us from wars. When, however, the events of 1939–41 demonstrated increasingly that this legislation was working against the best interests of America and when the danger that the United States alone might have to face a triumphant Germany and Japan became all too apparent, the American people became aroused to support its modification and finally its repeal.

During 1937 President Roosevelt took a stiffer attitude toward aggressor nations. Although he had accepted the neutrality legislation, he had protested against its failure to differentiate between aggressors and victims. When Japan found a pretense for attacking China in July, 1937, the administration followed as strong a line of action as possible. Since 1899 the United States had stood for the Open Door in China. At the turn of the century it added the doctrine of respecting the territorial sovereignty of China. With this stand the United States became the opponent of the Japanese desire to dominate that country. Tension soon increased between the United States and Japan. Japan was dissatisfied with the terms of the Portsmouth (New Hampshire) Conference which Theodore Roosevelt had called to end the Russo-Japanese War. During the first World War, the United States had objected to the twenty-one demands served by Japan on China and to the Japanese occupation of Shantung.

The Washington Conference of 1921 temporarily improved the relationship between the two countries when Great Britain, the United States, France, Japan, and five other nations signed a pledge to uphold the "sovereignty, the independence, and the territorial and administrative integrity of China." At this conference Japan accepted the 5-5-3 ratio on capital ships with Great Britain and the United States. As a reward, the United States promised that it would not strengthen the fortifications on any of its Pacific islands except Hawaii. In 1934, however, Japan denounced the limitation that had been placed on capital ships—and, as a matter of fact, competition in the building of smaller war craft had started even before this.

The agreement for the protection of the sovereignty of

China was openly violated by Japan in 1931, when her troops overran Manchuria. President Hoover denounced the aggression as "immoral" and agreed that the United States should co-operate with the League in support of the Nine-Power Pact. As to the question of whether America should go to war if the efforts of the League failed, President Hoover's stand was definitely "No." It was his opinion that Japan's acts "do not imperil the freedom of the American people, the economic or moral future of the people. . . . . We will not go along on war or any of the sanctions either economic or military, for these are the roads to war." Another factor hampering effective action by the United States was Secretary of State Stimson's feeling that if the more liberal leaders of Japan were not interfered with by outside threats, they would be able to check the military power and find a solution for the problem.

Secretary Stimson authorized the American consul at Geneva to attend meetings of the League dealing with this aggression. When the deliberations opened at Paris, Ambassador Charles G. Dawes was sent to observe them. At Paris it was agreed to send a commission to Manchuria to investigate and to report its findings to the League. While these steps were being taken, Japan crushed the last Chinese resistance in Manchuria. President Hoover and Secretary Stimson now moved to a stronger expression of their disapproval. On January 7, 1932, Stimson sent notes to China and Japan stating that the United States would not recognize any "situation, treaty, or covenant" brought about by means contrary to the Pact of Paris. This policy of the nonrecognition of territory acquired by force was to be continued later by President Roosevelt and Secretary Hull. The British Foreign Office failed to co-operate with Stimson's move. They issued a press communiqué stating that the British government would not take similar action.

Late in January, 1932, the Japanese attacked Shanghai. Closer collaboration between England and the United States seemed possible, and Secretary Stimson talked to British Foreign Minister Simon over the transatlantic telephone. Stimson wanted the League to impose economic sanctions upon Japan and hoped that Congress would do the same. He thought that Congress would be more willing to do this, however, "if it were recommended following the invocation of the Nine-Power Treaty than if it had been recommended solely by the League of Nations." Simon was wary of this suggestion and apparently was not willing to apply economic pressure on Japan unless he had concrete assurances that President Hoover and Congress would support Secretary Stimson. This, of course, was impossible because the President had stated that he was unwilling to apply economic sanctions, since he felt they would be a prelude to war—and Congress was isolationist.

The League Assembly soon adopted Stimson's doctrine of the nonrecognition of territory acquired by force. The League's commission late in 1932 brought in their report censuring Japan, which was concurred in by the American member of the commission. When the report was adopted by the League, Japan withdrew its membership. Japan, however, retained Manchuria and thus defeated the desires of the United States, Great Britain, and the League.

During the Manchurian crisis the American people failed to see the relation of the affair to American life. President Hoover's attitude that it did not imperil American freedom was echoed by the *Philadelphia Record* which stated that "the American people don't give a hoot in a rain barrel who controls North China." That this was the real beginning of the second World War was not realized by the democratic peoples of the world. Only now can we sadly agree that it would have been cheaper in lives and money to have co-operated in a military fashion to check the outbreak of aggression at that point, rather than wait to do it when the aggressors were far more powerful and better prepared for war.

When the Roosevelt administration was faced with the new Japanese aggressions in July, 1937, the international situation was extremely unfavorable from the American standpoint. The League had not been able to check Italy in Ethiopia. Great Britain was worried at the menacing developments in Europe. This left the United States alone to oppose Japan. Both Secretary Hull and President Roosevelt were anxious to assist China and hamper Japan, but not to the extent of using force. President Roosevelt did not invoke the Neutrality Act, since neither side had formally declared war. To have imposed an arms embargo would have struck a heavy blow at China, while injuring Japan but little. If the President had invoked the embargo, it would actually have placed the United States on the side of Japan. Such a step, regardless of the Neutrality Act, would not have been acceptable to the American people. In a poll conducted in October, 1937, the American people demonstrated that 59 per cent were in sympathy with China, 1 per cent with Japan, and 40 per cent with neither.

But in spite of sympathies for China the American people did not want to become involved in an armed conflict. A Gallup Poll taken in September, 1937, showed that 54 per cent of the people favored withdrawing American troops from China. On October 5 an advisory committee of the League dealing with the Far Eastern situation adopted a resolution declaring that Japan had violated the Nine-Power Treaty and the Kellogg Pact. Secretary Hull immediately made it known that the United States government concurred in that opinion.

On the same day President Roosevelt delivered a significant speech in Chicago, declaring that world peace was being threatened by international lawlessness. The countries that were contributing to gangsterism and disorder should be quarantined. Furthermore, he observed: "The peace, the freedom, and the security of 90 per cent of the population of the world is being jeopardized by the remaining 10 per cent, who are threatening a breakdown of all international order and law. Surely the 90 per cent who want to live in peace under law and in accordance with moral standards that have received almost universal acceptance through the centuries, can and must find some way to make their will prevail. . . . . There must be positive endeavors to preserve peace."

The wisdom of this speech failed to attract the American public, which, at this moment, thought that the United States need not pay any attention to what was taking place in the Far East. The conference of powers called by the League to discuss the Chinese situation ended in total failure. Only military action could stop aggression, and the peoples in the democratic countries shrank from such a step. The administration did, however, apply pressure upon Japan. In December, 1938, the State Department refused to countenance Japan's "New Order" in the Far East. A "moral" embargo was placed on the shipment of airplanes, and credits were extended to China for purchases here.

Speaking before Congress in January, 1939, President Roosevelt said: "There are methods short of war, but stronger and more effective than mere words, of bringing home to aggressor governments the aggregate sentiment of our people." This quarantine speech was aimed at the European aggressors as well as at Japan. By October, 1937, Mussolini had enslaved Ethiopia, Hitler had reoccupied the Rhineland, and both dictators had intervened in Spain. The German annexation of Austria in March, 1938, and the Munich crisis of September, 1938, which resulted in Germany's occupation of the Sudetenland, aroused America to high excitement. A poll revealed that 77 per cent of the American people thought that the German claim to the Sudetenland was not justified. When asked, if England and France had to go to war with Germany and Italy, which side they would favor, 65 per cent indicated England and France. Also, 86 per cent believed that in case of war England and France would win.

As war seemed to approach, farsighted internationalists were disturbed at the assumption of the Neutrality Act that the United States would stand aside in a conflict between the democracies and the totalitarian powers. If the democracies won a quick victory, then such a course would not be hard to follow. But if the war went into a stalemate or if the totalitarian nations threatened to crush France and England and, together with Japan, achieved domination of Europe, Africa, and Asia, the United States would be placed in an isolated, precarious position. If this were the situation, demand for American intervention to prevent totalitarian domination of the world would be inevitable. With this in mind, the internationalist position from 1937 to 1939 was that the United States, in order to prevent a war which might inevitably require American participation to prevent a totalitarian victory, should join in steps to prevent that war from arising.

Early in 1939, President Roosevelt reiterated his belief that collective efforts were necessary to achieve peace by pressing upon Congress the need for revising the Neutrality Act. On January 4 he told Congress: "At the very least we can and should avoid any action, or any lack of action, which will encourage or assist an aggressor. We have learned that when we deliberately try to legislate neutrality, our neutrality laws may operate unevenly and unfairly—may actually give aid to the aggressor and deny it to the victim. The instinct of self-preservation should warn us that we ought not to let that happen any more."

A bill to repeal the arms embargo was drafted, but the Senate Foreign Relations Committee by a vote of 12 to 11 on July 11 decided not to report the bill to the Senate. The majority of this committee were not willing to free the President's hands so that he could threaten the dictators and thus, as he hoped, prevent war from breaking out. In a final effort to persuade the Senate leaders that war in Europe was imminent, President Roosevelt and Secretary Hull called a group of them to the White House. Both the President and the Secretary of State were eloquent in their warnings that the arms embargo might encourage the dictators to start a war. Isolationist Senator Borah disagreed, however, with their contention that war was about to break out.

"I wish the Senator would come down to my office and read the cables," said Secretary Hull. "I'm sure he would come to the conclusion that there's far more danger of war than he thinks." To this Senator Borah petulantly replied: "So far as the reports in your Department are concerned, I wouldn't be bound by them. I have my own sources of information . . . . and on several occasions I've found them more reliable than the State Department." Shortly after this dogmatic statement, the meeting adjourned. Some six weeks later Germany invaded Poland.

II

The Nation Chooses Sides

ON SEPTEMBER 21, THREE WEEKS AFTER GERMANY HAD launched her invasion of Poland, President Roosevelt sent a message to Congress urging the repeal of the embargo forbidding the sale of arms and ammunition to nations at war and the substitution of a cash-and-carry plan instead. As he had warned eight months before, on January 4, the embargo aided the aggressor and hurt the victims, since Germany was prepared for war and the Allies were not. The Allies needed equipment of war which the embargo prevented them from acquiring from the United States. Therefore, the President believed that the United States should at once make it possible for the Allies to purchase the needed materials.

Five days after the President's message to Congress, Clark Eichelberger, director of the League of Nations Association and the Union for Concerted Peace Efforts, called a meeting of the executive committee of the latter group. This executive committee, composed of Hugh Moore, president, Henry A. Atkinson, chairman, Edgar J. Fisher, treasurer, James T. Shotwell, Charles G. Fenwick, Mary E. Woolley, G. Ashton Oldham, honorary vice-president, and Eichelberger himself, decided to organize a Non-partisan Committee for Peace through the Revision of the Neutrality Law, with the purpose of bringing to the attention of the American people the true facts of the situation regarding the embargo clause of this law.

The work of this new committee was to be done in the office of the Union for Concerted Peace Efforts in New York City, and the executive committee of the Union would serve as the executive agency for the new organization. After some discussion as to who the chairman should be, it was decided to ask a member of the Union, William Allen White, editor of the *Emporia Gazette* of Emporia, Kansas, to assume the position.

Eichelberger telephoned White and invited him to assume leadership of the Committee. White was told that at the Union's meeting everybody had agreed that he was the man who would attract the proper attention and whom thousands of people, now befuddled and discouraged because of so much false information and malicious propaganda, would listen to and believe. Charles G. Fenwick, an honorary vice-president of the Union for Concerted Peace Efforts, later wrote to White that the Union had asked him to head the new committee because "for many years your name has stood for the highest ideals of honor and integrity in American politics; . . . . we knew that around your name would rally a large number of people who, anxious to promote the best interests of our country but bewildered by the technical problems of neutrality, would recognize in your leadership the answer to their difficulties."

William Allen White was a logical man to select as chairman of this committee. He was from the Middle West, the traditional seat of isolationism; he was an outstanding liberal Republican who at the same time was on very good terms with Franklin D. Roosevelt; and by 1939 he had become something of a folk hero to millions of middle-class Americans. Ever since the Progressive days of Theodore Roosevelt the dominating force of White's existence had been a belief in the democratic way of life based upon reason and justice. In the country as a whole, as well as in his native Kansas, he had devoted his life to eradicating injustices from the social and economic system. Many years of that life had been spent in arousing public opinion to persuade the Kansas legislature, the Republican party, and the federal government to adopt progressive measures in social legislation and such democratic reforms as the initiative, referendum, recall, and the direct election of United States senators.

White first gained national prominence during the presidential campaign of 1896, when he wrote "What's the Matter with Kansas," an editorial bitterly denouncing the supporters of William Jennings Bryan. After that time his close association with Theodore Roosevelt, the many articles he wrote for popular magazines, and the novels and biographies he published won him an increasingly large following. From 1912 to 1916 he was a mainstay of the Bull Moose party, and when it collapsed he returned to the fold of the Republican party. During the 1920's he wrote two editorials—an obituary for his daughter, Mary White, and a Pulitzer Prize-winning editorial entitled "To an Anxious Friend," calling for freedom of speech in a time of stress and crisis—which widely increased his fame as a mellow, sane philosopher of American life. All during the 1920's he did everything within his power, including running for the governorship of Kansas, to destroy the bigotry and reaction of the Ku Klux Klan.

When the New Deal came to power, he felt that Franklin D. Roosevelt was wearing the old mantle of liberalism once worn by Theodore Roosevelt and Woodrow Wilson. His support of much of the New Deal legislation was gratefully received by the President, who on January 22, 1934, wrote him to say that "it gives me a great deal of pleasure to know that you are with us in these strenuous times." Frequently the editorials in the *Emporia Gazette* especially delighted President Roosevelt. He wrote to White on June 14, 1938, after one exceptionally good one and asked "Can't you bribe the *New York Times* and *Herald Tribune* to run them occasionally?"

President Roosevelt summed up the relation between White and himself when his special train stopped at Emporia during the 1936 campaign. He told the Emporians that "Bill White is with me three and a half years out of every four." No statement could have been more appropriate. For three and a half out of every four years the Emporia editor saw almost eye to eye with the President, but in the spring of the presidential year he would run back to the Republican party and support it through thick and thin.

In the three-and-a-half-year periods White freely criticized his party, and he always endeavored to see that the progressive wing had an ascendancy over the conservative. He candidly admitted the validity of the conclusion that his party loyalty at times took precedence over his personal convictions. He explained this by stating that in order to have influence in a state where the Republican party dominated, except when a split occurred between the standpatters and the progressives, one had to be a Republican. One sacrificed too much power as a local leader by bolting too often.

White was practical, and he felt that in this workaday world he could best mold public opinion to work toward what he considered his ideal and purpose in life through the Grand Old Party. He never considered himself a scout like Robert M. La Follette or Eugene V. Debs, always ahead of liberal opinion. He was usually ahead of his neighbors and most politicians, but he knew that to get too far out in front would cost him his influence among the people who counted—the great middle class for whom he had become a tradition.

The editor of the *Emporia Gazette* had had a consuming interest in the relation between foreign affairs and American life since the Progressive era. After the outbreak of war in Europe in 1914, he reached the conclusion that isolation was no road to peace for the United States. In 1915 he became a vice-president of the League To Enforce Peace, an organization founded with the purpose of providing machinery to replace slaughter as a means of settling future international disputes. When the United States entered the first World War, although he was too old for military service he went to Europe as an officer of the Red Cross. When the peace conference met in 1918–19, he was present as a reporter for a syndicate of American newspapers.

In his news dispatches he gave wholehearted support to Woodrow Wilson's plan for a League of Nations. He told his readers that there could be no world peace except under a league. On his return to the United States he was merciless in his assault upon such Republicans as Henry Cabot Lodge, who in their partisan intrigues against the League were "jeopardizing the peace of the world." The decade of the 1920's was a nightmare to William Allen White. He felt that the people of the world had lost faith in themselves and, in their fellow-men. During this decade he went so far ahead of public opinion as to advocate the recognition of Russia, although he did not agree with the Soviet philosophy; he also demanded respect for the rights of the Latin-American nations long before we had any "Good Neighbor Policy."

Japan's aggressions in China in 1931 and Italy's march into Ethiopia in 1935 convinced White that a world conflict might soon develop. If such a conflict came, he inclined to the belief that the United States could not stay out of it, in spite of the claims of a William Randolph Hearst or a Father Coughlin. We could not keep out of Europe's troubles any more than we could keep out of the world, White wrote in his

Courtesy of the "Los Angeles Times"

William Allen White
CARICATURE BY SALVADOR BAGUEZ

paper on July 20, 1935, because when "even one man's liberty is imperilled, all men's liberties are in danger." White's writings in the thirties revealed a mind deeply troubled over the foreign situation. He was torn between two poles—the desire for peace for the United States and the realization that internationalism was necessary for a real peace, although this internationalism meant danger of war. For a time his editorials reflected the pacifist feeling that was sweeping the United States, which culminated in the passage of the neutrality legislation (1935–37). To stop shipment of all war materials might keep war from the United States, but the Neutrality Act did not go far enough for White's logical mind. If America wanted to keep out of war, he observed in the *Gazette* on October 9, 1935, she must bottle up her entire export trade, not just the munitions trade to belligerent powers. One year later he had come to the conclusion that if we were to depend upon embargo to keep us at peace, we must forego the right to trade not only with the belligerents but with other powers who were trading with belligerents.

Even while he supported this step, designed to keep America out of war, White seems to have been aware that the fascism which was sweeping through Europe would some day threaten democracy in America. "During the next decade," he once said, "America must face the fascists." He called Father Coughlin a "perfect example of the American fascist." However, like the majority of Americans in 1935, he really thought that the Neutrality Act would work. He, too, failed to see that the assumption that the American people could allow the European democracies to be destroyed and yet preserve their own was false.

By the time of the Nazi invasion of Austria in March, 1938, White had regained his perspective. He clearly observed the danger that the United States would be in if the appeasers in England and France should submit to some kind of Fascist rule and leave the United States a lone democracy. Thus he wrote in the *Gazette* on March 3, 1938, that the United States was threatened with being completely isolated:

"We cannot forever be turning the other cheek. It will get bashed in the end and our head will be broken. . . . .

"If this country has one supreme duty it is to call the democracies of the world together and with their power before they crumble, to assemble a world peace conference. There demands of the underprivileged nations may be heard and considered. These underprivileged nations—Germany, Japan, Italy—are naturally motivating their hunger with a lust for war. America must either satisfy them in conference or on the battlefield. The supreme test of the doctrine of Jesus faces the western world. Are men really Christian sufficiently in their heart of hearts to bring justice to those who are underprivileged?"

When Hitler pressed his demands on Czechoslovakia in September, 1938, White supported President Roosevelt's indignation at Hitler's unnecessary use of force. But, having done this, he felt that we should "take a long breath and do something else with all our might and main. For if the wind blows this way we will catch the war." After England and France gave in to Hitler's demand on Czechoslovakia, White felt that the danger was only put off, not ended. He warned the United States to "gird up her loins for the inevitable strife." From 1933 to 1939, White not only opposed the aggressor nations by word, but he joined and actively participated in organizations that were formed to meet the challenge. In the fall of 1938, he joined the newly organized Union for Concerted Peace Efforts. For many years, he had been cooperating with Clark Eichelberger, James T. Shotwell, Nicholas Murray Butler, Frank Boudreau, and others in the League of Nations Association. He served as honorary vice-chairman of the American Committee for Non-participation in Japanese Aggression, was a member of the American Boycott against

Aggressor Nations, and was on the board of directors of the National Refugee Service.

The committees which the editor joined were organized to fight the American Fascist mind. With W. Warren Barbour and George Gordon Battle he was co-chairman of the Council against Intolerance in America. He was a member of the board of directors of the Association To Strengthen Free Government, other members of which were Louis Adamic, Albert Einstein, and Will Durant. He was a member of the National Conference of Christians and Jews, and he co-operated with Roger Baldwin and the Civil Liberties Union, serving as chairman of the Committee of Sponsors for a national meeting which the Civil Liberties Union held in New York City on October 13–14, 1939.

The day before Eichelberger invited White to be chairman of the new Non-partisan Committee for Peace through the Revision of the Neutrality Law, White had editorially supported President Roosevelt's cash-and-carry plan. He warned his neighbors that every day the President's plan remained in Congress there was increasing danger that such propagandist interests as the Germans, the Japanese, "the Coughlinites, who are thinly disguised Fascists," and the last-ditch pacifists would work on congressmen and frighten them into voting against the bill. The old threats of nonsupport in election year were still an excellent lever with which to move senators and representatives.

Although White once had stood for a complete embargo to warring nations, he did not permit this to deter him from taking a different stand when he considered such a move necessitated by changing events. It had now become evident to him that the President was absolutely correct in saying that the embargo clause worked to the disadvantage of the democracies, our natural allies, and to the advantage of the aggressor nations. Furthermore, as the embargo law stood, it was dangerous for the United States. Food was not embargoed, and American ships could carry it to the Allies. When Germany torpedoed these ships, indignation would be great, and we would be at war.

The cash-and-carry plan, of course, was another possible road to war, but White believed it to be a safer bet because it might help the Allies win quickly. And "if we don't back up the Allies," he warned in an editorial on September 26, 1939, "we can't escape with our hides, whether the war is long or short." The great danger to the United States was a war on two fronts, the European against Germany and Italy, and the eastern against Japan. At the heart of the turmoil, however, White saw the totalitarian threat to the Christian way of life—the right of man to live decently, to be kind and neighborly to whom he pleases.

Although White sincerely felt that the Neutrality Act should be revised, he demurred at first at Clark Eichelberger's request on September 26 that he become chairman of the new committee. He was seventy-one years old, and he had been trying gradually to relieve himself of his many committee duties that took time that he wished to devote to writing his long-awaited autobiography and several other books which he had promised. But Eichelberger would not take no for an answer and persuaded a number of White's New York friends, most of them newspapermen, to wire or phone to Emporia, asking the Kansan to head the committee. On September 27 Professor James T. Shotwell of Columbia University sent this wire, which summed up the situation: "Have just learned of Eichelberger's invitation to you to head National Committee for revamping alleged neutrality law. Believe this the right thing to do in the most important issue in years not only with reference to foreign policy but also with regards to preserving our form of government from being stampeded by demagogue use of mass telegrams and letters upon Congress. Have found Eichelberger wholly reliable after years of association with him and as clear headed as they make them."

The next day Eichelberger wired White that if he took the chairmanship he would have the support of these people on the Committee: Frank Graham, president of the University of North Carolina; Charles Fenwick, professor at Bryn Mawr College; G. Ashton Oldham, Episcopal bishop of Albany; Dorothy Thompson, newspaper columnist; Carrie Chapman Catt, lecturer; Mary E. Woolley, president emeritus of Mount Holyoke College; Father Maurice Sheehey, Catholic University; Frederic Coudert, New York lawyer; Roscoe Drummond of the *Christian Science Monitor;* Henry Atkinson and William Merrill of the Church Peace Union; Josephine Schain of the Cause and Cure of War group; Edgar Fisher of the Institute of International Education; Hugh Moore, president of the Vortex Cup Company; Frederick McKee of the West Pennsylvania Cement Company; Anne O'Hare Mc-Cormick, newspaper columnist; Mary Carter Jones; Dorothy Canfield Fisher, author; Raymond Gram Swing, author and radio commentator; and James T. Shotwell. As a matter of fact, the three friends who clinched White's acceptance were Betty Gram Swing; Irene Lewisohn, with whom he had worked on a Spanish children's relief project; and Dorothy Canfield Fisher, an old Kansas friend and daughter of Professor James Canfield of the University of Kansas, who had been White's favorite professor while he was at the university. It was to Mrs. Fisher that he finally said "Yes."

White accepted the chairmanship only on the condition that no munition-makers' money, no international bankers' money, and no money from the steel interests would be used in the campaign. On September 29, then, Clark Eichelberger went to Emporia, and plans were laid for what was to be a "purely propaganda job." Eichelberger, on October 1, sent telegrams to the first list of two hundred and fifty names which had been approved by Shotwell, asking them to join the Nonpartisan Committee for Peace through the Revision of the Neutrality Law. The League of Nations Association and the Union for Concerted Peace Efforts supplied this new committee with about one thousand additional names, to whom telegrams were sent or phone calls made. From Emporia, White released the story of the Committee to the press, and the New York group sent out a supplementary release containing their end of it.

The Committee was under way. Telegrams were immediately sent out under the chairman's name to professional men, college presidents, college professors, leading businessmen, and labor leaders, asking for their support in the enterprise. The first appeal was:

"Will you join me and several hundred others in a national Non-Partisan Committee for Peace through Revision of the Neutrality Law? The present Senate bill to revise the neutrality law goes as far as human ingenuity can to lessen the danger of American involvement. Moreover, by repealing the arms embargo our country is no longer aiding Hitler to the disadvantage of the democracies who are resisting the spread of dictatorship. Obviously debate may reveal places where the present Senate bill may be improved, but we are inviting you to join us on the principle of this bill and the international aims which will be secured by the application of that principle. The American Union for Concerted Peace Efforts will act as the Committee's secretariat."

The response to this telegram was immediate and almost completely favorable. Acceptances came from such people in the newspaper world as Colonel Frank Knox, publisher of the *Chicago Daily News;* Douglas S. Freeman, editor of the *Richmond News Leader;* Freda Kirchwey, editor of the *Nation;* Chester Rowell, editor of the *San Francisco Chronicle;* John T. Graves of the *Birmingham News;* and Herbert Bayard Swope.

College and university presidents joined, among them Mrs. Dwight W. Morrow, acting president of Smith College; William A. Eddy, Hobart; Ernest M. Hopkins, Dartmouth; Hamilton Holt, Rollins; Guy Stanton Ford, University of Minnesota; and R. G. Ham, Mount Holyoke College.

Religious leaders who lent their efforts to the Committee's work were Monsignor John A. Ryan, Catholic theologian; Henry S. Coffin, president of Union Theological Seminary; William T. Manning, Episcopal bishop of New York; Paul Kern, Methodist bishop of Nashville; G. Ashton Oldham, Episcopal bishop of Albany; and Rabbi Stephen A. Wise.

Also in favor of the Committee were outstanding businessmen like Henry I. Harriman, chairman of the board of the New England Power Association; Marshall Field, director of Marshall Field and Company; and Martin J. Collins, president of the Graham Paper Company, all of whom joined the organization.

Among the many others who joined were Robert Sherwood, playwright; Ida M. Tarbell, author; Anita McCormick Blaine, philanthropist; Quincy Wright, professor of international law at the University of Chicago; Max Lerner, professor of political science at Williams College; Alderman Paul H. Douglas, professor of economics at the University of Chicago; Edward G. Robinson, actor; Tallulah Bankhead, actress; Arthur Garfield Hayes, lawyer; Joseph M. Proskauer, judge; Frank Boudreau, doctor and president of the League of Nations Association; and Sherwood Eddy, author.

The members of this national Non-partisan Committee for

Peace through Revision of the Neutrality Law were by no means restricted to New York City and the eastern seaboard cities. They were from all sections of the country, though at first not all of the forty-eight states were represented. Although the headquarters of the Committee, for practical reasons, was in New York City, geographically it was a national organization.

A number of those who refused to join the Committee nevertheless supported its aims, although their position or the policy of their professions did not allow membership. Thus President James Conant of Harvard University; Henry S. Dennison, who was associated with the National Resources Planning Board; Harold G. Moulton of Brookings Institution; Karl Compton of the Massachusetts Institute of Technology; W. G. Carey, president of the United States Chamber of Commerce; Nicholas Murray Butler, president of Columbia and the Carnegie Endowment for Peace; and Henry Haskell, publisher of the *Kansas City Star*, consistently backed the Committee's work.

White's major purpose in heading the Non-partisan Committee was to keep the United States out of war if it were humanly possible. His secondary purpose was to see that the Republican party did not make the cash-and-carry plan a partisan issue and thus typify the Republican party as the party of isolation. Since 1919, as his actions have demonstrated, he had been fighting to make the Republican party internationally minded; and his work after September, 1939, was only a continuation of the struggle.

Colonel Frank Knox, Alf M. Landon's running mate in the presidential campaign of 1936, heartily concurred with White's attitude. He and White were in frequent communication on this point before and after the Non-partisan Committee was organized. Knox felt strongly that this country's relations with foreign nations in time of war should remain a non-partisan issue.

After a conference that President Roosevelt had with Knox and Landon over the embargo legislation on September 20, 1939, Knox wrote White that the President had gone even further, and was thinking in terms of a coalition cabinet in which anti-New Dealers and Republicans would be given representation. White replied that he thought this would be a splendid move in the effort to put foreign relations above partisan politics. "The President," he said, "needs someone to say no to him, and bang on the table, and a cabinet member might do it."

Landon, on the other hand, refused to join White's committee. He did not like the provision in the Administration's cash-and-carry proposal which would grant a ninety-day credit on purchases, and he felt that the Non-partisan Committee might not feel as strongly as he did about it. "I want to help and cooperate," wrote Landon, "with the foreign policies of the administration and present a united front as much as I can. But after all, the most an administration can expect from an opposition leader is silence when it is open to attack from flank and rear. It should not expect him to blaze the way, it should not use him for window dressing, at least without warning him in advance."

Later, when the Non-partisan Committee turned its pressure campaign on Congress, White asked Landon to send telegrams to members of Congress asking them to support the Administration measure. Landon refused again, because to scatter telegrams like this "among members of congress, when you don't know what their local situations are and what they are up against, is not a good thing for anyone to do."

Nor could Landon agree with White and Knox that it made any difference to the future of the Republican party what position members of Congress took on the bill, though it did make a difference to the country and on that ground he was willing to give such help and support as he could to the Administration. "I don't think that it is asking too much," he added, "if the administration wants me to help, that they should discuss the situation with me, or with Frank Knox, and tell us where they think we could give them some assistance."

While White remained in Emporia for the first ten days of October, 1939, the capable organization set up by Eichelberger and Shotwell prepared the ground for their campaign on Congress. Instructions were sent out to members to talk to their friends and neighbors and bring up the matter of adopting the cash-and-carry plan before their clubs and societies; to wire or write to their congressmen and senators; to organize meetings to discuss the issue; to write letters to local newspapers, calling for the passage of the cash-and-carry bill; and to send any suggestions and financial contributions to the Committee.

Sent to each member, over a period of time, were a Senate poll showing where various senators stood on the bill; copies of a speech by Professor Shotwell on "Fundamentals behind the Conflict"; reprints of Clyde Engleton's letter to the *New York Times* defending the legality of changing the Neutrality Act; reprints of letters by Henry L. Stimson and Nicholas Murray Butler to the *New York Times*, answering a speech by Senator William E. Borah against the cash-and-carry plan; copies of Alfred E. Smith's broadcast over the Columbia network on October 1, calling for repeal of the embargo clause; and reprints of Walter Lippmann's column of October 5, entitled, "Senator Borah Opens the Debate."

When White came to New York City in mid-October, the Non-partisan campaign was already progressing rapidly. At the Committee headquarters the chairman met two men—Hugh Moore of Easton, Pennsylvania, and Frederick McKee of Pittsburgh, both manufacturers—whom he considered to be "real patriots." They agreed to underwrite the initial expense of the campaign. (Later they made the same offer when the Committee To Defend America by Aiding the Allies was organized.) Hugh Moore, although he lived in Pennsylvania, spent a day or two every week at the office of the Union for Concerted Peace Efforts in New York City, where he saw to it that everything connected with the Committee was conducted by business-like methods.

On Sunday, October 15, White made a speech on the revision of the neutrality law over the Columbia Broadcasting System, entitled "The Hour Is Striking." In it he warned that materials such as steel, oil, copper, and scrap iron could go to the belligerents under the embargo act—and in American ships. Thus our sailors and ships were exposed to torpedoes. But, he pointed out, the cash-and-carry plan did not permit United States ships to carry anything to belligerent powers. The best protection for our country was in a neutrality law which gave the Allies the right to come with their own ships and with their own cash to buy the materials they needed. He observed that no law would keep us out of war, but involvement was less likely under the cash-and-carry principle. Also, only less than America's desire to keep out of war was her desire to see the Allies win, and the present embargo handicapped the Allies.

The European struggle "is not a contest of imperialist nations," he said, "struggling for place and power. It is a clash of ideologies. In Germany and in Russia, the state is the master of the citizen. In the democracies of Europe—France and England, Holland and the Scandinavian countries, the citizens control the state. The struggle of two thousand years for human liberty has been wiped out east of the Rhine. . . . . These European democracies are carrying our banner, fighting the American battle. These democracies west of the Rhine and north of the Baltic are digging our first-line trenches. We need not shed our blood for them now or ever. But we should not deny them now access to our shores when they come with cash to pay for weapons of defense and with their own ships to carry arms and materials which are to protect their citizens and their soldiers fighting for our common cause."

This speech was purposely delivered on Sunday from 1:40 to 2:00 P.M. to counteract the usual Father Coughlin broadcast. White received much favorable comment on the speech, including a letter from Clinton Howard of the International Reform Federation of Washington, D.C., who told White that his speech was the most convincing radio address he had yet heard on the subject of the Neutrality Act repeal.

White's speech was recorded, and on the other side of the record was cut a speech by Alfred E. Smith, a prominent lay Catholic. Further to offset Father Coughlin's opposition to the repeal of the arms embargo, the Committee had speeches broadcast by Monsignor John A. Ryan, General O'Ryan, Mayor Fiorello La Guardia, and Professor Charles Fenwick. These speeches, together with White's and Smith's, were sent to local stations which were not affiliated with the networks that had originally carried them.

The Non-partisan Committee also scattered over the country tens of thousands of statements supporting the cash-and-carry proposal, signed by leading Catholic, Jewish, and Protestant clergymen and by well-known college presidents. It released a poll of college presidents and deans which showed that 90 per cent favored revision of the neutrality law. The Committee did not operate directly on Congress. Instead, it had its members and their friends all over the nation deluge Congress with telegrams, letters, and postcards calling for support of President Roosevelt's cash-and-carry plan. Gifford Pinchot, old Bull Moose friend of William Allen White, co-operated with the Committee by sending out thirteen hundred letters to local papers, advocating repeal of the embargo clause.

Colonel Frank Knox, in the capacity of publisher of the *Chicago Daily News*, worked wholeheartedly with the Committee. All during the time that Congress was discussing the cash-and-carry bill, he was in touch with President Roosevelt. On October 18 he received a telegram from White in New York asking him to help in lining up the Republicans in the House of Representatives for the President's measure, and Knox made every effort to do so. He felt, according to a letter to White on October 18, that Landon was mistaken not to join him and White, because what was best for the country was best for the Republican party.

Five days later White wrote the Chicago publisher that the bill revising the neutrality legislation would have easy sledding in the Senate but not in the House of Representatives. In this letter he expressed fear that, if the Republicans in the House were responsible for killing the repeal of the embargo, it would make Roosevelt's re-election a sure thing. Knox agreed and wrote that he wondered "whether our party has not lost through inept and stupid leadership even the right to come back into dominance." On October 30 he ran a front-page editorial in the *Chicago Daily News* which he sent to every Republican member of the House and to the Non-partisan Committee for whatever use they wished to make of it. Landon still would not join in this move with White and Knox; on November 2 he refused to sign a joint statement with them to be sent to midwestern Congressmen calling for support of the President's bill.

On October 23, Chairman White wrote to Joseph Martin,

Republican minority leader of the House of Representatives, that he was worried by the report that a majority of the House Republicans were against revision of the neutrality law. Repeal should not be made a partisan issue. If the failure to repeal the embargo should be due to lack of Republican support and if such failure "should chance to have disastrous effects and might possibly even lead us into war, then the Democrats could properly charge us with responsibility for not repealing the embargo." Besides the political issue involved, there was also a moral issue, he told Martin:

"I would hate to have my party put itself in a posture where it can be charged that we played Mr. Hitler's game in the matter of the embargo. We have no reason to fear the effects upon us of a French-British victory. We have a whole lot to fear in the case of a Hitler victory. If we fail to repeal the embargo and Hitler should win, we, as a party, will be vulnerable, or if we refuse to repeal the embargo and then later we are dragged into the war, again, we would be, as a party, in a very vulnerable position."

On this same day, White had a half-hour's conference with Republican Representative James Wadsworth of New York. A week later he went to Washington to discuss his views with other members of the House of Representatives. He did not talk to the Kansas members, however, because "they are my personal friends and I don't like to put political pressure on them." All of the Kansas Republicans were opposed to the repeal of the embargo, even Representative Ed Rees from White's own district.

By the last week in October, the Non-partisan Committee had affiliates in thirty states. In order to support the growing enterprise, it had sent out requests from time to time to its members for financial contributions. On October 20, Frederic

R. Coudert, prominent New York lawyer, held a luncheon in White's honor at the Down Town Association in New York City. Among those present were Colonel Henry Breckinridge, lawyer; Nicholas Murray Butler; Clark Eichelberger; Thomas Finletter, lawyer; Lindsay Rogers, professor of public law at Columbia University; James McDonald, chairman of the board of directors of the Foreign Policy Association; Alexander J. Peet; Frank L. Polk, lawyer; Wendell L. Willkie; Thomas Watson, chairman of the American section of the International Chamber of Commerce; Archibald Watson, lawyer and publisher of the *United States Law Review;* Colonel Henry L. Stimson; Alexander Williams, New York correspondent of the *Christian Science Monitor;* and Coudert. White outlined to this group the activities of the Non-partisan Committee and told them that he needed some money right away to continue the work. He repeated that he did not want any munitions money, any international bankers' money, or any money in large chunks over a thousand dollars. After he had concluded, Wendell Willkie spoke up: "Well, if money is all that Mr. White needs, let's get it for him."

In the next two or three weeks enough money was received from the luncheon group and other sources to keep the campaign afloat. The majority of the contributions were in small amounts, ranging from five to fifty dollars. Approximately one-half of the total sum collected came from these small donors, demonstrating that the Committee had an appeal to other than wealthy citizens. The largest contributor was Frederick McKee of Pittsburgh, who gave $150.00 for general expenses, $574.00 for radio transcriptions, and $575.00 to operate a Washington office. The Union for Concerted Peace Efforts contributed $690.00. Theodore Pitcairn of Philadelphia and Henry R. Luce of New York City gave $500.00 each, and William F. Cochran of Baltimore gave $250.00. Eleven people gave $100.00 each. The total amount received by the Committee was $8,403.84, of which it spent $8,195.18.

On November 3, the bill to revise the Neutrality Act passed Congress. In spite of the work of such leading Republicans as William Allen White, Colonel Frank Knox, and Colonel Henry L. Stimson, only twenty Republicans in the House of Representatives voted for the Administration's bill. One hundred and forty voted to retain a law which was completely unrealistic and opposed to the best interests of the nation. Hamilton Fish of New York led the opposition to the bill, charging that revision was an act of war. It was, he claimed, "utterly unmoral, utterly un-Christian and vicious." Among other things, he stated that "this campaign of hysteria, emotionalism, hatred and poisonous propaganda has for its sole purpose sending American youth to the battlefields."

Another factor motivating many Republicans in their opposition to the bill was a dislike of supporting the President. It was held that any bill passed by Congress at the President's request would aid in making the President a dictator. Representative Youngdahl of Minnesota asserted that "repeal of the arms embargo is the first step towards the loss of freedom and democratic institutions on this continent." Some of those opposed to the President's bill also played upon distrust of Great Britain and France. Senator Gerald Nye stated that persecution by the British Empire was worse than the crimes of the Nazis. A number of congressmen denied that the United States was in any way threatened by Germany.

In spite of the work of these opponents, the neutrality revision passed the House of Representatives by a vote of 243 to 172. On November 1, when it was clear that the opposition in the House of Representatives would not be sufficient to defeat the President's bill, William Allen White left Washington for

Emporia. In the mail which awaited him at his office was a letter written October 31 by Cordell Hull, secretary of state, thanking him for the work he had done as chairman of the Non-partisan Committee. Hull said: "Nobody knows better than I do how great a contribution that was; and everybody here is warmly appreciative of your valuable help."

On his return home White wired Clark Eichelberger: "When vote seemed safe pulled out. Congratulations upon final issue. Give my warm regards to all your folks. It was a happy adventure. You were most efficient and I just an old friend and stuffed shirt." Eichelberger wired back: "Office staff at party to celebrate victory send you their affectionate greetings. We were deeply moved by your telegram but refuse to let you be so modest. It is probable that you were the decisive factor in the favorable Congressional vote." This belief that White's influence was the decisive factor was shared by many members of the Committee. White replied to their praise by writing Colonel Knox on November 10 that "it was a great fight but I fear I am merely the rooster on the cow catcher who mistakes his crow for the engine's toot and his power for the engine's steam. But the rooster and I always have a lot of fun."

That White was underestimating his influence on the repeal of the embargo can be seen in letters from Senator Claude Pepper and President Franklin D. Roosevelt. Senator Pepper felt that White had done the job that was necessary to stop the opposition. On the whole, concluded Pepper, the work that White had done in the past three weeks would have far more significance "toward a better and a saner world than anything you have done before." President Roosevelt wrote: "Dear Bill: You did a grand job. It was effective and most helpful! I am writing this note just to say: 'Thank you, Bill.' "

White's prestige as a sound, reasonable spokesman of American life had undoubtedly contributed greatly to the success of the Non-partisan Committee's campaign. A chairman from almost any other part of the country would have found it difficult to make the appeal to the middle western and western parts of the country that White's vigorous program did.

The Non-partisan Committee, of course, received a number of letters of opposition during the cash-and-carry campaign. Some were abusive, and some were simply letters of disagreement. But Chairman White, with his customary good nature, answered all of them politely and intelligently, always concluding with the following paragraph: "There are two sides to this question and each of us must respect the honesty and sincerity of the other side. I realize that your side has an entirely tenable position, and I hope you will finally see that my side is founded at least upon an honest opinion." The sincerity of what White said was the secret from which his great popularity sprang. Even those in disagreement with him were forced to admit it, and often his answers to condemning letters brought forth apologies for previous unfair accusations.

Shortly after the passage of the cash-and-carry plan, the United States Shipping Lines applied to the Maritime Commission for permission to transfer their ships to the Panamanian registry so that they could escape the new Neutrality Act prohibiting American ships from belligerent waters and, thus, continue their voyages to Europe. According to the Associated Press dispatches, the Maritime Commission on the afternoon of November 6 granted this permission, but in the evening announced that it was deferring action. Secretary of State Hull opposed the transfer as impairing the integrity of the Neutrality Act.

William Allen White vigorously denounced this transfer as "dirty work at the crossroads" and "a corrupt evasion of the law of the land." He warned that the transfer would bring war close to the United States because American seamen aboard these ships would be drowned by torpedoing or by a German attack on Panama, which we would have to defend under the Monroe Doctrine. White felt that the President and the Secretary of State should look sharply at this transaction and concluded editorially by asking: "Should the greed of American ship owners for blood money justify us in standing by and seeing a door to war open for no other reason in God's beautiful world than to allow a shipping corporation which we ordinarily protect and somewhat subsidize and certainly furnish with its normal business, to involve us, if not in war, in the danger of war?"

A copy of this editorial of November 8, 1939, was sent to Cordell Hull; and White told Hull, in addition, that he never would have worked for the Administration's neutrality bill if he had guessed that the Panama subterfuge was to be used. In a letter the next day he also told the Secretary of State that the "disillusionment in this country that will come from this Panama registration trick will be devastating politically to those who are responsible for it. It will be a surrender to the economic royalists that will be so palpable that it cannot be debated." At the same time he wrote Eichelberger that the transfer "stinks." Two days later he wrote to Secretary Ickes and to Senator Ernest W. Gibson in the same vain. He told his old friend Ickes that it was "a cheap trick" and he hoped that the President would see through it. His Irish temper was still aroused when on November 13 he wrote to Senator Claude Pepper and Ambassador Josephus Daniels, reiterating that he would not have worked for the repeal of the embargo if he had foreseen this development.

Secretary Hull replied to White's letter on November 13 by saying: "I think the ship transfer matter to which you refer in your last letter will work out to your satisfaction. I and others of my associates, from the day we learned of the proposal, have been emphasizing in effect the same views you express in your letter." On the same day President Roosevelt wrote White explaining the situation in the following words:

DEAR BILL:—

Cordell has shown me yours of November ninth. You were wrong in saying that the "subterfuge" or "registration trick" was adopted. The actual fact is that we heard of it just in time because it would have gone through under the normal powers of the Maritime Commission.

The simple fact is that while the transfer would have been legal, it would have been a mistake to furnish the means to a sister Republic to adopt a different form of neutrality from our own. Panama ought not to send Panama flag ships into the war zones any more than we do.

However, the sale to a European neutral—a bona-fide sale—is not only legal but lives up to the spirit of the law because a "laid-up" ship, for which there is no American use, can be sold as readily as Kansas wheat or California airplanes.

Now for a dirty dig at an old Kansas farmer by the name of Bill White. Do you honestly believe everything you read in the "tarnation" newspapers?

On receipt of this letter White wrote an editorial praising Roosevelt's stand against the transfer of the ships: " . . . . The American people will breathe a deep breath and then heave a sigh of rejoicing to know that President Roosevelt is frowning on the piratical act of changing flags on American ships. . . . . "

On November 14 White sent a letter to all of the members of the Non-partisan Committee for Peace through the Revision of the Neutrality Law, saying that the work of the Committee was at an end. In this letter he said: "The work of our Committee has seemed to me a constructive contribution to the cause of peace, ... a cause which will require the vigilant and continual efforts of its friends in the difficult days ahead."

Other members of the Committee, however, did not wish it

to be disbanded because they were convinced that grave questions would arise in the future requiring more congressional legislation to protect the peace, honor, and dignity of the United States. They convinced White of this, and he finally agreed to keep in touch with the members of the Committee so that he could call it into operation again if the occasion presented itself. For the time being, it was decided that the Committee should submerge and stay out of the public eye.

III

The Internationalists Organize

IT TOOK GERMANY JUST FOUR WEEKS TO CAPTURE POLAND. On October 6, 1939, Hitler celebrated this victory by announcing that, of course, Germany had no claims on France and England. "Why, therefore," he asked, "should there be war in the West?" Premier Daladier of France answered: "We have taken up arms against aggression. We shall not lay them down until we have certain guarantees of security, a security which will not be called into question every six months." Prime Minister Chamberlain, showing that he had at last learned something about Hitler, observed that "after our past experience, it is no longer possible to rely upon the unsupported word of the present German government." For the next six months there was little actual fighting.

In December, 1939, President Roosevelt sent Myron C. Taylor as his personal representative to the Vatican to merge parallel peace endeavors by the United States and the Vatican. A few weeks later, Summer Welles was sent to visit the belligerent powers and to report upon conditions in Europe. While the war was in its *sitzkrieg* stage and during the time when these diplomatic gestures were being made, the people who had conducted the Non-partisan Committee's campaign to revise the Neutrality Act were active in studying the problems of a lasting peace.

The Commission To Study the Organization of Peace was launched in December, 1939. The sponsoring organizations for this new commission were the American Association of University Women, the American Union for Concerted Peace Efforts, the Church Peace Union, the League of Nations Association, and the World Citizen's Association. The executive committee was composed of William Allen Neilson, chairman; Clark Eichelberger, director; and Lucius Eastman, Clyde Eagleton, Charles G. Fenwick, Roger S. Greene, Emily Hickman, and James T. Shotwell. Among its members were William Allen White, Frank Boudreau, Frank P. Graham, Thomas Lamont, Henry Atkinson, Esther C. Brunauer, Samuel Guy Inman, Quincy Wright, Max Lerner, Frederick McKee, Preston Slosson, Clarence Streit, and Charles P. Taft.

The Commission was planning to study such subjects as the world in which we live—including the social, economic, and cultural interdependence of people; the effects of war upon the world—upon both the belligerents and the neutrals; the aftermath of the war of 1914–18—investigating the peace treaties, the war debt, reparations, and the failure of disarmament; existing international organizations such as the League of Nations, the World Court, the International Labour Organization, and the Pan-American Union; and the world that we want, with a specific investigation of the problems of pacific settlement and social and economic justice.

William Allen White was especially concerned about the problem of a peaceful world after the present conflict. He felt that the Nazi idea of world domination by the "superior race" had set the clock of civilization back thousands of years. On December 14 he received a letter from President Roosevelt asking him to spend a night at the White House if he were to be in the East soon.

"I need a few helpful thoughts from the philosopher of Emporia," said the President. "Things move with such terrific speed, these days, that it really is essential to us to think in broader terms and, in effect, to warn the American people that they, too, should think of possible ultimate results in Europe and the Far East. . . . . Therefore, my sage old friend, my problem is to get the American people to think of conceivable consequences without scaring the American people into thinking that they are going to be dragged into this war."

White was quite flattered by President Roosevelt's solicitation of his advice, but he warned the President that he was not so wise as the President had been told. His feelings on the foreign situation were that he feared our involvement before the peace, "yet I fear to remain uninvolved, letting the danger of a peace of tyranny approach too near."

White also received a letter, filled with concern and anxiety over the world situation, from Robert E. Sherwood, the New York playwright who had served with the Canadian Army in the first World War. Sherwood felt that it was necessary for the United States to intervene in a military way to check aggression by the dictators. He concluded this letter, written December 11, 1939, by saying that he believed "it is readily within our power to save the human race from complete calamity, and that we should not hesitate any longer to assume our sacred responsibility." Sherwood's letter stirred White more than any letter that he had received in years. Several times he started to reply to it but was not satisfied with what he had written. White was in thorough agreement that the aggressor nations must be stopped for the sake of civilization. For years he had been worried by the growing menace of the dictators. Yet, as he put it, "old men have been leading boys to glory and death for thousands of years," and "old men who cannot fight shouldn't make wars."

The old man was baffled. He felt that he had no right to tell young men to go out and lose their lives, but, on the other hand, he knew he should not waste the knowledge of seventy-one years. As he wrote to Sherwood: "I have stood with you in spirit. Always I have been constrained by an old man's fear and doubt when it comes to lifting my voice for war." When he became chairman of the Committee To Defend America by Aiding the Allies, he did so in the hope that this might be a possible way to avert war for the United States, yet stop the dictators.

After Russia invaded Finland in November, 1939, White lent his support to the move to allow the United States to loan money to Finland. Although he felt strongly about aid to Finland, he refused to become co-chairman, with Major General John F. O'Ryan of New York City, of Fighting Funds for Finland. He took this stand only after consulting with some of his friends who had been in the neutrality campaign with him. He felt that if he joined this movement, isolationists would publicly discredit the neutrality fight and say that its leader was now trying to lead the United States into war, just as these isolationists had charged at the time of the embargo fight. White also felt that any such step on his part might impede the launching of another committee to aid the Allies in their war against Germany, in case such a committee became necessary. When Germany attacked Russia in June, 1941, White did not let his opposition in the Finnish affair prevent his urging the extension of Lend-Lease aid to Russia. He felt that Germany was the great menace to civilization and, as long as Russia was fighting Germany, the United States should be realistic enough to extend aid to Russia.

All during the winter of 1939, President Roosevelt's worry about the complacency of the American people toward the European war was shared by White. On January 15 Clark Eichelberger, on his way to Dallas, Texas, to deliver a speech, stopped off at Emporia and spent an afternoon discussing the state of the world with White. Both of them were agreed on the need of an organization to awaken the American people to the significance of the Nazi movement. Later they sounded out members of the administration and found approval for their idea. The Republican editor's relationship with the New Deal, always close, was even closer in these early days of 1940 because he frequently wrote editorials praising the Hull reciprocal trade treaties as a hope for future world peace. These treaties would check economic supernationalism and would be a step in establishing a world order based on economic freedom. Secretary of State Hull considered White's support a source of real gratification, and President Roosevelt wrote on January 23: "At this critical time in world affairs it is fine to know that there are strong voices like yours which are willing and ready, irrespective of any partisan consideration, to speak out courageously in defense of constructive and farsighted policies— policies that seek to build the future welfare of our country."

When Germany smashed into Norway and Denmark in early April, 1940, White went to New York with plans to go ahead and organize a committee with Eichelberger which would consolidate public opinion and show Congress that millions of Americans wanted to defend their country by keeping Great Britain armed while this country concentrated on its defense program.

"The ruthless invasion of the northern democratic countries and the obvious design to enslave them," wrote the Emporia editor in an unpublished manuscript, "gave the people of the United States a sickening sense of the reality of Hitler's purpose. By early spring, it was obvious that Holland was in danger and America began to see what kind of a war it was, the fanatical conquest of a pagan ideology which justified slavery, which exalted cruelty, which banished chivalry, scoffed at the equality of men, and was aimed straight at the dignity of the human spirit. It was then that the American people began to see, while it was not our war, it was our cause." Faced with this challenge to his democratic way of life, William Allen White needed no urging from anyone to organize a committee which would give the common man an opportunity to express his opposition to Hitler and his desire to aid Britain as our first line of defense.

The defeat of England's Army in Norway in April seemed to point conclusively to the need of American support in the Allied cause, but at no time was White a slavish admirer of England and the Tory aristocracy. He showed that when, in an editorial written in the middle of March, 1940, he said: "What an avalanche of blunders Great Britain has let loose upon the democracies of the world! The old British lion looks mangy, sore-eyed. He needs worming and should have a lot of dental work. He can't even roar. Unless a new government takes the helm in Britain, the British empire is done. These are sad words to say, but the truth is the truth." Regardless of the state to which the Tories had brought England, White's pragmatic feeling, in late April and early May, was that it was necessary to keep the British fleet afloat and to arm Great Britain, for behind the British fleet "we could have two years in which to prepare for the inevitable attack of the totalitarian powers upon our democracy, which must come unless Great Britain wins this war."

White and Eichelberger decided to use the same method of organizing their new committee as they had used in organizing the Non-partisan Committee for Peace through Revision

of the Neutrality Law. This was to gather together a list of influential people in all walks of life and write or wire them to
join the Committee. Eichelberger and White talked over their
plans with Hugh Moore and Frederick McKee, and these two
men agreed to stake the new Committee for a few weeks while
it was getting contributions through the John Price Jones
money-raising organization. From the men and women who
had supported the Non-partisan Committee, they selected
fifty names to serve as sponsors for this new committee.

With the support of these fifty people assured, the two men
began to write, wire, and telephone influential citizens whom
they wanted on the Committee. Not only did White and
Eichelberger want the support of college presidents, professors,
professional men, and prominent business figures, but they also wanted the active co-operation of labor leaders. At White's
suggestion, his partner talked with leaders of both the American Federation of Labor and the Congress of Industrial Organizations. When White was in Washington, April 18–20, he
himself conferred with William Green, president of the American Federation of Labor. Then White went back home for a
few days; but by the time he returned to New York City in
late April, the Committee had increased its membership to six
hundred names.

At first the two leaders did not name their new organization,
then, finally, White chose the name—the Committee To Defend America by Aiding the Allies—from among several suggested by Eichelberger. While White was in New York in late
April, Frederic Coudert held another luncheon in his honor at
the Down Town Association. Coudert had been asked to hold
this luncheon meeting because White wanted to discuss with
the group ways and means of keeping the Republican party
from adopting an isolationist attitude. Present at this luncheon
on April 29, in addition to White, were Dr. Henry Atkinson;

HITLER'S AMERICAN AMBITIONS

COMMITTEE TO DEFEND AMERICA

UNIFY OUR SPIRIT
SPEED OUR DEFENSES
AID THE ALLIES

UNIFY OUR SPIRIT ▬▬▬▬

SPEED OUR DEFENSES ▬▬▬▬

AID THE ALLIES ▬▬▬▬

COMMITTEE TO DEFEND AMERICA
45 DEVONSHIRE STREET
BOSTON, MASS.

KEEP THIS COPY MOVING! PASS IT ALONG! DON'T DESTROY IT!
Additional Copies $2.50 per hundred obtainable at Committee Headquarters.
Contributions — Any Amount Will Help To Carry On This Work.
Make checks payable to Allan Forbes, Treasurer

An early effort to unify the country against Hitler. These are the covers of a twelve-page leaflet

Dr. Frank Boudreau; Philip M. Brown, formerly professor of international law at Princeton University and on the board of editors of the *American Journal of International Law;* Nicholas Murray Butler; Frederic R. Coudert, Jr., New York Republican state senator; Clark Eichelberger; Victor Elting, retired lawyer and president of the English Speaking Union, New York City; Thomas Lamont; A. Warren Norton, of the Christian Science Publishing Society; Frank L. Polk, formerly undersecretary of state; James T. Shotwell; Alexander Williams; Colonel Henry Breckinridge; Colonel Henry L. Stimson; and Frederic Coudert, Sr. At this luncheon all agreed to try to do something to make sure that both parties would take a broad view of American interests and not adopt platforms which would prohibit aid to the Allies.

Colonel Stimson, particularly, was anxious that the Republican party should not follow an isolationist policy. White had served on three small platform subcommittees at previous Republican conventions, and he knew how platforms were made. He asked the assembled group to go to work to keep the Republican platform committee from making any definite declaration on foreign policy that would prevent the candidate in October from taking a stand on aiding the Allies. Many of these men had friends in high places in the Republican party, and they promised to work through them while White worked through Alf Landon. This group evidently succeeded in its purpose, and the plank on foreign affairs adopted by the Republican party in June did not tie the candidate's hands.

At this luncheon, the new White-Eichelberger committee was also discussed. Coudert declared, eight months later, that the luncheon group decided to maintain a permanent organization to educate the public on the need of aiding the Allies. White and Eichelberger, however, had decided this long before, and apparently all that the luncheon group did was to approve the idea.

Rush Holt and other isolationists were later to charge that these luncheons held by Coudert were made up of a sinister group "controlled by Wall Street" and that it was Wall Street that drafted White for the job. Father Coughlin's concept of the founding of the Committee, in *Social Justice* for June 24, 1940, was as follows:

"Like thieves who operate under the cover of night, there are in our midst those who operate beneath the cloak of protected auspices to steal our liberty, our peace and our autonomy. Frederic R. Coudert is one of these. 'The Committee to Defend America by Aiding the Allies' is a high-sounding name composed of high-handed gentlemen who are leaving no stone unturned to throw everything precious to an American to the dogs of war. Frederic R. Coudert organized this Committee. Sneakingly, subversively and un-Americanly hiding behind a sanctimonious stuffed shirt named William Allen White, these men form the most dangerous fifth column that ever set foot upon neutral soil. They are the Quislings of America. They are the Judas Iscariots within the apostolic college of our nation.

"They are the gold-protected, Government-protected, foreign-protected snakes in the grass who dare not stand upright and speak like men face to face. Eighteen prominent bankers met secretly on the 29th day of April in New York to set up this Committee. They were called together by Frederic R. Coudert, the legal adviser of the British Embassy and one who helped lead us into the last World War."

This, of course, was absurd. An examination of the people present at the October and April luncheons leads to the conclusion that Wall Street was almost without representation. A large majority of the people were professional men and businessmen who had long been interested in world peace, the League of Nations Association, and the Union for Concerted Peace Efforts. As White later wrote, Eichelberger and he, alone, figured out the Committee To Defend America by Aiding the Allies. The men in downtown New York did not even know it was being organized, as far as he knew, until he went to this luncheon and asked for their help in shutting off people like Hamilton Fish in the Republican platform committee.

Later on, after the Republican convention and just before the Democratic convention, White asked Coudert to gather this group together again to discuss what could be done to make sure that the Democratic platform called for aid to the Allies. According to a letter from White to Paul Hutchinson on November 7, 1940, "There was no secrecy about it. It was what any group of free born Americans had a legal right to do. This group has nothing to do with the policy of our committee. Only one of the group, as I recall it now, is on our policy committee."

When White returned home in early May, 1940, he warned his neighbors that as the war moved closer to the Atlantic highway, the United States lacked purpose and direction and was drifting into grave danger. When Germany invaded Holland and Belgium on May 10, he felt that the United States must give the Allies every possible ounce of economic strength. The next day he wrote in the *Gazette:* "If and when that hope fails, we must, despite our noble ideals of peace, fight gun with gun, force with force. This world cannot endure half slave and half free." It was a battle of ideology, not of empire. It was a clash of conflicting ideals of human life, based on malice and hate, versus a desire to establish decent relationships among men, based upon reason. The United States could not be neutral; it must give every possible aid other than war. White begged the country to unite behind President Roosevelt's foreign policy and national defense plans, with the people reserving the right to oppose the President only on internal affairs.

On May 10, when the tragic news of the German rush into the Low Countries reached New York, Eichelberger sent a three-page telegram to Emporia, suggesting an emergency statement to the country on the need of quick aid to the Allies. Later that day he called by long-distance telephone and talked the situation over. During the next few days White took some of these suggestions and incorporated them into a statement which he himself wrote. On May 17 this statement was sent to many of the country's leaders, asking permission to add their names to the small committee already organized. The organizers of the Committee To Defend America by Aiding the Allies realized that it would have to have more members and greater power to achieve its ends than the Non-partisan Committee for Peace through the Revision of the Neutrality Law had had. The emergency telegram that was sent out from Emporia—which for its complete sincerity and public spirit deserves to be quoted word for word—read as follows:

As one democracy after another crumbles under the mechanized columns of the dictators, it becomes evident that the future of western civilization is being decided upon the battlefield of Europe. Here is a life and death struggle for every principle we cherish in America, for freedom of speech, of religion, of the ballot and of every freedom that upholds the dignity of the human spirit.

Here all the rights that the common man has fought for during a thousand years are menaced.

Terrible as it may seem, the people of our country cannot avoid the consequences of Hitler's victory and of those who are or may be allied with him. It is childish to assume that so rich a prize as our beloved country could long remain immune. A totalitarian victory would wipe out hope for a just and lasting peace. The time has come when the United States should throw its material and moral weight on the side of the nations of western Europe great and small that are struggling in battle for a civilized way of life.

That struggle constitutes our first line of defense. It would be folly to hold this nation chained to a neutrality policy determined in the light of last year's facts. The new situation requires a new attitude. From this day on America must spend every ounce of energy to keep the war away from the Western Hemisphere by preparing to defend herself and by aiding with our supplies and wealth the nations now fighting to stem the tide of aggression.

This is no time for leaders to consider party or factional advantage. All men and all creeds and clans may well call upon our President to confer with leaders of all parties looking to a foreign policy providing for an increase in armaments to defend ourselves and for every economic effort to serve the Allies. In foreign affairs we must present an unbroken non-partisan front to the world.

It is for us to show the people of England, of France, of Belgium and Scandinavia that the richest country on earth is not too blind or too timid to help those who are fighting tyranny abroad. If they fail, we shall not have time to prepare to face the conquerors alone. Will you join with me and several hundred others in the formation of a committee which would carry these points of view to the American people?

In one hour alone telegrams of acceptance arrived from President Seymour of Yale University and President Conant of Harvard University; Robert Millikan of the California Institute of Technology; Catholic Bishop Lucey of Amarillo, Texas; Episcopal Bishop Sherrill of Boston; Alderman Paul Douglas, professor at the University of Chicago; Daniel Marsh, president of Boston University; Dwight Davis, former secretary of war; Robert Woods Bliss, former ambassador to France; Robert Lincoln O'Brien, federal tariff commissioner under Hoover; Thomas Lamont; Judge Samuel Seabury; Victor Elting; Ernest M. Hopkins, president of Dartmouth College; Bishop William T. Manning of New York City, on the theological right, and Reinhold Niebuhr, on the left; Edwin R. Embree of the Rosenwald Foundation of Chicago; and Thomas E. Burke, secretary-treasurer of the United Association of Plumbers and Steamfitters. Three days later the list had increased to many times this size.

On May 20 the story of the work of the past few days was

released to the country over the Associated Press teletype. The country was told of the number of telegrams that had been pouring into Emporia and the national headquarters of the Committee at 8 West Fortieth Street, New York City. As White said, "Public opinion as expressed by these telegrams from all parts of the country from people in all walks of life seems to be moving rapidly toward crystallizing every possible legal aid to the Allies."

With the formation of this large national committee, White, the chairman, and Eichelberger, the executive director, asked Hugh Moore to be chairman and Frederick McKee to be treasurer of its executive committee; and Thomas K. Finletter, Frank G. Boudreau, and Lewis W. Douglas, all of New York City, and Mrs. Emmons Blaine of Chicago, to compose the executive committee. White's job as national chairman was to form the policy of the Committee with the final "Yes" and "No" on all steps. Eichelberger, as executive director, was to take charge of the task of organization and personnel. As the Committee developed through the next few months, White and Eichelberger worked together very closely. According to the former, in the end he always accepted Eichelberger's judgment in organizational problems—and "he was equally generous in allowing me to take direction of the policies which we should espouse."

IV

"Stop Hitler Now!"

For days after the public announcement of the formation of the Committee To Defend America by Aiding the Allies, letters and telegrams poured into Emporia. White's old roll-top desk, already heavily laden with books and press clippings, creaked wearily under this additional burden. White himself kept three secretaries busy replying to all communications, whether friendly or hostile to the Committee's work; and it was months before his private secretary could catch up on her filing of this correspondence. Roughly nine out of ever ten letters and telegrams received were enthusiastic in their support of the Committee.

One of the most heartening letters came on May 26, 1940, from Felix Frankfurter, associate justice of the Supreme Court of the United States, saying: "Dear Bill White: The bench is partly prison; but not even the stuffiest notions of propriety preclude my expressing my gratitude to you for mobilizing our opinion so that our action may become effective in the challenge that mad brute force is hurling against the accumulated gains—oh! so painfully accumulated—of civilization."

There was no question but that support for the movement

was nation-wide. To all the people who asked what service they could perform, Mr. White suggested that they organize local committees, hold rallies, and urge people to write to their congressmen and the President, calling for all possible aid to the Allies short of war.

The national organization had to do very little proselyting to organize local chapters all over the country. Frequently the local League of Nations Association office served as a focal point for the formation of these chapters, as was the case in Chicago, for example. A few field workers were sent out; but on the whole the local chapters were formed spontaneously, expressing the deep desire of the American people for an Allied victory in the war—for example, Jerome Greben of the Off-set Gravure Corporation of New York City made and gave the Committee five thousand lapel buttons inscribed with "Defend America" on a red, white, and blue field. The local and national committees offered the average, isolated citizen a chance to make his private sentiment function as public opinion.

On the West Coast, William Allen White's friends, Chester Rowell of the *San Francisco Chronicle* and Guy Talbott, in-ternationally minded citizen, became the heads of a re-gional office. The office that was quickly set up in Boston in the last week of May, with former Governor Alvin T. Fuller as head and James Bryant Conant as honorary chairman, soon became the regional office for two hundred local New Eng-land chapters. In Kentucky, Barry Bingham, publisher of the *Louisville Courier-Journal*, and Mark Ethridge, general manager of the same paper, backed a state-wide organization.

During the month of April, while Clark Eichelberger and White were organizing the first committee, a meeting was held at the Town Hall Club in New York City to consider what could be done to help the French and the English. Members of this group—among whom were George Field, program director on station WEBD; Dr. Frank Kingdon, president of the University of Newark; Arthur J. Goldsmith, New York broker—naturally became the leaders of the New York City chapter.

This rapid expansion meant that by July 1 there were three hundred local chapters, representing every state in the Union except North Dakota. There were also chapters in Canada, the District of Columbia, and the Virgin Islands. Regional offices were established in Chicago, Chapel Hill, San Francisco, and Boston to correlate the work of the local chapters. In the first week of July, the Committee added another chapter—an "Americans in Britain" branch in London.

The local chapters were given a great deal of freedom by the national organization. As long as they adhered to the national policy, it was possible to carry it out as they pleased. In general, this resulted in the most efficient and valuable work by the local chapters, although several branches were later to cause the organization some difficulty and embarrassment. The national committee did not select the local officers, nor did it attempt to discipline the local groups. Each chapter became a center for distributing propaganda literature, holding public meetings, organizing debates between committee speakers and isolationists before clubs and professional groups, and sending letters to Congress asking for aid to the Allies.

White and the staff of the national organization reported that most of the good ideas for publicity and programs came from local committees. The Baltimore committee, for instance, prepared a popular pamphlet, *A Primer of National Defense*, which later became the subject of a movie short. The Boston committee organized a group to study means of revising the neutrality law and other legislation hampering aid to the Allies; while the local committees in cities like Chicago, Cleveland, and Louisville held great mass meetings attended by many thousands. In view of such energy the national organization felt that a great deal of local autonomy was fully justified. In most cases the local committees even raised their own funds.

Thus it may be said that the Committee To Defend America by Aiding the Allies would have been a paper organization without the local chapters. The workers in the local chapters rather than those at the national headquarters gave the Committee its strength and its influence. "It is a democratic process," wrote White, "furnishing a nucleus in each community to which like-minded people may turn for information, for a way to energize their will and so to implement their courage."

Professional groups organized their own branches within the Committee. Henry Steele Commager, professor of history at Columbia University, took the lead in organizing the historians' committee, which soon numbered among its membership Bernadotte E. Schmitt, University of Chicago; Albert Bushnell Hart, Harvard University, Winfred T. Root, University of Iowa; John D. Hicks, University of Wisconsin; Herbert I. Priestley, University of California; Andrew C. McLaughlin, University of Chicago; Allan Nevins, Columbia University; Carl Becker, Cornell University; Charles M. Andrews, Yale University; and E. C. Barker, University of Texas. Scientists likewise organized their committee; and artists, led by Harold Von Schmidt, Edwin Eberman, Fred Cooper, and McClelland Barclay, followed suit. The American Association of University Women, North Atlantic Section, gave its approval to the Committee's work.

One group whose support the Committee greatly desired was the youth of the nation. This was important, as part of the long-range program of establishing a strong sentiment for international co-operation in the United States after hostilities should cease. Again spontaneously, as in the case of many of the local chapters, youth groups organized to support the movement to aid the Allies. On May 24, the Aid the Allies Club of the University of Chicago, led by Hart Perry, Adele Rose, and Robert Merriam, sent this letter to William Allen White:

"About two months ago a group of us on the campus of the University of Chicago cognizant of the necessity of an Allied victory in Europe banded together informally into an 'Aid the Allies' club. The movement, originally a conception in the minds of several of us, has now been enlarged through informal conversation and persuasion to include a sizeable number. . . . . In this hour of crisis for world civilization we must all work to the utmost in the furtherance of the cause of right as opposed to might. The necessity of arousing student interest in this situation appears to be of special importance at this time because it is upon the college graduates of today that we must depend for leadership in the future. We aim to do all we can to awaken fellow-students to the overwhelming need for intelligent 'worldly' thinking at this time and to combat the present tendency toward utter moral irresponsibility as far as the rest of the world is concerned. . . . . "

White and Eichelberger welcomed the support of this youth group, and it received encouragement and literature from the national headquarters. The Chicago chapter, then being organized under Lucy McCoy, was requested to co-operate with the campus committee. And on June 6, without suggestion from the Chicago committee or the national committee, the student Aid the Allies Club held a rally attended by twelve hundred enthusiastic students.

Similar groups were organized on other campuses. During the last week in May, when the Germans were destroying French resistance, petitions were signed by Johns Hopkins

University students calling for more aid to the Allies. The New York chapter of the Committee (which should not be confused with the national committee, also located in New York City) formed its own youth division to carry on work in that city among young people. By the middle of June the Youth Division of the national organization was well organized and making great strides. The national organization suggested that all local chapters either form separate youth committees or have youth representation on their executive committee.

Many people, in offering their support to the Committee To Defend America by Aiding the Allies, also sent financial contributions to assist in carrying on the Committee's work. The money was used for organizing purposes—clerical work, expenses of field workers, and rent for office space; sending out literature; making and distributing radio transcriptions; organizing mass meetings; and printing petitions to be sent to Congress and the White House.

On June 7, Chairman White sent a letter to all members of the Committee asking for contributions. Also over White's signature, a letter was sent to a selected group of New York businessmen who might help in raising funds. These businessmen were asked to write to their business or professional friends on behalf of the Committee. White permitted this letter to be sent with the restriction that it go to no men "whose names you cannot proudly file with any critical investigating Committee."

The money that came in during the first thirty days averaged $23 a person. J. P. Morgan, Wall Street banker, sent a check for $500, as did David Dubinsky, president of the International Ladies Garment Workers Union. The gifts came from all parts of the country, representing the national dis-

tribution of the members. In June, the average total was perhaps $500 a day.

White was always cautious with donations made to the
Committee. He wanted no doubt to exist that the money was
used for the purpose for which it was solicited, because he realized that the Committee must never give even the appear-
ance of evil in such matters. Eichelberger was asked "to watch
this whole section of our activities with scrupulous attention."
Finally, at the end of July, White requested that his name not
be used on any more fund-raising letters, though it continued
to serve as the Committee's trade-mark except for financial
purposes.

As the Committee grew in importance, it needed more
specific goals than the vague phrase "aid to the Allies." Not
until it had something more substantial could it start a real
letter-writing campaign aimed at Congress. On May 25, therefore, White called the President. Six days later he wrote to
Justice Frankfurter that he had told Mr. Roosevelt that he was
all dressed up and had no place to go, and "would he please
send me a road map or something. I suggested trading back a
lot of army planes to the manufacturers and taking a due bill
for other planes from the manufacturers so that the manufacturers could sell these planes more quickly to the Allies. I also
suggested that so long as we had appropriated twenty million
dollars in 1918 and '19 to feed German babies it would be a
good idea to appropriate a hundred million to feed the French
and Belgian refugees now on the highways in northern France.

"I couldn't see his face and I don't know how he took it but
these are two objectives which might be realized by congressional acts if necessary or maybe the plane swapping deal
could be worked out with an executive order or a nod of the
head. . . . . "

The first policy statement of the Committee included these two points and a third calling for the United States to organize a defense scheme in co-operation with the Allied powers that owned islands in the Caribbean. The Committee wanted the United States to become a nonbelligerent ally of France and England, but White was afraid that it might be too late for the United States to be of much assistance. By late May, the Germans had cut the Allied armies in Flanders off from direct contact with France, and the English were in retreat toward Dunkirk.

White was aghast at the possible consequences to the United States if the English should be defeated and either scuttle their ships or turn them over to Germany. In an attempt to prevent the collapse of England and France, he wired the *Christian Science Monitor* that the Committee felt that the release of five hundred planes at once might possibly turn the tide. This act would not get us into war, and there was no question of credit involved, since France and England could pay for them. The United States government could trade planes to private manufacturers, who would sell them to the Allies. In return, the manufacturers would promise the government new planes to replace them. The United States would gain because these old planes, which might turn defeat into victory in Europe, would be obsolete before we ourselves could use them.

From his Emporia newspaper office William Allen White guided the policy of the Committee To Defend America by Aiding the Allies from May 20 to the middle of June. No statement was released by the national headquarters which he had not either written or read for approval. No day passed in these hectic weeks without long-distance telephone calls and lengthy telegrams between White and Eichelberger over the daily problems of the Committee. White's revisions of policy statements proposed by the national headquarters were frequent, and it is safe to say that he was the principal force in deciding the policy of this committee.

On May 27, the New York City chapter held its first big meeting. White wired that "America's supreme duty in this hour is to send every aid we can of credit and munitions, to those who are defending our liberty, who are holding the fort for our civilization and battling for our essential Christian philosophy." The New York chapter decided to send out petitions seeking a million names to send to President Roosevelt and Congress calling for immediate aid. Two days later, the Committee put James B. Conant on a national radio hookup, calling for support of the Allied cause. Local radio stations all over the country carried talks by various other members of the Committee. On June 1 the *Nation* commented: "The belief that sheer self-interest should persuade this country to help the Allies in every way possible 'short of war' is beginning to spread. . . . . "

Washington began to feel the impulse of the Committee's work, as letters, telegrams, and petitions arrived. On June 3 White was, as he told Conant, "semiofficially assured that two hundred planes left Newfoundland Saturday to fly to Allies. More soon." As further encouragement toward the release of planes to the Allies, White sent a telegram on June 4 to committee chapters all over the country, asking each of their members personally to wire President Roosevelt suggesting that "planes that can be spared go quickly to Allies whose need for planes is desperate."

On that same day Mrs. Dwight Morrow spoke for the Committee over the National Broadcasting system on the subject "Does America Deserve a Miracle?" Her call for aid to the Allies was an effective answer to her son-in-law, Charles Lindbergh, who was urging the nation to follow an isolationist policy. After Mrs. Morrow's speech, which the *Emporia*

Gazette carried under the heading "Listen to Mamma," fifteen thousand telegrams favoring the release of planes were deposited on President Roosevelt's desk. Two days later came the news that the government, through the manufacturers, was releasing fifty bombers for the Allies.

Mr. White at once wired Secretary of War Woodring: "I was delighted this morning to see the news that fifty bombers had started. You have the country behind you in this position and I want to thank you personally as a citizen for what you have done. I know you are hedged about. I know the home defense needs. But you have found a good and safe way to do the job. Congratulations. "

The epoch-making events in Europe were now definitely shaping America's attitude toward the war. The people began to realize that the Western Hemisphere was in deadly peril because of the German successes in France and the Low Countries. Although Charles A. Lindbergh, in a radio talk on May 19, charged the Roosevelt Administration with inspiring a "hysterical chatter of calamity and invasion," the public generally knew better. Though they were not yet willing to go to war, they did favor more effective defense measures and material aid to the Allies. Shortly after the President's request to Congress on May 16 for increased appropriations to arm the United States, Congress voted approximately two billion dollars for the Army and a billion and a half for the Navy. Before the close of 1940 the President's requests for defense, which Congress quickly granted, had exceeded ten billion dollars.

German panzer divisions cut through the French line near Sedan on May 15. In a cataclysmic week German forces reached the English Channel. British and French forces in Flanders were cut off from France. On May 28, King Leopold of Belgium surrendered. In the next few days 335,000 trapped English and French troops were evacuated from the port of Dunkirk. On June 5 the Battle of France began, and June 14 saw Paris surrender; eight days later France signed an armistice with Nazi Germany. The day after the Nazis crossed the Seine—June 10—Mussolini declared war "against the plutocratic and reactionary democracies who have always blocked the march, and frequently plotted against the existence, of the Italian people."

On that day the chairman of the Committee To Defend America by Aiding the Allies wired President Roosevelt: "My correspondence is heaping up unanimously behind the plan to aid the Allies by anything other than war. As an old friend, let me warn you that maybe you will not be able to lead the American people unless you catch up with them. They are going fast. But only you can and must keep them out of war by giving them some other economic equivalent in aiding the democracies. . . . . " President Roosevelt answered White's warning that he was falling behind the people in a commencement speech that day at the University of Virginia in which he clearly stood for the United States' extending its material resources to the nations that were fighting the Axis forces. The President said:

"Perception of danger, danger to our institutions, may come slowly or it may come with a rush and a shock as it has to the people of the United States in the past few months. . . . .

"Some indeed still hold to the now somewhat obvious delusion that we of the United States can safely permit the United States to become a lone island, a lone island in a world dominated by the philosophy of force. Such an island may be the dream of those who still talk and vote as isolationists. Such an island represents to me and to the overwhelming majority of Americans today a helpless nightmare, the helpless nightmare of a people without freedom; yes, the nightmare of a people lodged in prison, handcuffed, hungry, and fed through the bars from day to day by the contemptuous, unpitying masters of other continents. . . . .

"Let us not hesitate—all of us—to proclaim certain truths. Overwhelmingly we, as a nation,—and this applies to all the other American nations—are convinced that military and naval victory for the gods of force and hate would endanger the institutions of democracy in the Western world, and that equally, therefore, the whole of our sympathy lies with those nations that are giving their life blood in combat against these forces. . . . .

"In our, [*sic*] in our unity, in our American unity, we will pursue two obvious and simultaneous courses; we will extend to the opponents of force the material resources of this nation and, at the same time, we will harness and speed up the use of those resources in order that we ourselves in the Americas may have equipment and training equal to the task of any emergency and every defense. . . . . "

The French premier, Paul Reynaud, appealed to President Roosevelt for increased aid on June 10. Four days later—the day on which German troops entered Paris—Reynaud advised President Roosevelt that the only way to save France was to throw into the balance "this very day the weight of American power." The President replied that the United States was redoubling its aid, but that only Congress could make military commitments. Actually, by this time the military situation in France was beyond saving by any American action. Following the French surrender to the Axis, the American government informed France, Germany, Great Britain, and the Netherlands that the United States would not acquiesce in the transfer of any region in the Western Hemisphere from one non-American power to another non-American power.

During the early part of the second week in June, when France was tottering, the Committee To Defend America by Aiding the Allies was attempting to restate its policy in clear terms for the public. Wires passed back and forth between Emporia and New York, and the program formulated by the national headquarters was: "First, amendment of the policy of neutrality and the substitution of one of non-belligerency. Second, the manufacture of planes and war materials at top speed by the intervention and credit aid of the government of the United States and the sale of such supplies to the British and French, giving them priority. And, third, the repeal of the Johnson Act and the Neutrality Act." White fully approved of all but the last sentence. He felt that the Committee was moving too fast in asking for repeal of the Johnson Act and the Neutrality Act. When he read over the Associated Press teletype that President Roosevelt was going to adhere to the cash-and-carry program, he wired Eichelberger that the phrase about the repeal of these acts must be eliminated from the Committee's program: "It will be a mistake and a terrible one to get out ahead of the White House and the main body of troops." In this move White was following a lifelong policy of never being too far in advance of public opinion. Eichelberger concurred, and the phrase was eliminated.

The following day Eichelberger sent a memorandum to White and the executive committee, surveying what they had accomplished and suggesting future policy. He pointed out that the Committee had broadened its request for material aid to the Allies when it learned that the American government had enough rifles, 75-millimeter guns, and other equipment to re-equip the British Expeditionary Force rescued at

Dunkirk; and also that the Committee's experts had drafted a bill providing for food and supplies to be sent to refugees in France. This bill had the approval of the majority leaders of the House and Senate and the President and seemed likely to pass. He then informed his colleagues that the English wished to buy some reconditioned destroyers from the United States, and the Committee would need to prepare the public to support the idea; that the Committee should urge an expansion of American industrial production in war materials; and that, above all, if Germany was able to conquer the Continent, the Committee must prepare public opinion to reject isolationist opinion that we should accept the situation and return to business as usual with Germany.

To meet the cry of the isolationist group, Robert Sherwood prepared a full-page advertisement entitled "Stop Hitler Now," which he had inserted in the New York, Chicago, Los Angeles, Dallas, Des Moines, and Portland, Oregon, newspapers on June 10 and 11. The advertisement called for help now, before it was forever too late, to the nations fighting the dictators. It urged people to write to Washington telling the President, senators, and congressmen that the way to defend America was to aid the Allies now. It warned the American people that a Europe dominated by Hitler was a threat to American democracy, because the Western Hemisphere was the richest territory for exploitation on earth today. And the international gangsters wanted the Western World. Sherwood wrote: "Will the Nazis considerately wait until we are ready to fight them? Anyone who argues that they will wait is either an imbecile or a traitor."

Among the people who helped Sherwood finance this plea were Dorothy Backer, George S. Backer, F. D. Cheney, C. J. Churchill, Mrs. H. P. Davidson, George S. Kaufman, Henry R. Luce, Dwight D. Wiman, and C. V. Whitney. When Sher-

STOP HITLER NOW!

WE AMERICANS have naturally wished to keep out of this war —to take no steps which might lead us in. But—

We now know that every step the French and British fall back brings war and world revolution closer to US—our country, our institutions, our homes, our hopes for peace.

Hitler is striking with all the terrible force at his command. His is a desperate gamble, and the stakes are nothing less than domination of the whole human race.

If Hitler wins in Europe—if the strength of the British and French armies and navies is forever broken—the United States will find itself alone in a barbaric world—a world ruled by Nazis with "spheres of influence" assigned to their totalitarian allies. However different the dictatorships may be, racially, they all agree on one primary objective. "Democracy must be wiped from the face of the earth."

The world will be placed on a permanent war footing. Our country will have to pile armaments upon armaments to maintain even the illusion of security. We shall have no other business, no other aim in life, but primitive self-defense. We shall exist only under martial law—or the law of the jungle. Our economic structure will have to be adjusted to that of our gangster competitors. We shall have to change ourselves from easy-going individuals into a "dynamic race."

"Government of the people, by the people, for the people"—if Hitler wins, this will be the discarded ideal of a decayed civilization.

Is this "Alarmism"? Then so is the challenging scream of an air-raid siren, warning civilians that death is coming from the skies. We have ample cause for deepest alarm. It should impel us, not to hysteria, but to resolute action.

It is obvious that there is no immediate danger of direct invasion of the United States. Hitler doesn't strike directly when he doesn't have to. He edges up on his major victims, approaching through the territory of small and defenseless neighbors.

We have twenty-one neighbors in this hemisphere in addition to the colonial possessions of Britain, France, Holland and Denmark. We must not forget that however wide the Atlantic and Pacific oceans may be, the Canadian and Mexican borders are no barriers to invasion.

The Monroe Doctrine is not an automatic safety catch, securing the entrance to our hemisphere from all intruders. We have to enforce it—all the way from Greenland and Alaska to Cape Horn. Furthermore, we have to guard night and day against the manifold menaces from within. We can not ignore the fact that Trojan horses are grazing in all the fertile fields of North and South America.

The Western Hemisphere contains the richest territory for exploitation on earth to-day. And the international gangsters want it. They have already started the process of taking it. For many years the agents of the Nazis have been effectively at work in

THE FIFTH COLUMN

is led in this as in other countries by Nazis and Communists and their fellow travellers who are well trained in the dissemination of poisonous propaganda. Their object is to destroy national unity, to keep the United States in a state of confusion over all world issues so that we will be weak and helpless when our time comes. All Americans should beware the prevailing Nazi-Communist propaganda which attempts to capitalize our desire for peace by opposing all our moves toward national defense—sabotaging all aid to the Allies—preaching that Hitler has already won and we must meekly appease him.

Latin America, gaining ground by persuasion, bribery, intimidation. They have been fighting a trade war and a political war and what we have lately seen in Norway and Holland and Belgium proves to us that these agents are ready to fight a military war when the orders come through from home.

"Divide—and conquer!" has been the Nazi watchword in the insidious invasion of all countries. The preliminary work of division has been carried on here with devastating success.

We can and should and will devote ourselves to a vast program of defense. But we must not try to fool ourselves into thinking that security can be bought. It will be achieved only by unity of purpose among ourselves, by the spirit of sacrifice that we can summon from our own hearts and minds. Overwhelming destiny will not be stopped "with the help of God and a few Marines."

This is a job for *all of us!* It will take years for us to build the necessary machines and to train the men who will run them. Will the Nazis considerately wait until we are ready to fight them?

Anyone who argues that they will wait is either an imbecile or a traitor.

How long shall we wait before making it known to Hitler and the masters of all the slave states that we are vitally concerned in the outcome of this war—that we would consider a victory for them an unmitigated calamity for civilization?

Whatever our feelings about the tragic mistakes of statesmanship in England and France we know now that the free people of those nations are willing to fight with inspiring heroism to defend their freedom. We know now that such men will die rather than surrender. But the stoutest hearts can not survive forever in the face of superior numbers and infinitely superior weapons.

There is nothing shameful in our desire to stay out of war, to save our youth from the diver bombers and the flame throwing tanks in the unutterable hell of modern warfare.

But is there not an evidence of suicidal insanity in our failure to help those who now stand between us and the creators of this hell?

WE CAN HELP—IF WE WILL ACT NOW

—before it is forever too late.

We can help by sending planes, guns, munitions, food. We can help to end the fear that American boys will fight and die in another Flanders, closer to home.

The members of our government are your servants. In an emergency as serious as this, they require the expression of your will. They must know that the American people are not afraid to cast off the hypocritical mask of neutrality, which deceives no one, including ourselves.

Send a postcard, a letter, or a telegram, at once—to the President of the United States, to your Senators and to your Congressmen—urging that the real defense of our country must begin NOW—with aid to the Allies!

The United States of America is still the most powerful nation on earth—and the United States of America is YOU!

COMMITTEE TO DEFEND AMERICA BY AIDING THE ALLIES

(Composed of representative Americans from all sections. Sub-committees are already in existence in eighty-five cities and towns.)

National Chairman—WILLIAM ALLEN WHITE, Editor, The Emporia (Kansas) Gazette

NEW YORK OFFICE: 8 WEST 40TH STREET

THIS ADVERTISEMENT appearing in newspapers from coast to coast has been paid for, with funds contributed by a number of patriotic American citizens who believe in all sincereness and sincerity that the safety of our country, the whole future of our national faith, is gravely threatened by the world revolution of Hitlerism. The names and addresses of all those who contributed to the publication of this advertisement are being filed with the State Department, Washington, D C

IN A DICTATORSHIP, THE GOVERNMENT TELLS THE PEOPLE WHAT TO DO. BUT—THIS IS A DEMOCRACY— WE CAN TELL THE GOVERNMENT WHAT TO DO. EXERCISE YOUR RIGHT AS A FREE CITIZEN. TELL YOUR PRESIDENT—YOUR SENATORS—YOUR CONGRESSMEN—THAT YOU WANT THEM TO HELP THE ALLIES TO STOP HITLER NOW!

Courtesy of the "Chicago Daily News"

Robert Sherwood's famous advertisement

wood copyrighted the advertisement with the Library of Congress, he filed a list of the contributors with the library and the State Department to show that there was no foreign money involved. Some local chapters of the Committee paid for the advertisement's insertion in their home-town papers, and some newspapers gave it free space. A total of $25,000 was paid to newspapers carrying this advertisement, representing total circulations of 8,300,000.

At his press conference on June 11, President Roosevelt had a copy of the Sherwood advertisement on his desk. He indorsed it, saying that it was "a great piece of work." However, it stirred the wrath of people opposed to aid to the Allies. Letters poured into White's office at the *Emporia Gazette*, accusing Sherwood of warmongering and worse. Oswald Garrison Villard, for many years editor of the *Nation*, wrote in protest against the phrase, "Anyone who argues that they [the Nazis] will wait is either an imbecile or a traitor." He pointed out that millions like himself might be wrong in feeling that there was no danger to the United States from Hitler, but we are "just as loyal, just as sincere, and just as earnest Americans as Sherwood or anybody else."

Villard's letter carried great weight with White, and the next morning he replied that he was to blame for the objectionable phrase in the advertisement. He explained that he had not read the copy as carefully as he should have, and "there," he wrote Villard, "my foot slipped." But he warned Villard that he approved of all the advertisement but that one phrase.

On the same morning White wrote to Robert Sherwood, telling of the many unfavorable letters received and commenting, "You are bringing my gray hairs in sorrow to the grave." The unfavorable letters did not mean that the people had turned against aid to the Allies, but that the phrase had not been a diplomatic way to refer to the opponents of the Committee. If the advertisement was to appear again, White asked that another phrase be used.

Sherwood was shocked when he heard of the violent opposition to that part of his plea. He said in a letter to White on June 17 that he had not meant the phrase to apply to those who honestly held the isolationist view, it was "intended to apply to those who give solemn assurance (specifically Lindbergh) that Hitler is not going to attack the Western Hemisphere." If its meaning was not clear, he admitted, it was bad composition, and the phrase would be omitted in any future use of the advertisement.

When France sued for peace on June 17, the Committee redoubled its efforts to aid England, the last of the Allied powers still actively fighting the Nazi menace. To the heads of all local chapters, White sent this telegram:

"We need more energy and wisdom than ever in this fight to defend America by aiding the Allies. Defeatism of any kind is the first menace. It is a menace to democracy on this continent. We stand firm; we shall fight on for democratic liberties and to prevent war from coming to America. Please pass the word to your friends and be of good cheer. Democracy still is militant."

The fall of France caused the Committee to grow in strength and numbers. England now was left, a tragic figure in the world.

"Never before," wrote White, "has a nation been so beautifully dramatized as Great Britain was dramatized fighting alone. . . . . The wave of sympathy for Great Britain that washed across this country found our committee ready to energize its tide."

With the collapse of France many people implored White to change the name of the Committee. He and the other members of the executive committee refused and refused again after England was left alone in the battle. They felt that France, Holland, Belgium, and Scandinavia were still our allies, "that wherever men were fighting for national freedom and for the ideals of self-respect that are the care of democracy, there Great Britain had allies, there was our cause, our American cause." To his neighbors White pointed out that if Hitler got the French fleet it might bring war to our shores. In spite of what Colonel Lindbergh was telling the country, it was our war.

While the situation seemed desperate for England in late June, the White committee strengthened its efforts to aid her in resisting a Nazi invasion. That aid was more airplanes, arms, ammunition, ships. The President had just released to the manufacturers for sale to Great Britain twenty torpedo boats and submarine chasers soon to be completed. The Committee called on its members to assure the President that they supported him in this and in the transfer of some of the over-age destroyers and also to make it clear to Congress that they did not want such steps hamstrung by legislation. White and his executive committee were not sure that such aid would reach England in time, but they refused to accept the defeatist position and do nothing. If the worst happened, the White committee hoped that by getting some aid to England, enough good will would have been created between England and the United States to prevent England from scuttling her fleet or turning it over to the Nazis. White himself felt that England would not fall if aid from the United States could get there in time. But if Germany should get the British and French fleets, Hitler would soon be heading this way. To all national members and to the chairmen of local chapters the accompanying table was sent for circulation.

On June 21, White left Emporia for the East to visit President Roosevelt, report the Republican National Convention for the North American Newspaper Alliance, and work at the national headquarters of the Committee. The day before he started, President Roosevelt had created a coalition cabinet by appointing, as secretary of war, Henry L. Stimson (Hoover's secretary of state and Taft's secretary of war) and, as secretary of the navy, Colonel Frank Knox, Republican vice-presidential nominee in 1936.

IF HITLER GETS THE BRITISH AND FRENCH FLEETS

IF ENGLAND IS INVADED AND HITLER GETS THE BRITISH AND FRENCH FLEETS, THE TOTALITARIAN POWERS WILL HAVE COMBINED NAVIES MORE THAN THREE TIMES THE SIZE OF THE AMERICAN FLEET

Type	PRESENT WORLD NAVAL STRENGTH					
	Axis	British and French	Total	Japan	Grand Total	U.S.
Battleships........	12	21	33	10	43	15
Cruisers..........	28	76	104	39	143	35
Aircraft carriers...	0	9	9	11	20	5
Destroyers	175	239	414	119	533	129
Submarines.......	181	131	312	62	374	95

Ever since the outbreak of the European war White had wanted Roosevelt to take this step, but some other Republicans were not favorable to a coalition cabinet. John Hamilton, chairman of the Republican National Committee, read Stimson and Knox out of the Republican party. Some Republican senators on the naval and military committees of the Senate were vocal in their opposition to the appointments. In Washington, on Saturday, June 22, President Roosevelt told White that Stimson and Knox were in grave danger of not being approved by the Senate and asked him to help to change this situation.

White agreed to support this move, which he considered to be in the best interests of the nation, so the President sent him to Senator James Byrnes of South Carolina. Senator Byrnes told what he knew of the attitude of various members of the Senate; White took the names of the doubtful members and sent telegrams to influential constituents of these senators, asking that pressure be brought to bear for the approval of Stimson and Knox. On Sunday, June 23, telegrams began to arrive in Washington, and by Tuesday there was no doubt that Knox and Stimson would be confirmed.

In a letter on July 5 to Charles P. Taft about this and about the general propaganda work of his Committee, White said: "I feel like Father Coughlin or Frankenstein, and I am duly and properly scared, humble and a bit ashamed that one man should have such power!"

On Saturday morning, June 29, White conferred with President Roosevelt about the work of the Committee. At this meeting the President talked to White about trading destroyers to England for naval bases in the British possessions of the Western Hemisphere. This was the President's idea, not White's.

The relationship of President Roosevelt and the Committee To Defend America by Aiding the Allies was an important and close one. White has described it in these words: "My relationship to President Roosevelt has been more of a morganatic relationship. I knew I had his private support. . . . . I never did anything the President didn't ask for, and I always conferred with him on our program."

The approval of President Roosevelt was vital to the Committee, White added, for "he never failed us. We could go to him—any members of our executive committee, any member of our policy committee. He was frank, cordial, and wise in his counsel. We supported him in his foreign policy, many of us who voted against him in the election. . . . . He was broad-gauged, absolutely unpartisan, a patriot in this matter if ever there was one." Furthermore, as White has pointed out, none of the Committee's objectives was attained which did not have the approval of the departments of state, navy, and war. "Which," as he wrote, "is not bragging. The law requires it."

White also conferred with Lord Lothian, the British ambassador to the United States, regarding England's needs in the war. This had no particular significance. Anybody who was not suspected of being a German agent could go to the British Embassy and find out what the British considered their needs of the moment. The official British position was that Britain was glad to receive any aid that this country might decide to give.

At the White House meeting the President also brought up the matter of conscripting men for the Army. White was not wholly in favor of it. The National Committee To Defend America by Aiding the Allies never took a definite stand on conscription, although the Boston chapter advocated the passage of such a bill. On July 31, 1940, White wrote Eichelberger that he hoped that the Boston committee would cease to advocate the Selective Service Bill. Actually, the need for such an act (which was finally passed by Congress and signed by the President on September 16) was extremely great. America's professional volunteer army was far too small for adequate defense even within the United States proper. White, in his opposition to conscription, was displaying a lack of foresight akin to that of the opponents of aid to the Allies.

In July the Committee To Defend America by Aiding the Allies formulated four major objectives. The first was to secure all moral and material aid which might legally be given to maintain England as the United States' first line of defense—

planes, guns, ships, food supplies, removal of difficulties prohibiting Americans from volunteering in the Allied armies,
and assistance in bringing mothers, children, and old people
from the British Isles to the Western Hemisphere; second, to
stimulate the expansion of industry and the building-up of our
national defense; third, to defend the Bill of Rights and civil
liberties (although the Committee favored action against
fifth columnists under the law); and, last, education for the
preservation of liberty—people must be made to realize that
sacrifice is sometimes necessary in order to retain liberty, and
appeasement and defeatism must be exposed at every turn.
This restatement of policy omitted the phrase "aid to refugees
in France," which had appeared in the early pronouncements
of the Committee. After the fall of France, efforts to aid
French refugees would only have played into Hitler's hands.
The feeding of Europe was no longer a measure of humanity
but one of military strategy in which we could not interfere.

White received assistance in formulating this policy from
his executive committee. Frequently he sought advice from
people all over the country and from the heads of the local
chapters. He also received a great deal of unsolicited advice,
some of which was valuable and some impracticable. To men-
tion only a few of the suggestions, a number of people wanted
the Committee to advocate the Clarence Streit plan of "Union Now" with the European democracies; others wanted a
declaration in favor of war.

Now, feeling the need of counsel on policy from influential
and devoted citizens throughout the country, White sent the
following telegram on July 6 to a select group of people:

"The Committee To Defend America by Aiding the Allies
has grown so large and its potentialities for influence weigh
heavily upon me—so heavily that I feel the need of the advice
of citizens from all over the country. The problems of public

policy are too grave for one man and a small executive committee to face and to solve with the intelligence that is necessary. The times are too terrible. So, as you will imagine, I am asking you to serve on that policy committee. Matters of public policy—major aims and temporary objectives—I hope may be submitted to that committee for quick consultative advice."

This telegram received almost universal approval from the people who received it, and the Policy Committee was formed with twenty-eight members, among them well-known scholars, lawyers, and businessmen and women from all over the country. White planned to have this Policy Committee meet regularly once a month and as many times as was necessary in between regular meetings.

By the first of July, the Committee To Defend America by Aiding the Allies could look with satisfaction upon the work that it had already accomplished. *Fortune*'s poll in its July issue indicated that 67.5 per cent of the people of the United States favored aid to the Allies; a poll taken by Market Analysts, Incorporated, of the delegates to the Republican convention showed that 60.6 per cent were for extensive aid, short of war. Some of the credit for this trend in public opinion undoubtedly belonged to the Committee and to the work of its local chapters. Petitions with approximately two million signatures had been sent to the White House, plus thousands of telegrams, postcards, and letters to senators and representatives. Nation-wide radio broadcasts, the "Stop Hitler" advertisement, and local rallies had gone far to crystallize the public conviction that halting Hitler at the English Channel was "just plain, ordinary common sense," as one of the Committee's bulletins put it.

An important way in which the White Committee brought

its message to the people was through the prominent figures in our Army and Navy who advocated the cause. Rear Admiral Harry Yarnell, Retired, addressed a great rally at Faneuil Hall, Boston, on June 28. At this same rally the following telegram from General John J. Pershing was read:

The time has come for all Americans to lay aside partisanship and work together to build up the defenses of their country and the defenses of our democracy against the greatest peril with which America has ever been faced.

We need material equipment of every kind for our Army and Navy at the earliest possible moment. Our only chance of security lies in the wholehearted and energetic co-operation of all who can contribute in any way to the arming of democracy.

Without such team-play and readiness to make sacrifices we cannot hope to get what we need when we need it and cannot use it effectively when we get it.

So long as Britain stands the danger may be kept at a distance. Therefore, while organizing and equipping ourselves it is sound sense to do all that we can to keep Britain supplied with the food, arms and munitions of which she must have a continuous supply if that outer bulwark of democracy is not to crumble. If we do that the last sacrifices may not be demanded of us.

British manpower is far from exhausted, but there is desperate need for the products of our farms and factories.

Earnestly hope that you may be successful in awakening our people to the real situation, for I am sure they will then play their part worthily, as they have always done throughout our history.

There is no time to lose.

In late June, the Macmillan Company, publishers, in co-operation with the Committee, published *Defense for America*, a book in which the arguments for aid to the Allies were presented in clear and forceful articles by men in the academic, religious, newspaper, and business worlds. Among the contributors were Quincy Wright, Henry Sloan Coffin, James B. Conant, Monsignor John A. Ryan, Chester Rowell, Lewis Douglas, Rabbi Stephen Wise, and Rupert Hughes. In general they all put forward the principle that Europe's war would be ours unless we gave the maximum aid and did it soon. The problem was approached from many angles, and the viewpoints presented ranged from the moral to the purely pragmatic, from historical to economic, from personal to international.

This book was distributed far and wide. Senators, congressmen, teachers, governors, lawyers, clergymen, and prominent businessmen received free copies. When they had read it, they were asked to pass it along to someone else. Stanley Walker, in the *New York Herald Tribune Books* on July 7, 1940, said of this volume: "What they have said should be read and pondered by all thoughtful citizens, and every man in public life, particularly between now and next November, should be ashamed to open his mouth until he has digested the arguments set forth here. For here, written by a group with clear minds and unquestioned patriotism, is a distillation of the answers to the question of just where the United States stands in the world of today. . . . . This little book may be potential dynamite—and that, too, may be a good thing. Certainly it is a tremendous jolt to smugness, complacency and softness." Most of the book's other reviews echoed Walker's sentiments.

By the time that *Defense for America* was published, the White Committee had grown to be a powerful organ for arousing public opinion. With the fall of France and the approaching Battle of Britain, the Committee's efforts against the isolationists were redoubled. Its members realized that the coming struggle in the British Channel and in the air over England might well decide the fate of democracy in the world.

V

"First Europe....Then America"

CORDELL HULL SPOKE TO THE PEOPLE OF THE UNITED STATES on August 6, 1940. He warned them that great forces of lawlessness, conquest, and destruction were moving across the earth "like a savage and dangerous animal at large." For the protection of America, the Secretary of State said, every citizen must be ready for real sacrifices. "We cannot pursue complacently the course of our customary normal life."

Yet many still insisted that we could isolate ourselves from the effects of the German domination of Europe and the menace of Japan in the Far East. The *Chicago Tribune*, Charles A. Lindbergh, the Communist party of Earl Browder, and the Socialist party of Norman Thomas clamored that this was not our war. Their position, incidentally, was enthusiastically acclaimed by the Nazi and Fascist organizations in this country and abroad. The debate raged on, but the course of events outside the Western Hemisphere was inevitably leading the majority of Americans into a realization of their responsibility to the Allies.

Our people watched with deep sympathy as England prepared to withstand the shock of German air attacks and possible invasion. Churchill's magnificent leadership of the British people in this time of their greatest peril made a great impression in the United States. When one Englishman—Professor Richard H. Tawney—was asked why his countrymen were willing to fight against seemingly overwhelming odds, he dramatically replied: "We prefer dying on our feet to living on our knees." In spite of certain defeatists and appeasers in both England and the United States, the British doggedly went ahead with their plans to defend their island. Churchill echoed this spirit when he spoke on July 14 to American and British audiences:

"Should the invader come to Britain, there will be no placid lying down of the people in submission before him, as we have seen, alas! in other countries: We will defend every village, every town, and every city. The vast mass of London itself, fought street by street, could easily devour an entire hostile army, and we would rather see London laid in ashes and ruins than that it should be tamely and abjectly enslaved. . . . . All depends now upon the whole life strength of the British race in every part of the world and of all our associated peoples and of all our well-wishers in every land, doing their utmost night and day, giving all, daring all, enduring all, to the utmost, to the end."

During July and August, United States newspapers carried story after story of the increased sinkings of British supply ships on the Atlantic Ocean by German airplanes and submarines; of continual German bombing raids on English ports, intended to disrupt the landing of American supplies; and of the preparations being made by the Nazis to carry out an invasion of England. The Committee To Defend America by Aiding the Allies, in order to meet the threat of increased sinking of Allied shipping and to ward off the danger of an invasion, began to place the emphasis of its campaign on the release of fifty or sixty over-age but recently reconditioned American destroyers to England.

It issued a new four-point program on July 23, calling, first, for action under a congressional resolution, if necessary, to make it possible for the United States to return the destroyers to the manufacturers for sale to Great Britain; and, second, for ships to evacuate British children, to be provided by the President under whatever plan he deemed satisfactory and wise. In the third place it asked for legislation which would make it possible to arrange terms of credit by which the United States could sell its agricultural surpluses to Great Britain, the terms of the sale to be defined in pending legislation. The fourth point asked everyone to urge the President to use his authority to prohibit the sale of oil to Spain, to help prevent raw materials from reaching aggressor nations. A dispatch in the *New York Times* of July 20 had said that "there is every reason to believe that far more oil has been reaching Germany from America since the war started than Hitler has obtained or can hope to obtain from Russia. Statistics would indicate that this oil is now going through Spain."

The Committee felt that it must conclusively demonstrate to President Roosevelt that the country as a whole wanted the destroyers to go to England. "If the President really wants to do it," wrote White in a press release, "it can be done. But we must show him that the country will follow him in this matter." The question of evacuating English children to the Western Hemisphere was also of immediate and paramount importance, and the Committee tried to find a way in which the President and the Pope jointly might ask Hitler to permit United States ships to sail for this purpose—but the most immediate issue was that of the destroyers, and it received the Committee's first attention.

President Roosevelt's inaction in the issue disturbed White.

They had talked it over late in June, and White felt that, since President Roosevelt had won his third-term nomination, "he had, as it were, lost his cud." Since the Democratic convention, he thought the President had seemed more or less hazy about what to do next. Therefore the work of the Committee during the next few weeks was principally to demonstrate to the President that the public would support such a move—and that if anything he was behind, not ahead of, public opinion. On July 23 White sent the following telegram to a long list of people:

"Confidential information highest authority convinces me British Government desperately short of destroyers. Successful defense of Great Britain may depend upon release through sale by the United States of fifty or sixty over age but recently reconditioned destroyers. President already has authority or could secure Congressional authorization if necessary. Urge you wire President immediately advocating this action."

Members of the Committee worked day and night to determine the legal procedure necessary to permit this sale, but their feeling was that the President and Congress would find the necessary means if public opinion supported this course. On July 30 the Committee ran an advertisement in the *New York Times* and the *New York Herald Tribune* entitled, "Between Us and Hitler Stands the *British* Fleet!" The following day it appeared in the *Washington Post* and the *Chicago Daily News*, and on August 1 it appeared in the *Kansas City Star*.

"First Europe . . . . then America," it read. "So says Adolf Hitler! He has promised his followers—'It will be a simple matter for me to produce unrest and revolt in the United States so that these gentry will have their hands full with their own affairs. . . . . —We shall soon have storm troopers in America . . . . we shall have men whom degenerate Yankeedom will not be able to challenge.' "

It went on to point out that the British Isles and the British fleet served as a fortress "stopping the international gangsters from reaching the loot across the Atlantic Ocean." Britain's most vital need was destroyers, and as a measure of American self-defense the public was called upon to write or wire the President, senators, and representatives that it wanted the over-age destroyers sold to England. A chart, showing the strength of the American and British fleets as contrasted with the dictators' and Japan's, was inserted in the advertisement with the warning, "Think where we'd be if the British fleet fell to the Dictators and was used AGAINST us." An appeal to the public to contribute money to the Committee or form a local chapter completed the advertisement.

To co-ordinate the work of local chapters, Professor Theodore Smith of Massachusetts Institute of Technology volunteered to devote his summer to touring the country, without remuneration, strengthening the work of the local branches and helping to establish new ones. He visited cities from Cleveland to Omaha and Dallas. He met a few key people in each place, held a larger meeting for the public, gave one or more radio addresses, and attempted to secure publicity in local newspapers. Frequently new headquarters for the chapters were set up in important business buildings.

In order to stimulate the flow of letters and telegrams to Washington, the Committee sponsored rallies and radio addresses by prominent people. Probably the most influential radio address was delivered by General John J. Pershing on August 4. He spoke to America in the following words:

"No war was ever prevented by arguing that the danger does not exist. . . . . More than half the world is ruled by men who despise the American idea and have sworn to destroy it. . . . . It is not hysterical to insist that democracy and liberty are threatened. . . . . By sending help to the British we can still hope with confidence to keep the war on the other side of the Atlantic. . . . . Today may be the last time when, by measures short of war, we can still prevent war. . . . . It is my duty to warn you that the British navy needs destroyers and small craft to convoy merchant ships, to escort its warships, and hunt submarines, and to repel invasion. . . . . If a proper method can be found, America will safeguard her freedom and security by making available to the British or Canadian governments at least fifty of the over-age destroyers, which are left from the days of the World War. If the destroyers help save the British fleet they may save us from the danger and hardship of another war."

Transcriptions and reprints of this speech were made and widely distributed.

Late in June, William Allen White and Clark Eichelberger had discussed the possibility of getting General Pershing to broadcast in favor of the release of the destroyers. White had forgotten about the incident when Eichelberger called him on August 4, while he was taking a short vacation in Colorado, and said that General Pershing was to speak that evening. White assumed that General Pershing was broadcasting under the auspices of the Committee To Defend America by Aiding the Allies. He told reporters that the Committee had put the General on the air, and it was not until some months later that he learned the true facts. General Pershing had spoken without sponsorship, although Herbert Agar, editor of the *Louisville Courier-Journal* and a member of the Committee, and members of the Washington chapter of the Committee had been largely responsible for persuading him to speak.

As White later explained, the boss on his vacation made a mistake about an office deal. But whether the speech was sponsored by the national committee members or the Washington members made little real difference. Nonetheless, White was accused by Columnist General Hugh Johnson of writing this speech for General Pershing.

Three retired sea dogs soon added their voices to that of Pershing, seeking release of the destroyers to England. On August 9 Rear Admiral Harry E. Yarnell, commander-in-chief of the Asiatic Fleet in 1936–39, spoke at a Boston rally of the Committee. The next day Admiral William H. Standley, chief of naval operations from 1933 to 1937, went on record in favor of the transaction. The third to speak out was Rear Admiral Yates Sterling, Jr., who on August 10 summed up the sentiments of the other two in these words:

"The British Navy is all that stands between Hitler and his ultimate goal—the resources of the Americas and the enslavement of their peoples. The destroyers in question are of little use to us as long as the British Navy remains undefeated. They will be fighting for America most effectively by being added to the British Navy." The statements by the three admirals were sent, along with excerpts from General Pershing's speech, in handbill form to national committee members and to the local chapters for distribution to the public.

Four days later Clark Eichelberger sent to national committee members and chairmen of local chapters this telegram:

"News from England that Blitzkrieg has started leads us to believe matter of destroyers to Great Britain should come to head this week. Therefore urge telegrams from you and important friends you can reach. Statements, editorials in your local press, every possible expression of opinion to the President, your Senators and Representatives that way must be found immediately to get destroyers to Great Britain."

A number of people in the public eye also openly advocated the Committee's objective—among them were Elsa Maxwell; Dr. Robert A. Millikan of the California Institute of Technology; Chester Rowell of the *San Francisco Chronicle;* Douglas Fairbanks, Jr., who was vice-chairman for the Southern California chapter of the Committee; Dorothy Thompson, who spent most of the summer speaking in New England; Governor Lehman of New York; Senator Ernest W. Gibson of Vermont; Maury Maverick, mayor of San Antonio, Texas; Edgar Ansel Mowrer, foreign correspondent of the *Chicago Daily News,* who was in France during the weeks before the surrender to Germany; and the late William Lyon Phelps of Yale University.

Two more speeches which were nearly as influential as General Pershing's in stimulating the people to show President Roosevelt that they wanted destroyers to go to England were delivered by Ambassador William C. Bullitt, just returned from four years in France, and William Allen White himself. On August 18 Ambassador Bullitt addressed the American Philosophical Society of Philadelphia with the text "America Is in Danger."

"It is my conviction," he said, "drawn from my own experience and from the information in the hands of our government in Washington, that the United States is in as great peril today as was France a year ago. And I believe that unless we act now, decisively, to meet the threat we shall be too late.

"The dictators are convinced that all democracies will always be too late. You remember Hitler's statement: 'Each country will imagine that it alone will escape. I shall not even need to destroy them one by one. Selfishness and lack of foresight will prevent each one fighting until it is too late. . . . .'

"They [the dictators] are not yet in a position to attack America by military means; but their campaign of befuddlement, their preparatory assault, is following the same lines in America that it followed in France. Do not imagine that the French citizen was less intelligent or cared less about his country than the American citizen. The honest French patriot did his best, but he just could not see through the smoke screens of bribery, propaganda, lies and threats which the dictators spread in his country. . . . .

"The Americans who believe that the Nazis will not have to be stopped but will stop of their own accord are indulging in the fatal vice of wishful thinking. They want to believe this. Therefore they believe it. . . . .

"The men and women who tell you that the dictators will not attack the Western Hemisphere may be honest wishful thinkers or they may be agents of the dictators; but in either case, by lulling you into a false feeling of security and retarding your preparations for defense, they are keeping the way clear for an assault on America by the dictators. They are enemies consciously or unconsciously, of our country and our liberties. . . . . "

When the Committee To Defend America by Aiding the Allies distributed reprints of this speech to the nation, Bullitt was vilified by the isolationists. Senator Clark of Idaho stated that the talk was "very little short of treason," while Congressman John Schafer of Wisconsin declared that Bullitt should be "locked up."

Over the Columbia Broadcasting System on August 22, William Allen White called upon the whole nation to help send the destroyers to Great Britain. In this speech he said that the real strength of the Committee To Defend America by Aiding the Allies was its six hundred local chapters and thousands of volunteer workers. "They have been the steam in this engine of publicity and propaganda," he said. "I am only the rooster on the cowcatcher, crowing lustily sometimes at the crossroads." The speaker was certainly underestimating his own work. He and Eichelberger had worked day and night on Committee affairs, and White's name and respected position as a prairie philosopher and elder statesman had won many to the cause of the Committee.

In the course of his speech he, too, pointed out that the United States would be in mortal danger if the British fleet were conquered. If Great Britain fell, the shipbuilding facilities of the world's dictators would outnumber the shipbuilding capacities of the United States five to one. He asked:

"How can we sleep comfortably in our beds until we know that for some just, honest, and legal return, either for cash or for air and naval bases or in some other honorable legal bargain, those destroyers are on the high seas, manned with British sailors, hurrying to our first line of defense? . . . . If Great Britain falls, a new phase of civilization will dominate Europe and will menace the United States and the Western Hemisphere. It is not a question of form of government between Great Britain and the European dictators. It is a way of thinking, a way of life, a social order, a slave economy that menaces the world, and the world cannot live half slave and half free."

In this speech White, "as a partisan Republican supporting Mr. Willkie," paid a sincere tribute to President Roosevelt as one whose "vision, more than that of any other ruler in the world, has seen from the start the meaning of this conflict. We may agree or disagree with him on domestic policies, but I think no American statesman of the first order has risen to deny that his leadership pointed steadily in the only direction of safety for the American people." In concluding the talk, White reminded the public of the long-range purpose of his Committee To Defend America by Aiding the Allies, a purpose to which both he and Clark Eichelberger had devoted many years of their lives: that of defending democracy, so that after the war a world order could be set up among free people.

White was not, and never claimed to be, an orator. It was

DESTROYERS FOR BRITAIN MAY
MEAN AMERICAN SAFETY

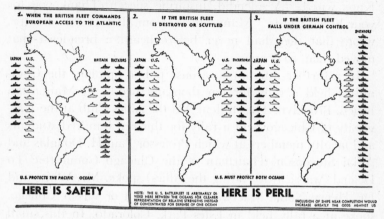

1. WHEN THE BRITISH FLEET COMMANDS EUROPEAN ACCESS TO THE ATLANTIC

JAPAN   U.S.   BRITAIN   DICTATORS

U.S. PROTECTS THE PACIFIC OCEAN

HERE IS SAFETY

2. IF THE BRITISH FLEET IS DESTROYED OR SCUTTLED

JAPAN   U.S.   U.S. DICTATORS

U.S. MUST PROTECT BOTH OCEANS

HERE IS PERIL

NOTE: THE U. S. BATTLEFLEET IS ARBITRARILY DIVIDED HERE BETWEEN THE OCEANS FOR CLEARER REPRESENTATION OF RELATIVE STRENGTHS INSTEAD OF CONCENTRATED FOR DEFENSE OF ONE OCEAN

3. IF THE BRITISH FLEET FALLS UNDER GERMAN CONTROL

DICTATORS

JAPAN   U.S.   U.S.

INCLUSION OF SHIPS NEAR COMPLETION WOULD INCREASE GREATLY THE ODDS AGAINST US

OUR SAFETY is protected now by the British Fleet..............
— BUT —
Britain's most vital naval need now is.....................
MORE DESTROYERS.

The United States has 162 over age destroyers (over 16 years old) available. We could safely spare 60 of them.

These ships can defend America now by guarding Britain's lifelines.

Write or wire your representatives in Washington urging that these old destroyers be made available to Britain immediately.

THE COMMITTEE TO DEFEND AMERICA BY AIDING THE ALLIES
WILLIAM ALLEN WHITE, *Chairman*
8 WEST 40TH STREET   NEW YORK, N. Y.

Reasons for the "destroyer deal" pictured in a folder by the Committee To Defend America by Aiding the Allies.

not the way he delivered this speech that impressed his audience, but what he had to say. A flood of congratulatory letters and telegrams descended upon him in Emporia. Mrs. Frank Knox wired, "A splendid, inspiring speech. Thank you for your brave words." Many others, from all over the country, wrote that they had never before heard a broadcast that moved them so deeply.

In a further attempt to arouse public opinion, the Committee held a rally for ten thousand people at Manhattan Beach, Brooklyn. The student Aid the Allies Club at the University of Chicago held a rally for thirteen hundred students and faculty members at which Professor Paul H. Douglas and Adlai Stevenson (chairman of the Chicago Committee To Defend America by Aiding the Allies) spoke. Mr. White and Dr. Henry Noble MacCracken, president of Vassar College, spoke at a rally held in Estes Park, Colorado. In this small village, twenty-seven miles from a railroad, with one weekly newspaper and no local radio station, chapter workers filled the local auditorium with eight hundred summer visitors. A Western Union telegraph operator was engaged to stand at the door of the hall, and, as the audience streamed out, they sent telegrams to the President.

To improve the Committee's work among the women of the nation, a Women's Division was organized with Mrs. Rushmore Patterson as chairman. The plan was to establish a women's group in each of the 3,070 counties in the United States. An Aviation Division was likewise organized, the members of which included Rear Admiral Byrd, Bernt Balchen, Clyde Pangborn, and Roscoe Turner. Their purpose was to make a nation-wide tour. The New York chapter also sent out a Youth Caravan of young speakers on a thousand-mile tour of New York and New England towns to plead for aid to Great Britain.

One important phase of the question of releasing the over-age destroyers to Great Britain was the legal aspect. Section 23 of Title 18 of the United States Code reads:

"Whoever, within the territory or jurisdiction of the United States, fits out and arms, or attempts to fit out and arm, or procures to be fitted out and armed, or knowingly is concerned in the furnishing, fitting out or arming of any vessel with intent that such vessel shall be employed in the service of any foreign prince, or state, or of any colony, district, or people, to cruise or commit hostilities against the subjects, citizens or property of any foreign prince or state, or any colony, district or people with whom the United States are at peace, or whoever issues or delivers a commission within the territory of the United States for any vessel, to the intent that she may be so employed, shall be fined not more than $10,000 and imprisoned not more than three years. . . . . "

Four lawyers, led by the onetime undersecretary of the Treasury, Dean Acheson, stated that this law did not apply in the case of the over-age destroyers. They cited the United States Supreme Court decision in "The Santissima Trinidad" case (7 Wheat., 283) to the effect that the statute "did not apply to the commercial sale of an armed vessel to a belligerent when there was no evidence that it was originally outfitted contrary to law."

However, Section 3 of Title V of the Espionage Act of June 15, 1917, also had to be dealt with:

"During a war in which the United States is a neutral nation, it shall be unlawful to send out of the jurisdiction of the United States any vessel built, armed, or equipped as a vessel of war, or converted from a private vessel into a vessel of war, with any intent or under any agreement or contract, written or oral, that such vessel shall be delivered to a belligerent nation, or to an agent, officer, or citizen of such nation, or with reasonable cause to believe that the said vessel shall or will be employed in the service of any such belligerent nation after its departure from the jurisdiction of the United States."

The same lawyers held that this law, too, was "inapplicable to armed vessels, like our old destroyers, which were not built, armed or equipped as, or converted into, vessels of war with the intent that they should enter the service of a belligerent." Furthermore, they cited many precedents which gave the President power by executive action alone to release the destroyers. Their brief, distributed by the Committee To Defend America by Aiding the Allies, carried great weight with the President, and Attorney-General Jackson leaned heavily upon it for his argument in support of the transaction.

The Committee To Defend America by Aiding the Allies appointed a subcommittee on July 25, 1940, to study this question. Lawrence Curtis, Boston lawyer, was chairman; and the other members were Dean William G. Emerson, Clark Eichelberger, Quincy Wright, James B. Conant, Cornelius Wickersham, Cloyd Laporte, George K. Gardner, Denys P. Myers, and Charles Wyzanski, Jr. Professor Quincy Wright did not like the legal reasoning of the Acheson group. He felt that the United States was "entitled to make reprisals against Germany because she had violated the Pact of Paris. . . . . Assuming that Germany is at war in violation of the Pact of Paris, under the Preamble of that pact Germany 'should be denied the benefits furnished by this treaty,' which means that the United States is not obliged to use only pacific means in dealing with Germany and that Germany is not entitled to have her military operations regarded as legal war. The United States is thus free to take such measures of coercion against Germany as seem expedient. In other words, the way is open for 'all measures short of war' or even war itself in aid of the Allies so far as international law is concerned." The subcommittee in drawing up its report on November 19, 1940, accepted Quincy Wright's position. Later, at the time of the passage of the Lend-Lease Act, Congress also accepted his position.

However, to the Committee To Defend America by Aiding the Allies the destroyer question was not one of legal technicalities. Their argument was based on the simple fact that the destroyers in the hands of England would be defending the United States. While White was still on his vacation in Colorado, in August, he phoned President Roosevelt, Secretary of State Hull, and Secretary of War Stimson and Wendell Willkie about the destroyer deal. He helped arrange an interview on August 1 between the President and three Committee members—Clark Eichelberger, Herbert Agar of the *Louisville Courier-Journal*, and Ward Cheney of Washington. When some people wrote expressing fear that what the Committee favored was unwisely stripping the United States of its defenses, he replied:

"Your letter contains a most intelligent question which I have considered seriously every time I have made a move in the direction of helping to defend Great Britain: 'Can we spare all this material?' I have made no move without first consulting the Secretary of War, the Secretary of the Navy, the the President and the Secretary of State. . . . . We have made no recommendation that has not been approved by the general staffs of the two military organizations and by the State Department. . . . . I have felt safe in walking under the guidance of the administration and its military staffs."

A Gallup Poll, taken in the middle of August, revealed that the majority of the American people supported the release of the destroyers to England. Two questions were asked in the poll, the first of which was: "General Pershing says the United States should sell to England fifty of our destroyer ships which were built during the last World War and are now being put back in service. Do you approve or disapprove of our government selling these destroyers to England?" Those expressing an opinion voted 62 per cent for and 38 per cent against the sale.

The second question was: "England needs destroyer ships to replace those which have been damaged or sunk. The United States has some destroyers which were built during the last World War and are now being put back in active service. Do you think we should sell some of these ships to England"? The answers in this case were 61 per cent "Yes"; 39 per cent "No."

In the end, on September 3, President Roosevelt by executive authority announced the release of fifty over-age destroyers to Great Britain in exchange for naval and air bases in English possessions in the Western Hemisphere. The Committee To Defend America, of course, hailed the transaction as an important step in our defense and in nonpartisan fashion expressed its gratitude to the President.

The British possessions which we received in the exchange were immediately fortified and later served as important forward positions in the United States' defense against overseas aggression. The destroyers were invaluable to England in protecting her line of supply. After the great evacuation at Dunkirk nearly half of the British destroyer fleet was laid up for repairs. It was estimated that in June, 1940, 269,000 tons of British shipping went to the bottom of the ocean; in July, 290,000 tons. The British, in order to protect their shipping, had to keep a full fleet of destroyers; they probably could not have continued the war without food and supplies from overseas.

Leasing of bases as payment for the destroyers had been suggested in earlier discussions between Knox and Roosevelt. The day before the destroyer-base affair was announced, President Roosevelt stated that "the greatest attack that has ever been launched against the liberty of the individual is nearer the Americas than ever before. To meet that attack, we must prepare beforehand, for preparing later may and probably will be too late." On September 3 the President in his press conference compared the destroyer-base exchange to the Louisiana Purchase. Both, he said, had added to the country's strategic resources and both had had to be concluded in an emergency before informing Congress.

The White Committee's work in arousing public opinion to advocate the release of these destroyers had been successful in showing the President how the country felt. The Committee, in this case as well as in subsequent ones, afforded the citizens of the United States an agency through which they might express their intense desire for an Allied victory in the war.

During the period of agitation for the release of the destroyers and after the actual exchange, the Committee To Defend America by Aiding the Allies had exhibited various shades of political, economic, and diplomatic opinion. Some members were rabid New Dealers, and some were as rabid in their dislike of the New Deal. Some were extremely conservative about the amount of material that they felt should be sent to England, while others wanted the United States to declare war at once. In between these two poles of thought were White, Eichelberger, and a majority of the Committee members.

The middle-of-the-road group advocated all possible aid to Great Britain, hoping that this might keep the United States out of the war. They did not deny that aid to Britain might lead to war, but their argument was that the alternative—isolationism—would more surely lead us to war because it would mean the defeat of England, which would leave us without Allies in a world of hostile dictators. If there could be any escape from war, they sincerely and honestly believed that aid to the Allies would bring it.

White received many letters urging the Committee to support a declaration of war; but, as he always pointed out, such a step would dissolve the Committee because he and the vast majority of its members were against war. His belief, as stated in a letter to W. M. Harrison on September 3, was that if the United States were armed to the teeth, no dictator would challenge us in a war. Therefore the thing to do was to arm as fast as possible, and at the same time to keep England in the fight so that we would not have to fight Hitler alone before we were properly prepared.

During these vital and tragic months, from June through September, 1940, an amorphous group of individuals operated along parallel lines with the Committee or at times in collaboration with it. It had no fixed name or organization, but it was mentioned in the press as being the "Century Club group" or the "Miller group." This group sometimes thought it wise to express an opinion in advance of the views of the Committee To Defend America by Aiding the Allies. Some of its members were members of the Committee, but it was an independent organization of distinguished citizens formulating their own views. As a body, it was not affiliated in any way with the Committee. White in describing the Miller group said: "There must be half a dozen such committees in existence. They are made up of people on our committee and other committees in the interlocking directorate of internationalism with various degrees of agreement from three cheers to war. They have no affiliation with us. We have no Blue Lodge, no Shriners, no Royal Arcanum."

The Monday morning papers of June 10, 1940, carried a public statement signed by thirty citizens calling for a declaration of war. These people acted in order to arouse the American people to the danger of permitting a Hitler victory in Europe. There was no meeting of the signers. The petition was drafted on June 2 and sent around to a selected list of people. Francis P. Miller of Fairfax, Virginia, author and an organization director of study groups formed by the Council on Foreign Relations, sent the petition to William Allen White. White refused to sign, in these terms: "By advocating the declaration of war you get about four jumps ahead of my group. And I cannot afford to seem to be crowding my own mourners at the funeral." Six of the thirty signers were members of the Committee—Herbert Agar, William H. Hessler, Bishop H. W. Hobson, Calvin B. Hoover, George Fort Milton, and Lewis Mumford.

Some of these thirty thought that it would be a fine idea if a group could be brought together who agreed that it was necessary for the United States government to take steps to prevent Germany from gaining control of the North Atlantic. As a result, Lewis W. Douglas was host at a dinner in New York City on July 11, at which he and his eleven guests drew up a program (which is reproduced in the notes at the end of this book) composed of eight general conclusions about the war situation.

Francis P. Miller sent these conclusions to William Allen White—but it is clear that White was honestly opposed to war and that he was aiding Britain on that basis. He could not favor the state of war indicated in the Miller group's suggestion that "planes and ships of our navy join in the protection of the British Isles."

Although the Miller group was unorganized and entirely fluid, it was decided that a central office should be established to facilitate the arrangement of future meetings and the possible execution of plans. Miller himself was selected to do this.

He first obtained a leave of absence from the Council on Foreign Relations, in order not to mingle their activities with his propaganda organization. On July 22 he opened an office at 11 West Forty-second Street, New York. Ward Cheney, silk manufacturer, and other members of the group or their friends supplied him with a total of $3,500 for two months' office expenses.

On July 25 this group held another meeting, at the Century Club in New York, to discuss the matter of destroyers for England. They agreed that destroyers should be transferred to England by executive action on the part of the President. Among the steps they advocated were that, regardless of private representations which might be made to the President, the campaign of education concerning the vital importance of the British fleet to us should be immediately pursued through the press, radio, public platform, personal correspondence with influential individuals, and through all other effective channels; that certain individuals be designated to see the President; that a radio program of education be launched immediately; that the group co-operate fully with the William Allen White Committee, and the Committee with the group; that a newsletter be prepared by three or four outstanding special writers; that moral backing and practical support for the Committee for the Release of Ships for European Children be provided; and that the group meet again in the near future.

There was nothing in this platform that differed from the program of the Committee To Defend America by Aiding the Allies, except that the Miller group wanted the release of one hundred destroyers, while the Committee had spoken of fifty or sixty. Only Hill, Hobson, Miller, Shepardson, and Standley of this Century Club group had signed the public statement of June 10 favoring an immediate declaration of war. During July and August the members of the Miller group co-operated with the William Allen White Committee to prepare the way for the release of the destroyers. Admiral Standley spoke for the Committee. Herbert Agar, Ward Cheney, and Francis P. Miller held personal interviews with President Roosevelt and his cabinet members on the need of transferring the destroyers to England. Herbert Agar and Joseph Alsop helped persuade General Pershing to make his broadcast on August 4. Alsop had also talked to Admiral Stark, chief of naval operations. These men told the President and his aides that the government was trailing behind public opinion, which would favor the release of the destroyers.

The importance of the work of such editorial writers as Agar and Parsons, and columnists Allen of the "Washington Merry Go Round" and Alsop of the "Capital Parade," which received wide circulation in daily and weekly newspapers all over the country, cannot be minimized. They aided greatly in crystallizing public sentiment for the release of the destroyers and in helping the President to discover how best to fulfil the wishes of his people.

The work of the Francis P. Miller group dovetailed completely in one instance with the work of the William Allen White Committee. Under Miller's direction John L. Balderston (former London correspondent of the old *New York World*, playwright, and movie script-writer) prepared a newsletter to be sent out to papers all over the country. Miller then persuaded White to issue the newsletter under the auspices of the Committee To Defend America by Aiding the Allies. The various members of the Century Club group backed Balderston's newsletter by putting him in touch with the highest authorities knowing accurate and complete facts about the material needed by England and what the United States had to spare. Balderston himself, having been a London correspondent for many years, knew a great deal about England's needs.

The purpose of this release was to clear up a general misconception among newspapers as to the President's attitude on the destroyer deal and to supply the figures that many editors did not have, showing why England so desperately needed ships, planes, and guns to re-equip her forces after Dunkirk. White was in complete accord with Miller in this project. The newsletter was to be wired to newspapers from time to time as events warranted. Balderston contributed his services free, and the cost of sending the wire was met by members of both the Miller group and the Committee To Defend America by Aiding the Allies. The contributors and the amounts of their contributions were filed with the State Department.

The service cost the newspapers nothing; but it was decided not to furnish it for the Washington or New York papers or radio commentators, because they were already in close touch with confidential information. Fifty papers, all with a circulation of over one hundred thousand, were selected to receive the service. Before any newsletter was sent out over the Committee's name, it was agreed that White, Eichelberger, or a third person would check it. Any one or all of these three people could delete any item that they did not like. A copy of each newsletter went to Francis P. Miller, who mimeographed it and mailed it to the members of his group and others in sympathy with the cause.

William Allen White sent the following telegram to the fifty selected editors, announcing the news service and pointing out its distinctive features:

Our Committee To Defend America by Aiding the Allies is considering working out an occasional news letter service to a preferred list of American newspapers. It is not propaganda service. Yet it will consist of facts bearing on issues which we are interested in getting before the public and of course will bear on the causes we are trying to further. Mostly it is background material for private use of editors. We shall try hard to make it timely and accurate. At the moment, for instance, we are greatly interested in securing for Great Britain through some kind of negotiation, horse trade or sale the fifty destroyers for which they are asking. If our service had been in operation two weeks ago we should have been able to set editors straight giving them certain tips without violation of confidence. We could have given also secret figures indicating the crucial urgency of the destroyers which was largely due to the fact that the British have concealed damage which makes their situation much worse than they permit to be known. And of course they nor we cannot make those facts public. But that background is a basis for comment and could be given to our friends without violation of confidence. You may be assured that so far as I am able to gauge the truth there will be nothing but the truth and all the truth in this service. A little later we may take up the British need for planes. Mr. John Balderston, whom you knew perhaps as chief European correspondent of the old New York World until it died, is collecting this data and will write the daily or semi or tri-weekly bulletins from the New York office after I have read and okayed them, and we shall with all earnestness try to give a true and accurate picture. These letters will be sent to you personally without cost by wire for ten days. After which I shall ask you: first, if the service has any value; second, if you have any suggestions; and third, if you want to continue. It is entirely without price. I don't need to tell you I have every faith in Mr. Balderston. I shall be most happy if you will give this service your personal attention.

During the next few weeks a number of newsletters went out, some of them straight news releases, others background material not intended for publication. Several times, however, the latter were published, causing the Committee some embarrassment.

The press published on September 5, on the basis of a Balderston newsletter about the needs of Great Britain, the statement that the William Allen White Committee had a new seven-point program. What Balderston actually had written was that the English needed the following: (1) twenty torpedo boats at once; (2) flying boats for scouting and convoy service over the North Atlantic; (3) a number of United States Flying Fortresses to carry bombing to Germany; (4) tanks; (5) airfields in the United States to train English pilots because the cold weather of Canada impeded training there; (6) two hundred and fifty thousand more Lee-Enfield rifles; (7) the American bombsight. Balderston said about this last item:

"Finally there comes the bomb sight. At this point this dispatch hastens to censor itself, and the subject would not be mentioned except that it affords a perfect example of the two ways of thinking possible about any or all of the British requests.

"If we give a secret weapon to a friend, that weapon sooner or later may be captured by the enemy and used against us. That's one way to look at it. That's the way all of Hitler's victims have looked at similar problems. The other way to envisage the problem, of course, is to concede that if your friend is fighting alone, and protecting you while he does so, it is neighborly to give him whatever help you happen to have available, and if this involves risk to yourself, to take that risk in the interest not merely of sound strategy but of your own self-respect."

In this newsletter, Balderston also called for public pressure to be put upon any Army and Navy officials who were opposed to these steps. If the staffs were opposed to the release of this material, he said that they should be overruled by executive or legislative action backed up by public opinion.

When this newsletter was published as the Committee's new program, William Allen White disavowed it. Neither White, his executive committee, nor his policy committee had sanctioned sending any materials which the Army and Navy authorities felt were vital for American defense. He explained that the Balderston program was an inventory of English needs, not the objectives of the Committee. Balderston had released this seven-point program without White's indorsement. This was the only Balderston release which White had not indorsed before release. After reading it, he had wired Balderston that it was "superb and . . . . just what our papers and Committee need," but requested that the release be held until the following morning, when he would be in Washington to discuss it.

Both White and Eichelberger felt that such a release should not come too soon after the news of the destroyer deal, because the public might feel that they were being hurried into a new position. Balderston, apparently fearing that White was planning to change the wording of the newsletter, released it on September 4. When White and Eichelberger arrived in Washington on the fifth, White called the *New York Herald Tribune* and repudiated the Balderston release. On September 26, Balderston was accused by Senators Clark and Holt of being in the pay of the British Ministry of Information, a charge which he denied in a privately printed pamphlet entitled, *The William Allen White Committee News Service and a Little "Smear Campaign" in the Senate*, which is in the national Committee files.

Eichelberger opposed White's repudiation of the Balderston release, which caused some trouble within Committee ranks. A number of members wrote that they would not support the transfer of any equipment that was regarded by the Army and Navy as essential to the defense of the United States. The national Committee, disturbed by such protests, drew up an office memorandum on Balderston, on September 16. This memorandum pointed out that his zeal was such that they were never sure when he would commit them to something that was not wise. On the other hand, his services were valuable because of his writing ability and his contacts. In spite of the friction, Balderston continued as head of the Committee's news service for several more weeks, until he had to return to Hollywood. Later, the Committee tried to secure his services again.

When new objectives of the Committee To Defend America

by Aiding the Allies were officially published on September 12, they included the "immediate dispatch of twenty-five flying fortresses and as many pursuit planes as possible, and twenty mosquito boats." Two of these three items—Flying Fortresses and mosquito boats—had been on the Balderston list. The new policy also mentioned that tanks might be necessary, but no word was said of pressure on the heads of the Army and Navy staffs to release the flying boats, the bombsight, the Lee-Enfield rifles, or to permit the training of English pilots on American airfields. In the course of the next few months, however, all of the points on Balderston's list were adopted by the Committee except that of putting pressure on the heads of the Army and Navy staffs.

By this September, with the beginning of the Battle of Britain, substantial aid to the Allies had become our firmly established policy. Although no legislative steps had yet been taken, the Committee To Defend America by Aiding the Allies had given the popular desire to assist the opponents of Hitler a definite and powerful means of expression. The months to come would require further steps, but the actual decision to render aid had already been reached.

VI

War Decides the Election

On SEPTEMBER 7, 1940, THE GERMAN AIR FORCE LAUNCHED its all-out blitz on Britain. Although the next few months saw vast destruction in English cities from continued heavy bombings, Germany failed to gain supremacy of the skies over England. Buildings, factories, docks, and fortifications may have been widely damaged, but the morale of the English people was fortified by the ordeal. In the United States, before a public that was watching the reports of this great blitz with intense interest and sympathy for the English people, a presidential campaign was being waged. William Allen White correctly predicted in the *Chicago Daily News* on July 18, 1940, that "Hitler rather than either Roosevelt or Willkie will settle the real issues of this campaign. The American people cannot witness the horrors of this war in England and split hairs over the wording of the National Labor Relations Act or the shortcomings of the federal control of Wall Street. Domestic issues will be out after the *blitzkrieg* starts. . . . . "

At the Republican nominating convention in June, the Committee To Defend America by Aiding the Allies exerted its efforts to insure that the platform committee did not accept an isolationist plank. The Committee asked all its local chapters to have their members wire the delegates urging them to incorporate into the Republican platform planks favoring continued aid to the Allies. The platform committee did finally adopt a plank which asked for extended aid to all peoples fighting for liberty—but aid which was not in violation of international law or inconsistent with national defense.

In his daily North American Newspaper Alliance dispatches about the convention, White did the best he could to aid Wendell Willkie. The candidate, in White's eyes, was of greater importance than the platform. As early as May he had begun to toy with the idea of supporting Willkie. He liked Willkie's courage and his unequivocal stand for aid to the Allies. Here, he felt, Willkie differed from Robert Taft, Thomas Dewey, and Arthur Vandenberg, who were all isolationists or dangerously close to it. Although White privately favored Wendell Willkie during May and early June, he refrained from any public indorsement until June 13, when he stated in the *Gazette* that Willkie was the best man that the Republicans had. He was a middle-class man; he was forthright.

However, White did not believe that Willkie had a chance of securing the nomination. On June 15 he wrote an article in which he gave Willkie a boost; and just before he left Emporia to attend the Republican convention he published an open letter to Willkie in the *Gazette*. It counseled Willkie to keep his independence, to "blurt out" whatever he wanted to, and, above all, warned him not to become a political hypocrite. "Our democracy has been waiting for a man like you," wrote White.

Shortly after Wendell Willkie's nomination, White called on him and warned him against the influence of such conservative Republicans as John Hamilton, Joe Pew, and Sam Pryor. White told Willkie that Hamilton, probably with the aid of

Pryor, Republican national committeeman, had been responsible for the foolishness of repudiating Colonel Frank Knox and Colonel Henry L. Stimson for accepting appointments in President Roosevelt's cabinet. Although White approved of Willkie's selection of Representative Joseph Martin to serve as manager of his campaign, he disliked the appointment of Pryor as head of the campaign in the eastern part of the country.

A few days after the termination of the Republican convention, the Democratic convention assembled in Chicago. On July 15, the first day of the Democratic convention, the White Committee ran a half-page advertisement in the *Chicago Daily News*, entitled "Help Britain To Stop Hitler Now!" The advertisement again cited figures showing the importance of the British fleet to American defense and called upon the public to write or wire the candidates of *both* parties to support aid to the Allies. White and Eichelberger appeared before the platform committee and urged an unequivocal plank for aid to the Allies. Eichelberger cited the program of the Committee and continued:

"The Democratic party is in a position to tell the American people the truth concerning the present international situation because the party traditionally has been in favor of all efforts for prevention of war and cooperation for the maintenance of peace. The President and the Secretary of State labored long and persistently to prevent the present war and limit its scope. In this crisis the Democratic party has the right to remind the nation that, had the dreams of Woodrow Wilson for permanent peace been realized, the world might enjoy the golden era of peace instead of the tragedy of a second world war. . . . . The Committee To Defend America by Aiding the Allies believes that the United States must continue to hold the torch of democracy high for all the world to see. It agrees with the President that an effort to appease the totalitarian way of life, politically, morally or economically, would be doomed to failure. Defeatism now is treason."

White and Eichelberger asked members of their committee to wire the members of the Democratic platform committee and the convention delegates from their communities and states urging a strong plank for Allied aid. The Chicago chapter of the Committee opened a temporary office at the main convention hotel—the Stevens—and distributed literature to the delegates. This office was picketed by opponents of aid to the Allies, who carried signs reading, "I'm 20—William Allen White is 72." White was greatly amused by the pickets, and he pattered back to his room at the Blackstone Hotel to fetch his young niece to see them.

When the Democratic convention adopted a plank calling for material aid to the victims of "ruthless aggression," both parties were on record as favoring all legal aid to the Allies. However, throughout the campaign the editor of the *Emporia Gazette* was for Wendell Willkie. Since both candidates stood for aid to the Allies, his opposition to Roosevelt centered around the third term. He felt that a third term was dangerous because it was not wise to keep one party in control for twelve years. The party out of power for twelve years might disintegrate, and the country would have a one-party system. White also thought that Wendell Willkie, because of his executive training, was better equipped to do the job of arming America and that he had more political courage than Roosevelt. To those ardent Republicans who wanted him to criticize President Roosevelt's honesty and sincerity, however, he answered:

"I hate to question motives of men whom I know. I like to assume their honesty and disagree with them on other matters and so when I saw things that raised my gorge in Roosevelt I just assumed that maybe he knew more than I did about it and maybe it would come out all right in the wash. I suppose on the whole that is about the only way to keep friendship, and I think perhaps friendship is more important than the wisdom of consistency. I don't know. The older I get the less I know."

On the issue of foreign affairs, Chairman White continued to support the President loyally. During the last part of July he called upon the nation to back President Roosevelt and Secretary Hull in taking over the French islands in the Western Hemisphere. When he went on the radio on August 22 to advocate the release of the destroyers, he enthusiastically praised the President's foreign policy (see chap. v). Letters poured into Emporia from many people who could not understand how he could praise the President and support Wendell Willkie. He pointed out to these people that, as head of the nonpartisan Committee To Defend America by Aiding the Allies, it was fair to speak justly of the President's leadership.

To his good friend Edna Ferber he wired: "Sure I'm for Willkie stronger'n horseradish. Ask your friends why a man can't pay a decent and deserved tribute to the President on one side of his work without the presumption that he agrees with all sides of his work. I would be for Willkie for a dozen reasons but if for no other because of the swell sock he took at Coughlin the other day. . . . . " Because of his continued support of Roosevelt's foreign policy, White and the *Gazette* staff all through the campaign had constantly to deny that White was for Roosevelt.

White's relations with Wendell Willkie during the campaign were those of a trusted adviser. The last time that White saw President Roosevelt, he told the President that he must talk with Willkie as frankly as he had been talking to the President. On August 1 and 2, then, he had conferences with Wendell Willkie at Colorado Springs, where Willkie was preparing his speech accepting the Republican nomination. Willkie showed White a draft of the speech, and White encouraged him in his unequivocal stand for aid to Britain. The two men saw each other several times at Colorado Springs, and White devoted his efforts to bringing Willkie and Roosevelt together in a common statement on sending the over-age destroyers to England. On August 11 he wired the President:

"It's not as bad as it seems. I have talked with both of you on this subject during the last ten days. I know there is not two bits difference between you on the issue pending. But I can't guarantee either of you to the other, which is funny for I admire and respect you both. I realize you in your position don't want statements but congressional votes. Which by all the rules of the game you should have. But I've not quit and as I said it's not as bad as it looks."

The same day he sent a wire to Chester Rowell of the *San Francisco Chronicle*, which revealed the work that he was doing and the difficulties facing him:

"Most confidentially here is the story: various people have been sent from the White House and officially as emissaries to Willkie hoping to get Willkie to support Roosevelt in Congress on his plan to send fifty aged destroyers to England. Willkie ducked for various fairly good reasons. First the legislation has not been introduced; second whatever Willkie's personal views are he has not conferred about the specific proposed legislation with House and Senate Republican leaders Martin and McNary and he feels a natural diffidence about assuming Congressional leadership before his ears are dry.

"As Chairman of our Committee I talked to both Roosevelt and Willkie on this matter. Also with Hull and Stimson and find not the least fundamental difference between them as you will see Saturday by Willkie's acceptance speech. But a public agreement is politically difficult to bring about because it is political dynamite, and a private agreement which would gradually leak out is even more hazardous. I have not lost hope. It is a tough assignment in which I agree with both sides and respect each but can find no way to overcome the rather silly but terribly real and practical obstacles to candid agreement. Have you any suggestions and remember this is absolutely under your hat."

Although William Allen White could not bring the two men together on a joint public statement or even a private agreement on the destroyers, he could advise the President that his competitor was for the plan. When the release of the fifty ships was at last announced to the public on September 3, Willkie approved the result but opposed its being consummated by executive action, feeling that Congress should have approved the transaction first. White and the Committee To Defend America by Aiding the Allies let it be known at once that they agreed with the President's executive action. White sent the following telegram to Committee members:

"Believe it important today's splendid news release of destroyers and acquisition naval-air bases for American defense be greeted by nation-wide indication of approval. Suggest existing sentiment favoring action be expressed in thousands of congratulatory messages to President Roosevelt; also messages to Senators and Congressmen approving President's act: also local statements to press, letters to editors, radio talks and other activity indicating public's favorable attitude. What is done next few days may have significant effect advancing other of our objectives."

White further demonstrated his support of President Roosevelt's executive action by drawing up a statement to the President signed by fifty citizens who indorsed the destroyer transaction. Three important pro-Willkie names headed the list—William Allen White, James B. Conant, and Lewis W. Douglas, president of the National Democratic Willkie Clubs—and a majority of the signers were Willkie men.

With the destroyer transaction successfully completed and both presidential candidates openly favoring aid to the Allies, the Committee concentrated its efforts on securing the release to England of twenty-five Flying Fortresses, as many pursuit planes as possible, and twenty mosquito boats. To carry out this objective, it repeated some of the devices that had been used in the destroyer campaign. White cabled General Douglas MacArthur, in charge of the defense of the Philippine Islands, to ask his opinion on further aid to Britain. General MacArthur's reply, widely circulated by the Committee, was, in part:

"The history of failure in war can almost be summed up in two words, too late. Too late in comprehending the deadly purpose of a potential enemy. Too late in realizing the mortal danger. Too late in preparedness. Too late in uniting all possible forces for resistance. Too late in standing with one's friends.

"Victory in war results from no mysterious alchemy or wizardry, but entirely upon the concentration of superior force at the critical points of combat. To face an adversary in detail has been the prayer of every conqueror in history. It is the secret of the past successes of the axis powers. In this war it is their main hope for continued and ultimate victory.

"The greatest strategical mistake in all history will be made if America fails to recognize the vital moment, if she permits again the writing of that fatal epitaph 'Too Late.' Such coordinated help as may be regarded as proper by our leaders should be synchronized with the British effort so that the English speaking peoples of the world will not be broken in detail. The vulnerability of singleness will disappear before unity of effort—not too late, not tomorrow, but today."

The Women's Division of the Committee enrolled five hundred volunteer women workers from each of New York's five boroughs as "Minute Americans" to serve at a moment's notice. Each "Minute American" was given a page from a telephone directory with instructions to call the names in order to explain why aid for Great Britain was essential to national defense and to enlist the subscriber as a new "Minute American" who, in turn, would recruit others. The "Minute Americans" were called upon from headquarters to write or wire the President and their congressmen and senators urging immediate action when a specific need arose. By the first week in October, the "Minute Americans" had talked with some five hundred thousand New York City housewives.

More rallies were held all over the nation to crystallize public opinion to bring pressure on Washington so that the Flying Fortresses, pursuit planes, and mosquito boats might be sent to Great Britain at once. The most important mass meeting was held in Chicago under the auspices of the Chicago chapter on September 18, with Adlai E. Stevenson, head of the Chicago chapter, Rear Admiral Standley, Dorothy Thompson, Maury Maverick, and Douglas Fairbanks, Jr., addressing a capacity audience.

William Allen White spent the first two weeks of September at the New York headquarters, and he also spent some time in Chicago discussing the Committee and its objectives with representatives of the middle western chapters. These were busy weeks for a man of seventy-two, weeks filled with talks, conferences, and luncheon discussions. He returned to Emporia in the middle of September with a cold, which gradually grew worse and began to hamper his usual active existence.

SEND THOSE BOMBERS!

Stop Hitler Now and Keep War Away From America

In favor of American bombers for Britain. A cable from General MacArthur and an editorial in the "New York Herald Tribune" are the basis of this broadside.

For ten days White was confined to his home. On October 11 he made a speech at a memorial program for former Chancellor Lindley at the University of Kansas, and he almost collapsed. His physical exhaustion can be seen from what he wrote Jack Harris of the *Hutchinson* (Kansas) *News* on October 16: "I again was aware of the fact that I have no business making speeches. Mine was only seven minutes and it kicked me like a government mule." White's doctor forbade him to go back to New York until November, and he had to cancel numerous talks and conferences that had been planned for him at national headquarters.

In spite of his poor health, White was alive to the meaning of the German, Italian, and Japanese agreement which was signed on September 27. He felt that the Committee now would be obliged to arouse the American people to the totalitarian danger in both the Atlantic and the Pacific and show them that the war in the two oceans was really our war—that it was part of the battle for a world democracy. Nevertheless, he felt that while the American people were being awakened to the menace of Japan, they should not take their minds off aid to England, for "if Great Britain wins (and we are arming her to win) we shall have to fight no war. France will be free; so will Belgium, Holland and Scandinavia, and we need have no worry about Japan and her Axis. The Pacific fight will be won in the Atlantic."

The Triple Alliance of September 27, 1940, was, in the words of the Berlin Foreign Office, its "answer to the destroyer deal." The published document stated:

The governments of Germany, Italy and Japan, considering it as a condition precedent of any lasting peace that all nations of the world be given each its own proper place, have decided to stand by and cooperate with one another in regard to their efforts in Greater East Asia and regions of Europe respectively. . . . .

Accordingly, the governments of Germany, Italy and Japan have agreed as follows:

1. Japan recognizes and respects the leadership of Germany and Italy in the establishment of a new order in Europe.

2. Germany and Italy recognize and respect the leadership of Japan in the establishment of a new order in Greater East Asia.

3. Germany, Italy and Japan agree to cooperate in their efforts on aforesaid lines. They further undertake to assist one another with all political, economic and military means when one of the three contracting powers is attacked by a power at present not involved in the European war or in the Chinese-Japanese conflict. . . . .

The United States thus found itself menaced by a war in two oceans. Undoubtedly the Axis nations felt that this statement would serve to check American aid to England and China. They were mistaken, however; and Cordell Hull observed that the alliance "does not, in the view of the Government of the United States, substantially alter a situation which has existed for several years." Japan, long before signing this pact, had taken steps to increase its domination of the Far East. It had demanded in June, 1940, that France permit Japanese "inspectors" in French Indo-China; and under duress, on September 22, Vichy France signed an agreement with Tokyo providing three Japanese air bases in Indo-China and allowing Japanese troops entry. Yet, in spite of these aggressive actions on the part of Japan, the *Chicago Tribune* (June 5, 1940) went so far as to assert that "under Mr. Roosevelt our foreign policy . . . . has been provocative. We have succeeded in irritating the Japanese by such proposals as the project to fortify Guam. . . . . "

Hitler gave his approval to the Japanese steps, and in return a secret section of the Triple Alliance pact of September 27 committed Japan to a war against the United States and the British Empire when the circumstances seemed appropriate. Any doubt that such an agreement existed was dispelled by the Tokyo *Asaki*, which declared that "a clash between Japan and America now seems inevitable."

Shortly before the signing of the Triple Alliance, the American Export-Import Bank announced another loan of $25,000,-000 to the Chinese, and on October 17 England reopened the Burma Road (which she had closed in the trying days after Dunkirk) for the shipment of arms to China. President Roosevelt in a Columbus Day address declared that "the Americas will not be scared or threatened into the ways the dictators want us to follow. . . . . No combination of dictator countries of Europe and Asia will halt us in the path we see ahead. . . . . No combination of dictator countries of Europe and Asia will stop the help we are giving to almost the last free people fighting to hold them at bay."

The United States government, meanwhile, sent reinforcements to its own bases of Hawaii and the Philippines. On October 16, an embargo on the export of scrap iron and steel to Japan became effective (earlier in the summer, on July 31, an embargo had been placed on the shipment of aviation gasoline). This embargo on metal did not include steel rails, class-A steel, or other forms of iron and steel, but it did cover all forms of scrap. Oil products except aviation gasoline, however, could still be sold to Japan.

The situation in September and October, 1940, was indeed foreboding. If the Japanese should strike at Singapore, the Dutch East Indies, the Philippines, and Australia, there would be little opposition in their path. England was fighting for her life in the Atlantic, in the Channel, and in the air over the British Isles. The Dutch had only a few colonial troops, and Australia was largely unprepared. America's defense efforts were just being launched; and a two-ocean navy, although authorized by Congress on July 19, was still in the blueprint stage.

According to Davis and Lindley in their semiofficial *How War Came*, the Far Eastern policy of the United States government after the Triple Alliance was:

"1. We pick no quarrels with Japan.

"2. We back down from no issue with her.

"3. We reserve the right to use economic pressure in the hope of bringing the Japanese to reason.

"4. The door, meanwhile, is to be left wide open for discussion and accommodation within the framework of our historic position in the Far East."

On October 15 the Committee To Defend America by Aiding the Allies let it be known that its policy had not changed as a result of Japan's adherence to the Axis alliance. Clark Eichelberger stated the Committee's view in a release of that date:

"The following policy seems clear: the key to our entire future is survival of Great Britain. If Britain wins, the Pacific area can be taken care of. If Britain loses, the aggressors will be victorious all over the world. Under no circumstances, therefore, should the American people be swerved from their purpose of giving all possible aid to Britain as quickly as possible. The purpose of the axis treaty was, in part, to discourage the United States from giving further aid to Britain. Our answer should be increasing aid. . . . ."

White had only scorn for those people who felt that the United States should appease the Axis as a result of this new combination of powers. Charles A. Lindbergh, he felt, was not frank with the American public and misunderstood the menace of Hitler. In an editorial on October 15 he stated that Lindbergh "is blind to the fact that the longer the United States can arm Britain and keep her fighting, the more time we shall have to prepare to meet Germany. . . . . All but France tried to be neutral, as Lindbergh advises. And what did it buy them? And our arming Britain will have nothing to do with the attack which Hitler will make upon this country. Why? Because Hitler's whole philosophy, his idea of government, his economic setup, his insatiable ambitions, all make it impossible for a free country and a free people to live beside Hitler's world enslaved. To that Charles Lindbergh shuts his eyes. So when he opens his mouth, he utters folly and people shake their heads and walk away."

It was quite natural, as the presidential campaign reached great intensity in the month of October, for the Committee To Defend America by Aiding the Allies to become embroiled in politics. The official stand of the Committee was nonpartisan. White was for Willkie, Eichelberger was for Roosevelt, and the policy committee was split about half and half between the two candidates. On the whole, the national committee retained its nonpartisan stand quite well, but the trouble came from the enthusiasm of members of some of the local chapters.

In Los Angeles a Mrs. Verbeck, chairman of the Women's Division of the Los Angeles chapter, sent to local members, over the name of the Committee To Defend America by Aiding the Allies, two statements supporting Wendell Willkie. One of these statements was a reprint of a *Gazette* editorial entitled "Willkie for President," and the other was a statement by Winston Churchill in 1937 that the New Deal was vicious toward private enterprise and was leading the world back into a depression. Some reform, Churchill contended, was good, but the dangerous world situation needed prosperous times to avert calamity, and the United States should lead the way in this. Mrs. Verbeck distributed these to members on October 26, with this statement: "As Chairman of the Women's William Allen White Committee I have run across these articles which I find have clarified many things for me in the Anglo-

American situation, so I am enclosing copies to you which I know you will find valuable."

Immediately irate Rooseveltians sent William Allen White copies of this material and asked him publicly to denounce Mrs. Verbeck's action. White wrote back to all these people that he was sorry it had happened. "This organization, as an organization, has no choice for President. Personally I am for Willkie because he has said a dozen times in this campaign that he would favor giving every aid to Great Britain even to slowing down our own defense program. But I wouldn't think of sending out my own personal views on Committee stationery. Nor would I countenance it!" He was shocked and disturbed at Mrs. Verbeck's use of his editorial, but since the Committee permitted local chapters to elect their own officers, he could do little but voice his disapproval.

The chairman lost considerable sleep over another episode in the campaign, involving Hamilton Fish, belligerent isolationist congressman from Roosevelt's home district in New York. Late in September Arthur J. Goldsmith of the New York City chapter of the Committee wrote White urging him to have the Committee publish the records of isolationist candidates Hamilton Fish, Bruce Barton, and David I. Walsh. White's answer was that if the Committee published the record of one congressman, it would have to do it for all congressmen, and this would be a tremendous task involving a considerable expenditure of money. Furthermore, such a step might mean that the Committee would have to oppose almost all Republicans because of their isolationist records in Congress. When the Committee did this it would lose its nonpartisan character, and this would be the end of its existence.

In mid-October, however, White read in the column of Bruce Catton, Washington reporter, the statement that the Committee To Defend America by Aiding the Allies was out to defeat Hamilton Fish for re-election to Congress. He immediately wrote to Catton repudiating the statement, pointing out that though many people had wanted the Committee to go after Fish, he had prevented the move as being unfair. The same day he also wrote a letter to Hamilton Fish stating that if any members were using the Committee's name against Fish, it was being done without authorization. In this letter White made the following statement to Fish, which later was to cause him grief: "However you and I may disagree about some issues of the campaign, I hope as Republicans we are united in our support of the Republican ticket from top to bottom in every district and every state." He added, furthermore, that this was not a private letter.

White also wrote to Eichelberger that he did not like the activities of the New York City chapter in the Fish campaign. Fish's isolationist record was no worse than that of the Kansas congressmen and some other Republican congressmen. To the secretary of the Dutchess County chapter of the Committee, White repeated his statement that if the Committee fought Fish, it had to fight nearly every Republican congressman, which would "land us squarely into the Democratic camp and absolutely annul our influence. . . . . We would be nothing but a Democratic side show." He added that he had written to Fish and personally had wished him victory as a Republican.

Actually, it appears that, although the people fighting the re-election of Fish were members of the Committee To Defend America by Aiding the Allies, and the candidate against Fish, Judge Hardy Steeholm, was chairman of the Dutchess County committee, they were acting as individuals and did not use the name of the Committee in the campaign. They seemed to be trying to disassociate their political activities from their Committee membership as completely as possible. Probably they were as successful in this as White was in supporting

Willkie as editor of the *Gazette* and yet remaining the head of a nonpartisan Committee.

Dr. Frank Kingdon, Arthur Goldsmith, Christopher Emmet, and George Field, of the New York chapter, formed a Non-partisan Committee To Defeat Hamilton Fish and on October 23 distributed the following mimeographed statement:

"National issues and the international crisis have absorbed our attention so as to cause us to overlook local situation affecting major policies. Hamilton Fish's campaign for re-election to Congress deserves the immediate attention of every American citizen who supports the policy of defending America by strengthening our own defenses and aiding Britain. According to the rules of seniority, Mr. Fish is in line to become Chairman of the Foreign Relations Committee or of the powerful Rules Committee if his party gains control of Congress. Consequently, we urge you to communicate with your favorite radio commentators and the editors of newspapers, to voice your disapproval of the activities of Hamilton Fish and to call for his defeat. Letters to the reader's columns of your favorite newspapers will be valuable. We submit the record of Hamilton Fish as the basis for your immediate action."

The record of Fish which accompanied this statement pointed out that he had organized the Committee To Keep America Out of Foreign Wars in order to fight repeal of the embargo in 1939; that he had been feted in Germany and given a German plane in which to fly to Oslo; and that he had said that the German claims against Poland were just. It also listed his recent work to prevent aid to Britain.

During the campaign Fish himself read to the public White's letter of October 18 to him. The Non-partisan Committee To Defeat Fish was upset and indignant at this. Its members wired White on October 24 that they had loyally fought for aid to the Allies for months, and Fish was against this aid. They were not using the name of the Committee in the campaign, and they were not all Democrats. Many good Republicans were in the movement fighting Fish because of his isolationist record. The telegram concluded with this statement: "If you feel obliged to point out that the National Committee sanctions no political action we could have understood but when you send him your warmest regards and express your hope for the straight Republican ticket we feel that you have let us down badly . . . . you have lent aid and comfort to the enemy. Will you not consider how you can undo the damage you have done?"

Frederick McKee and Hugh Moore, both of the national executive committee of the White organization, wired White that he should do something about Hamilton Fish's use of his letter. They, too, pointed out that the individuals opposing Fish were not using the name of the Committee. Furthermore, the national committee had returned money contributed to fight Fish. Hugh Moore stated, however, that he felt that if a poll of the Committee were taken throughout the country, White would find that the members approved of action against isolationist congressmen regardless of party.

Clark Eichelberger wired White that his letter to Fish made it appear that the Committee would support any Republican candidate, no matter how bad he was, and that this was an absolute violation of White's own position that the Committee was nonpartisan. He advised White to wire Mrs. Lewis Mumford and others working against Fish. Realizing that he had slipped up, in this case, White immediately sent the telegram which Eichelberger suggested:

"Our Committee is nonpartisan. As such we wish to see the Republicans and Democrats elected who support a program of aid to Great Britain. Our Committee naturally wishes to see appeasers, isolationists and pro-Germans defeated irrespective of party. You may make the widest use of this you wish."

In spite of the efforts of the Non-partisan Committee To Defeat Hamilton Fish, Fish was re-elected and during 1941 was one of the most vigorous foes of the Committee. William Allen White's refusal to permit the Committee officially to oppose isolationist Republicans in the election was probably largely motivated by his Kansas background. The Republican party in Kansas, to him, most adequately expressed the fundamental traits of his middle class—honesty, industry, and thrift. An early editorial of his in the *Gazette* for August 11, 1896, emphasized that the Democrats had not been a party of constructive legislation in the past twenty-five years. In *Collier's*, August 9, 1924, he summed up the Democratic party as a party of disorder and emotion in adjectives that remind one of the charge used after the Civil War that it was the party of "rum, Romanism, and rebellion." On February 23, 1940, he wrote in the *Gazette* that along with the sensible Kansas Democrats were "the others, the psychopathic cases, the great unterrified, unregenerate and moronic sections of the Democratic party."

If, in 1940, the Committee had opposed isolationist congressmen up for re-election, White would have had to oppose all the Kansas Republican incumbents and support their Democratic opponents. To do this might have jeopardized the re-election of Republican Governor Payne Ratner, personal friend and political ally of White's, and also it might have so confused the issues in Kansas as to lead to the defeat of a constitutional amendment permitting the state to have a civil service system. The Emporia editor had spent many years nursing this bill along until it was finally placed upon the ballot in the 1940 election. During the last two weeks of the campaign, he suspended his work for the Committee To Defend America by Aiding the Allies and toured Kansas, making numerous radio addresses in favor of the constitutional amendment.

This local situation in Kansas and the fear that the Committee would become an adjunct to the Democratic party if it opposed all the isolationist Republicans seem to account for White's refusal to permit the Committee To Defend America by Aiding the Allies to fight isolationists up for re-election. Some of the most bitter isolationist opposition to the objectives of the Committee in 1941 might have been prevented if the opposite course of action had been followed. Clear thinking about the security of America would have required strenuous opposition to all isolationist candidates regardless of previous party affiliation.

There can be no doubt that the campaign was a headache to White. Irate Rooseveltians disliked his editorials in support of Wendell Willkie, and ardent Willkieites disliked his praise of the President's foreign policy. During October he was worried that the Committee's work to stimulate aid to Britain was operating in favor of the election of Roosevelt. He did his best to prevent this from occurring. When Raymond Clapper, Washington columnist, stated that the Committee To Defend America by Aiding the Allies was a campaign sideshow for Franklin D. Roosevelt, a hot denial came from White. In a letter to Clapper on November 25 he explained his relations and the Committee's relations to the two candidates thus:

"All summer I was talking over the telephone, or seeing personally, Mr. Willkie. During the whole destroyer deal Mr. Willkie knew what was going on. On Sunday the 17th, before Mr. Willkie went to the South and before I called at the White House, Mr. Willkie and I went over everything that I discussed at the White House. Let me repeat, my dear Ray, that

I have never talked to Mr. Willkie that Mr. Roosevelt didn't know about it, nor talked to Roosevelt that Willkie didn't know it. Each knew what I was saying to the other. I give you this on my personal word of honor.

"At the White House I am received purely as the head of our Committee. But you may bet your bottom dollar that I go and come in entire self-respect as member of his majesty's loyal opposition."

In the midst of the problems created by the presidential campaign, the New York City chapter of the Committee To Defend America by Aiding the Allies became a source of irritation to White as chairman of the Committee. To Eichelberger he confided that "The New York Committee is my hair shirt." White felt that this chapter was going after side issues and endangering the main objectives of the national organization. During October it had come out for a complete boycott on all goods from Japan; it had asked the State Department to force the German government to recall surplus personnel in the consulates; and members of the chapter had gone after isolationist candidates Bruce Barton and Hamilton Fish. On October 4 a party was held at the night club Monte Carlo in New York City for the benefit of "Funds for France." On the day of the benefit, Dr. Frank Kingdon, Dr. Schieffelin, William Loeb, and Christopher Emmet sent the following telegram to the sponsors of the affair, and also published it:

"Are you aware that by attending Mrs. Harrison Williams' Monte Carlo party tonight you are unwittingly being made a part of the opening wedge to weaken the British blockade? Ambassador Haye who is the guest of honor tonight has been known for years as the great Nazi apologist in France and the intimate friend of the notorious Herr Abetz. The British do not want to inflict unnecessary suffering on the French people.

They will lift the blockade if and when it can be done without helping Hitler. But the blockade is their greatest weapon. They cannot lift it now and any American pressure for relief in France weakens the British cause which is the only hope for French freedom."

That evening the benefit was picketed. Neither the telegram nor the picketing were done in the name of the William Allen White Committee; but, since the leaders were members of the New York City chapter, White received a telegram from Mrs. Harrison Williams and George Harrison Phelps, her public relations counsel, protesting the public telegram and the picketing. Although White might feel that such activities were commendable in themselves, he believed they distracted the Committee's attention from the main purpose of crystallizing public sentiment to aid Great Britain. He wrote to Frederic Coudert of the need to control the extra-curricular activities of the New York chapter. Coudert, Frank Polk, and Thomas Lamont agreed to devote their efforts to quieting "the misdirected gyrations" of some of the members of the chapter.

The last three weeks of the presidential campaign took the eyes of the country off the Committee, and for the first time since May the organization went into a temporary eclipse. Also, for the first time, contributions ceased almost entirely. This temporary setback was not unexpected, nor was it a case for concern, since both candidates supported the Committee's objectives. On behalf of the Committee, its chairman sent a telegram to the Associated Press and the United Press on October 24, reminding them that the Committee was nonpartisan in the election.

The results of the presidential election did not find the old Kansas editor bitter or disillusioned with American democracy. He called for great unity mass meetings in celebration of the election, at which there would be a public burning of campaign literature and buttons, "not in any spirit of exaltation on the part of a victorious party but with the idea that we destroy the symbols of partisan bitterness and unite now on a national program for safeguarding American democracy and keeping war away from America by all possible aid to Britain and other nations resisting aggression." National unity, concentration upon national defense, and acceleration of aid to Britain, he felt, should now be the watchwords of America.

VII

The Isolationists Organize

By NOVEMBER, 1940, THE COMMITTEE TO DEFEND AMERICA BY Aiding the Allies had 750 local chapters, in which about ten thousand people were doing active work. In addition to the chapters in the forty-eight states, there were branches in London, Honolulu, Manila, San Juan, Puerto Rico, St. Thomas and St. Croix, the Virgin Islands, Hong Kong, and Montreal. By this time over ten thousand donors had contributed roughly $230,000. The average gift was $25. The smallest was 12 cents in stamps from a W.P.A. worker. Only one gift was over $2,000; it was from Dr. and Mrs. Wells P. Eagleton of Newark, New Jersey, with whom neither Eichelberger nor White was acquainted. Since the source was unfamiliar to them, it was investigated before the check for $3,000 was accepted. Among the other donors of large gifts were Henry Luce of New York; Harry Scherman of New York; Mrs. William H. Moore, Pride's Crossing, Massachusetts; Mrs. Walter G. Ladd, Far Hills, New Jersey; and Edith Root Grant, Cleveland, Ohio.

The Chairman felt that none of the gifts of over $1,000 came from munitions-makers or from any "unsocial or improper source." To those people who charged that the Committee was financed by international bankers or munitions-makers, he always wrote that the books of the Committee were open for investigation. The books were regularly audited by New York accountants, and any responsible person could see them. "We would be glad," wrote White about his accusers, "if they would trace the checks to see if any checks come from unsocial sources, from people who have the slightest self-interest in this war."

During the last two weeks of the presidential campaign the contributions to the Committee almost ceased, but after the election they resumed their normal flow. The Committee was never secretive about its funds. It published a list of its leading contributors—a policy which was in sharp contrast to the secret policy of its most important opponent, the America First Committee. White himself followed the policy of telling the story of the contributions to any person who inquired.

The Committee, of course, did not accomplish its work without protests from a vocal opposition. Although the polls of public opinion demonstrated that the majority of Americans favored aid to the Allies short of war, the minority was active in its protests. In the great horde of letters that poured into Emporia and the national headquarters in New York City after the Committee was launched, there was roughly one unfavorable letter for every ten that approved. The unfavorable letters varied in tone, ranging from intelligent dissent from the Committee's purpose to violent personal abuse of William Allen White. Many letters called him a warmonger trying to draw the United States into Europe's wars. Others told him to wake up, that America was no longer a colony of Great Britain, and then proceeded to criticize England as undemocratic and an oppressor of others peoples, particularly Ireland. Some people charged that White's willingness to risk war could be laid entirely to the fact that he was too old to fight himself.

"In your mercenary reason for advocating help for Allies," wired one individual, "it might be well for you to state that you and your friends are too old and physically unfit to serve in front line trenches in France but you want to speak for the youth of our country to see that they are killed maimed and crippled while you live in comfort and become a great dollar a year patriot."

A few people suggested that White should go to England if he wanted to fight. One of them put it in this fashion, typographical errors and all: "Dear Mr. Warmonger: If you and the rest of your kind of lice are so anxious to help England, why dont you go to Canada and join the army. they have a lot of nice new riffles up there and I am sure they would be glad to let you and Professor Conant, have one. . . . . If we just had some legal means of hanging such war mongers as you and Conant, America would be alot better place to live."

A number of the letters warned White that he had no qualifications, lacking a knowledge of history, geography, and international relations, to speak on the foreign situation. One person asked: "Why don't you old Fogs listen to An American like Lindberg who knows what he talks of, whilst you do not. . . . ." From a man in Chicago came this statement along a similar line:

"I presume I should say Colonel White and salute, to satisfy your ego, but I just want to say to you—'I thank God we have in our midst one strong individual who has the courage to speak up and help quiet any hysteria brought on by such so-called culture groups that you belong to.' I refer to Mr. Lindberg—a man who has always given us truthful statements. . . . ."

A minister from Georgia made the mistake of wiring White:

"Please reread the Sermon on the Mount and presume not to lead Christian ministers into ways of evil." He had met his match, for White was quite a student of the Bible and replied succinctly, "Matthew 7: 21." This verse reads: "Not every one that saith unto me, Lord, Lord, shall enter into the kingdom of heaven; but he that doeth the will of my Father which is in heaven."

Miss Patricia Kane, a niece of White's, wrote him from her college that she was greatly disturbed by the foreign situation. She had been a pacifist, but now she did not know what to believe. Her uncle's five-page reply contained a great deal of enlightening information on his state of mind. He pointed out that neither the isolationist nor his own side was right philosophically—there was no absolute right or wrong in the situation. But if Hitler won, the peace he would make would be unjust. If the Allies made the peace, the United States would have some say in it, and we could work to prevent an unjust peace.

Furthermore, if Hitler won he would take over the colonies of the defeated nations in the Caribbean and also their trade in South America. Having the Germans in the Caribbean and in South America would be a threat to the Panama Canal, the key to our national defenses. A victory for Hitler would also rob the younger generation of all hope in sharing fairly in an equitable distribution of our wealth.

These were practical things. They could not be justified philosophically or idealistically, but at the same time no man or group of men should "put their blind idealistic judgment and their faith in non-resistance where that judgment and faith will imperil so much that is fine and worth saving.

"So my dear, with many a conflict, many a doubt, as the old song says, I who am a philosophical pacifist have yielded to my practical sense of the realities of a terrible situation. I believe I am right, but I am not sure. No one can be sure. You must not be sure. But you must do what in your own heart you think is wise and just."

To all of his critics, whether they were gentlemanly and intelligent or merely abusive, White had one general answer similar to the reply that he had had for critics of the Non-partisan Committee for Peace through Revision of the Neutrality Law.

"I have your kind letter and have read it with great interest," he would say. "There are, of course, two opinions held honestly by intelligent people in the United States. One is that to help the Allies keeps the war away from America by letting them fight the war in Europe rather than to wait until the Germans conquer Europe and turn their greedy eyes westward. The other opinion is your opinion and many fine, wise people hold it. There being two sides, perhaps the best thing each of us could do is to respect the honesty and integrity of each other's opinions and realize that there must be differences if there is to be progress in the world.

"All that you say I had considered before taking my position and felt that on the whole I was right, yet not without doubts as probably you have in holding yours."

To this form answer White added a sentence or two to meet specific statements made by his opponents. For instance, to the ministers who claimed his movement was un-Christian, he sent the names of ministers like Reinhold Niebuhr, Henry Sloane Coffin, and Bishop Manning, who were on his Committee. To those who stated that Lindbergh had the only answer to the foreign situation, he wrote: "As the Germans get nearer the coast they answer Lindbergh best." When he was accused of being a warmonger because he was too old to go to war and had nothing to sacrifice, he pointed out that he had a son of military age.

In addition to private individuals, some magazines and newspapers also went after White when the Committee was publicly launched. Senator Arthur Capper of Kansas in his newspaper, *Capper's Weekly*, wrote on June 8, 1940: "There is a very active minority officially headed by my good friend William Allen White, which insists we must take part in the European war." On reading this, White sadly wrote to Capper: "It was unfair of you to say that I insist we take part in the European War. You know I don't believe in getting into war. I believe in aiding the Allies to keep out of that war, and you know it. Why, after fifty years of affectionate friendship, do you care to drag me in in this unfair way?"

In Fact, a newsletter edited by George Seldes, in its first issue on May 20, 1940, stated that there was an unnamed organization, sponsored by Thomas Lamont of Morgan and Company, formed to prepare the United States for entrance into the war. Another news publication which kept up a continual attack on White's Committee was *Uncensored*, edited by Sidney Hertzberg and including among its editorial sponsors such isolationists or pacifists as John T. Flynn, Oswald Garrison Villard, and Harry Elmer Barnes.

The greatest number of critical letters came to William Allen White not at the launching of the Committee To Defend America by Aiding the Allies but after the nation-wide publication of Robert Sherwood's "Stop Hitler Now" advertisement on June 10 and 11, 1940. Oswald Garrison Villard's reaction to the phrase in the advertisement that everyone who did not agree was an imbecile or a traitor has already been mentioned. This letter was only symptomatic of the many that were received.

A few people wrote demanding to know what international bankers and munitions-makers paid for the advertisement.

Some letters charged that the advertisement was stirring up hysteria to lead the country into war. One individual accused White of being a fifth columnist; if he were so strong for the Allied cause, why didn't he go over on the first boat? "It certainly will be good riddance. . . . . Anyone who would stoop so low as you have done is a disgrace to Americanism. . . . . A traitor to your country of the most vile and sinister type. A man without principle, without decency, honor or virtue of the slightest degree. A snake in the grass trying to draw America into the war and sacrifice possible millions of American lives and because you are the puppet of financial interests who do not dare show their names for fear of immediate defeat of their most vicious propaganda."

To those who charged that Wall Street was financing the "Stop Hitler Now" advertisement and the Committee's work, White described Robert Sherwood's sponsoring of the advertisement and analyzed the gifts received by the Committee, pointing out that they were not from big financial crooks but from small-town citizens. Senator Rush Holt stated on the floor of the Senate that the advertisement and the funds of the Committee came from Wall Street, pointing out that contributors to the advertisement were members of such international banking firms as J. P. Morgan and Company, Drexel and Company, the Guaranty Trust Company, and so forth. Then, however, he had to admit that there were other contributors— Henry Luce, Robert Sherwood, Maxwell Anderson, Fred Astaire, Irving Berlin, Douglas Fairbanks, Jr., Lynn Fontanne, Myrna Loy, Alfred Lunt, and Paul Muni, just to name a few. He could not demonstrate that these people were international bankers, so he implied that they were suckers. The Committee did not feel that it was necessary to send a personal reply to Holt; its books were open, and that was the best refutation to the charges. The *Portland* (Oregon) *Journal* on

June 14 summed up the case by saying: "As between the hysteria of the young senator from West Virginia and the calm poise of William Allen White, public opinion will string along with the latter."

Soon after the Committee's advertisement appeared, an interesting exchange of letters took place between William Allen White, on one side, and, on the other, Verne Marshall of the *Cedar Rapids* (Iowa) *Gazette*, who later headed the short-lived No Foreign Wars Committee, and Burton K. Wheeler, isolationist senator from Montana. Marshall wired to find out the contributors who paid for the advertisement. He was grateful for White's reply, but added: "I am still against War Mongering." White carefully pointed out that he did not want to go to war or to send troops to Europe and even that he would not be in favor of it under any circumstances that he "could imagine now." Marshall accepted the statement but said: "I fear, my dear friend, that the eastern seaboard warmongers have used the name and prestige of a venerable and widely beloved mid-westerner to further ends which are poisonous to the American way of life." To this White answered that the two of them saw things differently and that it took a lot of people to make this world.

Senator Wheeler, meanwhile, openly charged that Wall Street was the most active force behind the White Committee. These and other such attempts to smear the Committee by asserting that international bankers were behind it were the product of a widespread misunderstanding of the forces that took the United States into the first World War and that were drawing the United States slowly and inevitably into the second World War. The public in general, however, was far wiser in most instances than the outspoken isolationist leaders, and the majority of the American people somehow sensed that their fate was bound up with what happened in the European and Asiatic conflict. They knew, too, that they had, of their own will and without the aid of international bankers' money, seen the necessity of sending aid to the Allies.

After reading *Defense for America*, Senator Wheeler next published a letter to White in the *New York Times* on June 30 in which he denied that America's first line of defense was in Europe and held that White was stirring up war hysteria. White replied that time would tell, and meanwhile why call each other names?

The "Stop Hitler Now" advertisement did not escape without some newspaper criticism. the *San Francisco News* commented: "The appeal, like the prohibition experiment, was 'noble in purpose.' Otherwise it was not so good. The Committee, for whose personnel and high purpose we have the greatest respect, might be called the 'Committee to get America into the war by the back door.' "

The isolationist *Chicago Tribune* ran the advertisement on page 17, but the editorial page pointed out that it did not agree with the advertisement and that it considered that William Allen White was an honest man but a "simple" one for not understanding that measures short of war usually led to war. This editorial was clipped and sent to White by an Illinois editor, to whom White replied: "Thank you for your clipping. I would be surprised and deeply shocked if the Chicago Tribune would ever agree with me."

The Tribune continued to be a vitriolic critic of the Committee To Defend America by Aiding the Allies. One of its editorials on September 5, 1940, asserted that "William Allen White's Committee To Defend America by Aiding the Allies keeps repeating the statement that 'the British fleet is our present chief defense.' That is a monotonously chorused untruth." After a particularly caustic attack in the morning issue of August 28, 1940, John A. Morrison, director of the Chicago chapter, sent the editorial to White and asked if he would answer it. White said that he had made it a point all his life never to answer such attacks—"And anyway who cares what the Chicago Tribune says one way or another."

The only time that White apparently was pricked into answering the campaign of abuse carried on by the *Chicago Tribune* was in a barbed editorial in the *Gazette* (October 22: 1940), when, in his own distinctive editorial style, he observed:

"Another funny thing about going to Chicago is to read the papers, the Hearst paper and the Tribune. In policing of the news they are the worst offenders in the United States. Saturday afternoon the Kansas papers printed in the middle of the front page under a four or five line head the story that the British minister to Rumania was burning his papers and getting out of town as the Germans came in. It wasn't much of an item. The event had been predicted for two or three days in all newspapers. But look: both Sunday morning papers in Chicago carried a banner clear across the page to the effect that the 'British flee in the Balkans' or its equivalent. Anyway, both said the 'British flee,' leaving the impression that there had been a great rout of British soldiers. Which is policing the news, giving the impression that the Germans are winning the war. One sees that sort of idiocy in the morning papers of Chicago time and again, over and over, year after year. .... This doesn't happen in any other town in the United States. It is a Chicago disease and why the Chicagoans stand it, heaven only knows! These morning papers reek with unfairness. It is papers like that that make the freedom of the press a joke. There are precious few of them, but enough to give many dumb readers the notion that the freedom of the press is a private snap to make money or arrogate power to the editors and owners. Which is too bad."

During the period in which White was national chairman of the Committee, he received many letters stating that he was destroying the civil liberties of the people. Actually, the civil liberties of the nation had found a vigorous supporter in the editor of the *Gazette*. As early as May 27, 1940, he editorialized against a spy-hunt hysteria like the "folly that descended upon this nation when we entered the World War!" He refused to become a sponsor of "America Preferred," an organization to make patriotic speeches and report agitators to the Federal Bureau of Investigation, because it seemed to him likely to menace liberals fighting for civil liberties and to lead attacks on foreigners.

In the campaign for the release of the over-age destroyers, however, the opposition was particularly noisy and belligerent. Senator Nye charged on September 1, 1940, that "the sale of destroyers would be a belligerent act making us a party to the war and would in addition weaken our own defence." One newspaperman from Pennsylvania accused White of being a fifth columnist and added that he was surprised that the attorney-general of the United States had not prosecuted him for being un-American. "Report me as often as you will," White replied jovially, "and God bless you for your enthusiasm, but you are enlisted in a lost cause. If I am put in jail, Alf Landon, Mr. Willkie and Franklin Roosevelt will all go with me. And I hope that you and Bert Wheeler will poke some food through the bars occasionally as we pine and languish in durance vile."

A few people went so far as to write White after his radio speech on the release of the destroyers, stating that he was senile and in his second childhood. W. H. Montgomery of Salina, Kansas, wrote a letter to Clyde Reed, one of his senators, expressing his conservative Kansan's view of White. It is impossible to resist quoting it, especially in view of the fact that a copy of it was also sent to White himself.

"You know Bill White and you know how Kansans regard him," wrote Montgomery. "I'm typical myself. I lived the first twenty years of my life in Emporia and I love him . . . . his autographed picture hangs on the wall of my office. I've read practically everything he's written and I'm proud of him . . . . but I realize that while fifty percent of the time he's right, good, and kind, and wise . . . . the other fifty percent he's wrong, good, and kind . . . . but nuts. Always he means well . . . . but he dearly loves to find some maudlin, half-baked idea and go into ecstasies of action over it . . . . just like a young kitten with a very dead little mouse . . . . you've watched him . . . . side starts and capers . . . . fierce pouncings and energetic shakings . . . . toss it in the air and then shadow box . . . . then after a while you notice the mouse is gone and the kitten asleep. Well, that's Bill White. He can't help it . . . . he's just got to fluff out his tail, arch his back and walk stiff legged and sideways about every so often. It's relaxation for him, and out here in Kansas we don't mind . . . . we're used to it . . . . and we love him.

"But every now and then Bill gets on something that the rest of the country, not knowing him intimately as we do . . . . may take too seriously. . . . . So you just tip the boys off . . . . Bill White and his emotional committee and the emotional folks who respond to their advertisement aren't to be taken too seriously.

"Here's something that is serious, though. Don't adjourn Congress and give Franklin a chance to follow the dictates of Bill's committee. You boys just stick around and see that Franklin and Bill don't get our neck out too far."

After the over-age destroyers were traded to Great Britain in September, 1940, many people vented their anger on White.

A Pennsylvanian stated that, as a man whose family had been in the United States for two hundred years, he was protesting against the traitorous and callous Committee To Defend America by Aiding the Allies, which was un-American. White's answer was that his family had been here for three hundred years, and he inclosed a list of names—Willkie, Pershing, Admiral Yarnell, Conant, Seymour, etc.—asking if he thought that all these people were traitors and crooks. To a person who said that he had no words to express his "resentment and disgust and utter disdain" at White's attitude, White replied, "In which case, why try?"

Shortly after the destroyer transaction, Charles G. Ross of the *St. Louis Post-Dispatch* wrote an article for the Sunday issue of September 22 called "Inside Story of 'Propaganda Engine' To Send U.S. Army and Navy Equipment to Britain." Although the title left the impression that the story was an exposure, actually it was a good reportorial account of the White Committee, the Miller group, and the relations of John Balderston with the White Committee. Ross came to the conclusion that White was no figurehead for Wall Street but the very real leader of the Committee.

The title of the article came from White's own words that the Committee was an "engine of publicity and propaganda." Evidently for this reason alone Senator Bennet Champ Clark of Missouri had the story read into the *Congressional Record* on September 23. Father Coughlin's *Social Justice* on October 7 printed an excerpt from the article apparently under the impression that it was an exposure. When a reader of this paper asked White why he did not reply to the charges, he answered: "You ask about the article in the Post Dispatch. I can only answer that I wrote to the Post Dispatch thanking them for the article. I thought it was fair, accurate and intelligent. I saw nothing to question in the article."

White Christmas

Let us hope that the new Congress will turn deaf ears to the war propaganda storm and consider again WHAT IS BEST FOR AMERICA!

Courtesy of the "Los Angeles Examiner"

As the isolationists saw it. A cartoon from an editorial page.

The *Christian Century* on November 6, 1940, also reprinted excerpts from the article but felt that the study was incomplete because it did not show up the fact that the Committee had had its origin "among a little group of New York lawyers and business men—Wall Street insiders—who chose the Kansas editor as a respectable prairie state 'front' for their efforts to break down the nation's neutrality." White immediately wrote a long letter to Paul Hutchinson, managing editor of the *Christian Century*, explaining the luncheon meetings with Federic Coudert's group. He stated that these men in no way formed either of his two committees or ever told him what to do. He declared that he, White, rather told them what to do!

About this time a series of isolationist committees were organized to oppose the work of the White Committee; among them was the Citizen's Keep America Out of War Committee, which was set up by Avery Brundage, a Chicago businessman. In August this committee held a rally at which Charles A. Lindbergh was the featured speaker. Three other committees—the War Debts Defense Committee, the Make Europe Pay War Debts Committee, and the Islands for War Debts Committee—were founded under the sponsorship of certain isolationist senators and representatives; but the inspiration for these committees came from George Sylvester Viereck, the Nazi agent. Prescott Dennett was selected to run the committees, and they were all supplied with German funds. The congressmen (including Senator Lundeen, Senator Robert R. Reynolds, and Representative Martin L. Sweeney of Ohio) who accepted offices in these committees, however, were not aware of the source of their financial backing. Congressional franking privileges were used by all these groups to send out heavy amounts of isolationist propaganda.

Viereck's job, apparently, was to keep America out of the

war and to try to stop any aid from going to the Allies. According to Sayers and Kahn in *Sabotage*, Viereck did his best to get isolationist material—anti-British articles, anti-Administration editorials, anti-Russian articles—inserted in the *Congressional Record*. Once the material was in the *Record*, Prescott Dennett paid Congressman Hamilton Fish's clerk, George Hill, to have the Government Printing Office reprint these articles. Then, using the frank of various congressmen, Dennett mailed out this propaganda, postage free, to hundreds of thousands of American citizens. From March to September, 1941, George Hill bought over half-a-million reprints from the *Congressional Record*, the majority of which had been delivered by isolationist and anti-Administration congressmen. These congressmen, "no matter how patriotic their motives may have been," write Sayers and Kahn, "were thus creating propaganda material of use to George Sylvester Viereck."

An extraordinary example of the way in which Viereck was able to use certain congressmen is found in the case of Stephen A. Day, Republican representative-at-large from Illinois. Day wrote a diatribe against Great Britain, entitled *We Must Save the Republic*, which was published in 1941 by Flanders Hall, Incorporated, Viereck's publishing house. Certain parts of this book were considered unsuitable by Viereck, and Day allowed them to be revised and edited by the Nazi agent. William Stratton, the other Republican representative-at-large from Illinois, permitted his frank to be used by the Islands for War Debts Committee. When these two men again sought office in the 1942 elections, the *Chicago Daily News* (March 7, 1942) remarked:

"Their association with the activities of the leading Nazi agent in this country is susceptible to only two explanations: either they were in complete sympathy with Viereck and the agencies through which he operated, or they were so simple-minded that they were completely taken in. . . . . In either case, Illinois cannot afford to permit such men to represent the State. We cannot afford to permit Illinois to be represented by simpletons."

The No Foreign Wars Committee was organized in late October, 1940, as an attempt to unite the activities of all the isolationist committees, and the main speaker at the meeting which inaugurated the new enterprise was Charles A. Lindbergh. Verne Marshall, the isolationist newspaper publisher, was selected to serve as the head of the committee, which had a brief existence, punctuated by hectic rallies and a deluge of printed propaganda. Marshall's antics in seeking publicity so discredited his committee in the public's eye that Lindbergh and the other leading backers soon withdrew from it.

By December of that year, the leading committee opposed to aid to the Allies was the America First Committee. R. Douglas Stuart, Jr., wealthy and socially prominent Chicago student at Yale, had organized the first chapter of this group among isolationist or appeasement-minded fellow-students, and on September 18, 1940, the committee was formally incorporated in Chicago. General Robert E. Wood, chairman of the Board of Sears, Roebuck, and Company, became the national chairman. Up until the time of Pearl Harbor this committee sponsored rallies and radio speeches, distributed literature, and used many other means of disseminating its point of view.

Although its leaders undoubtedly had no intention of aiding the Axis, Nazi agents like Viereck and Japanese agents like Ralph Townsend nevertheless made use of the America First Committee. For instance, the committee received many mailbags of isolationist propaganda from the Prescott Dennett headquarters for use all over the country. One of the leading speakers at America First rallies was Laura Ingalls, who continuously harangued her listeners to fight President Roosevelt and his "war program." A few days after the attack on Pearl Harbor, she was arrested by the Federal Bureau of Investigation and subsequently sentenced to jail for having failed to register with the United States government as a paid agent of Nazi Germany. Baron von Gienanth, the Gestapo chief in the United States, told her at one time that "the best thing you can do for our cause is to continue to promote the America First Committee."

The point of view which was expressed by the America First Committee showed little realization of the actual menace of naziism to Western civilization. The New York chapter stated in a bulletin which it released near the end of September, 1941, that "we have nothing to fear from competition with Hitler for markets outside this hemisphere and a Nazi-dominated Europe. . . . . We have nothing to fear from a Nazi European victory." Charles A. Lindbergh, speaking before an America First rally in New York City, October 30, 1941, charged that "President Roosevelt and his administration have never taken the American people into their confidence. They preach about preserving democracy and freedom abroad, while they practice dictatorship and subterfuge at home. . . . . This war we are asked to enter would be the greatest and most devastating conflict in all history. And what have we to gain from either a material or an ideal standpoint? . . . . There is no danger to this nation from without. Our only danger lies from within." A few weeks before at Des Moines (September 11, 1941) Lindbergh had asserted that "the three most important groups which have been pressing this country toward war are the British, the Jewish, and the Roosevelt Administration."

Dr. Goebbels' Propaganda Ministry had hailed the America First Committee on January 2, 1941, by broadcasting over the short-wave to America, "The America First Committee is truly American and truly patriotic!" On May 1, 1941, the leaders of the German-American Bund had urged all its members to join the America First Committee. The leaders of this committee, however, repudiated the Bund's support—although they did not refuse the support of William Dudley Pelley's Silver Shirts or Father Coughlin's Christian Front. Certain other groups, among which were the Ku Klux Klan, the American Destiny Party, the American Guards, the Patriots of the Republic, the National Copperheads, and the Gray Shirts, also rallied around the America First banner.

Following an investigation of Axis agents that were in the America First movement, the American Legion in California publicly stated in October, 1941, that its committee found that in local meetings "processes are at work whereby a person attending merely to seek information, may unwittingly be transformed into a Nazi sympathizer, and even into a potential traitor to his country." It went on to assert that "the subversive infiltration into America First in California has not only confused the minds of the people it attracts, but also has poisoned the minds of persons of outstanding community reputation who have participated in its activities."

During late November and early December, 1940, the America First Committee openly attacked the Committee To Defend America by Aiding the Allies and stated that it was leading the nation into war. General Thomas S. Hammond, chairman of the Chicago chapter of the America First Committee, declared that the White Committee was purposely preparing the public mind for a declaration of war. The Reverend J. A. O'Brien of Notre Dame made the same statement. John T. Flynn, speaking at a rally sponsored by the America First Committee, felt that "tonight we can say that this great free American people which so generously gave its sympathy to Britain is in the grip of a conspiracy, a conspiracy in which the American government, the William Allen White Committee, and agents of the British government are plotting to take America into an actual declaration of war."

Verne Marshall loudly agreed, and Guy Fowler wrote in his column in the *Whittier* (California) *Reporter* on December 12 that "nobody with brains or heart wants war. William Allen White, who once was a good country editor of the *Emporia Gazette*, is sending up senile thunder for American entry, but he no longer hears the voices of little people who were so important when he was striving for circulation and advertising. He has been blown up by the bankers and the Big Money crowd until he is no more than their loud-speaker service trumpeting in the midst of doubt and confusion."

These attacks were serious matters to White. They bothered him a great deal and were one reason why he gave his now famous interview to Roy Howard on December 23, 1940. Less serious than these attacks were the demagogic tactics of Rush Holt in the Senate. On December 4, Holt took up the time of the Senate unearthing a clue as to why White wanted "to enlist the United States as a British ally in the European War." The clue was to be found in White's book *The Martial Adventures of Henry and Me*, published in 1918. According to Holt, a good portion of the book was taken up with glowing descriptions of lavish entertainment by London society during the first World War. Holt's conclusion was that the author was perhaps "seeking to return to those delightful fields as the hero who helped shove the United States for a second time into war as Britain's ally." The *Chicago Tribune* gave this story some play, and Paul S. Mowrer, editor of the *Chicago Daily News*, sent it on to Mr. White. The answer he received was that "Holt is such a nut I can't think that anyone would seriously be affected by what he said and that particular story. Aren't they hard up for argument?"

Although because of his illness White had been unable to go to New York in October, 1940, to take personal charge of the Committee's headquarters as he had planned, he spent a great deal of time in Emporia pondering the policy for the Committee to advocate after the presidential election. Letters were sent to various members of his policy committee suggesting some thought about the Far Eastern situation, increased American production, and delivering the goods to Great Britain. When Ray Tucker, Washington columnist, mentioned in October that the Committee stood for the repeal of the Johnson Act, White sent him a long letter stating that it was not so. Some members of the New York and Washington chapters might have advocated this, but not the national organization. He told Tucker that he had the support of men like Thomas Lamont on this question.

Livingston Hartley, writing pamphlets for the Committee, on October 30 sent Mr. White a draft for his approval, which contained the phrase "revision of neutrality act." White's attitude was: "I don't feel we should take that up at this time and I don't want this thing to turn up in the congressional investigation as our attitude at this time. I also don't like nonbelligerency as a term to describe American attitude. And anyway I don't think we should go on the record even to our executive committee until after election."

On Monday, November 11, White made a trip to Chicago to discuss the policy of the Committee with Clark Eichelberger, John A. Morrison, regional co-ordinator of the middle western chapters, and delegates from chapters in Ohio, Michigan, Indiana, Illinois, Minnesota, Wisconsin, Iowa, and Missouri. By this date the course of the war had shifted somewhat. In September the Italian army had attacked Egypt from Libya and advanced as far as Sidi Barrani. Italian planes had bombed Alexandria, Port Said, and Suez. The British had built up their army in Egypt to meet this Axis threat and had also fought to keep the Mediterranean Sea open for their supply ships. Then on October 28 an Italian army invaded Greece. Meanwhile, the Nazis had reduced Hungary to an Axis satellite and had infiltrated into Rumania.

In view of these events, Chairman White pointed out at the Chicago conference that with the movement of the war to the Mediterranean there would be a let-down in the American people's interest unless the Committee kept the public informed of the consequences of a British defeat in the Mediterranean. "We must not let down," he said, "as long as the war continues." For that matter, he also emphasized that he hoped the Committee would work energetically for a lasting peace once the war was over.

From Chicago, White traveled to Montreal and spent a day there consulting with the Montreal chapter. He then went to Boston for a day and addressed a Boston committee dinner at the Hotel Somerset. The other speakers were Senator Styles Bridges of New Hampshire and Frank Knox, secretary of the Navy.

At the end of that week he reached New York City, and for the next week or more his time was completely occupied with Committee matters. He held many conferences and attended luncheons in his honor. On November 18 he had a luncheon meeting with a group of writers who favored the objectives of the Committee. At this luncheon he appointed several of those present to serve as a nucleus committee to co-ordinate their services to the Committee: Stephen Vincent Benét, John Farrar, Allan Nevins, Henry Pringle, and Mrs. Sophie Kerr Underwood. At this luncheon he dismissed the argument that aid to Great Britain was leading the United States to war by saying:

"If Hitler finds it advantageous at any time to make war on us, he will find a reason; make an incident a cause of war. We shall not be attacked because of our moral attitude, whatever that may be. Did it help Czechoslovakia to capitulate, or did it help Norway to carefully guard her neutrality? Make no mistake, we shall not be attacked, if we are attacked, because of an attitude—it will be because of our worldly goods."

White's arduous activities, however, were beginning to tell. He wrote Frank Clough, managing editor of the *Gazette:* "I'm having a busy time. Every hour seems to be scheduled. This committee job is both getting my goat and renewing my youth. When you get to be in your seventies you'll know what I mean." His mind was troubled by complaints from the New York City chapter that they did not have enough influence on the determination of the policy of the Committee. Furthermore, he was worried by the failure of England to prevent supply ships from being sunk and was wondering how this country could give her more help "short of war."

In addition to the vexing problem of getting supplies to England, the Committee was faced with the problem of what position to adopt in connection with Herbert Hoover's proposal to feed the peoples of occupied Europe. During the previous summer Hoover had revealed that he was negotiating with Great Britain in an effort to persuade her to lift the blockade so that food could go to the peoples of Poland, Norway, the Netherlands, and Belgium. This plan, it turned out, would have defeated the main purpose of the British blockade and would have been of great value to the Nazis, who were taking possession of the food supplies of the conquered regions. The British refused to lift the blockade and pointed out that the

German war industries were using potatoes for alcohol, fats for nitroglycerin, and milk for aircraft plastics.

On October 24, then, White wired Hoover that he was opposed to feeding the peoples of Europe, because it might aid Germany. The next day the Committee released a statement that "under no circumstances should American public opinion urge the British to weaken their blockade. . . . . We cannot afford to feed populations who are engaged in producing the means of threatening our safety. And it will be extremely difficult if not impossible to feed any part of the populations which Germany controls without running the risk of indirect diversions which will have the effect of strengthening Germany through those who must do her bidding. For our own sakes we should not take the risk."

While White was in the East in November, he and Thomas Lamont talked with Hoover about the opposition of the Committee to the Hoover plan. They attempted to talk Hoover out of his plan but failed. White, in view of this failure, felt that the Committee should soft-pedal its opposition to the Hoover plan. Immediately following this conference, he told Eichelberger that "we don't want to get Hoover down on us. Let someone else carry this fight, not us." It now became White's opinion that it was not the job of his Committee to speak against Hoover's proposal, but that, on the other hand, the Committee would not put pressure on Britain to let supplies through the blockade. England would be left free to make her own judgment on this question.

Before his policy committee met on November 25, White went to Washington to have a conference with President Roosevelt, which took place on November 19, 1940. He went to see the President, as he had earlier written Clark Eichelberger, because "I don't want to get crossways with the White House on national policies." In their talk, according to White,

President Roosevelt supported him in his opposition to the repeal of the Neutrality Act and against convoys. White also talked with Secretaries Knox, Hull, Stimson, and Morgenthau and later stated that they all agreed that his stand against these two things was right.

The policy committee, which met on White's return to New York, decided upon a statement which was issued publicly on November 26. This policy statement called for increased aid to the Allies, which could be accomplished only by greatly increasing American production. If it were necessary, the Committee suggested that the President declare a state of national emergency to mobilize our industrial resources for maximum production. In the Pacific area the Committee urged that the United States give all possible material and financial help to China and place an embargo on all war materials destined for Japan. There were three statements in this policy release that are worth quoting in full:

. . . . The life line between Great Britain and the United States is the sea route to the Western Hemisphere. Under no circumstances must this line be cut and the United States must be prepared to maintain it. The United States should supply Great Britain with all possible merchant vessels to fly the British flag. The United States should produce boats as rapidly as in the World War days, for lease or rent to the British. A shipping pool should be developed so that American ships could operate in the Indian and Pacific Oceans and thus release Britain's shipping for service in the Atlantic.

The time has come when Congress should assume a larger share of responsibility, with the President, for the policy of aid to the Allies. Consequently, we favor through Congressional action a revision of our international policy. This would include a repeal or modification of restrictive statutes which hamper this nation in its freedom of action when it would cooperate with nations defending themselves from attack by nations at war in violation of treaties with the United States. We ask immediately the repeal of laws regarding recruiting and enlistments as far as Canada is concerned in the interests of the mutual defense pact with Canada. . . . .

The United States should establish a clear naval understanding with Great Britain which will permit the two fleets to be placed in the most advantageous position to protect the Atlantic for the democracies and to stop the spread of war in the Pacific. The world's future is secure if the British and American fleets control the seas.

All of the implications of this program were not entirely clear, and many of the chapters inquired as to their meaning. On December 7 the national organization issued a further clarification of its policy:

In the light of inquiries which have been received from branches regarding two points in the Committee's last Statement of Policy, it is desirable to clarify these points by fuller explanation than could be given in so condensed a statement.

The first point which has caused such inquiries is the following passage:

"The life line between Great Britain and the United States is the sea route to the Western Hemisphere. Under no circumstances must this line be cut and the United States must be prepared to maintain it."

It is clear that if this life line were not maintained, Britain could not survive. Since the Committee believes that the successful survival of Britain is now essential to the successful defense of the United States, it holds that this life line must be maintained. At present it is being maintained by Britain. But the United States must be prepared to maintain it if a time should come when Britain cannot maintain it herself.

This principle concerns a contingency which might arise. Only if it should arise would action by the United States Government become necessary to maintain this life line. How far such action should go cannot be decided now. Suggestions have been made in the press that more over-age destroyers be released to Britain and that the Neutrality Zone be extended many hundreds of miles east from Newfoundland.

At the present time, when such a contingency must be prepared against, the Committee has limited itself to advocating in its Policy Statement immediately after the passage quoted: "That the United States must supply Britain with all possible merchant vessels to fly the British flag."

The second point concerning which inquiries have been made was the following passage.

"The United States should establish a clear naval understanding with Great Britain which will permit the two fleets to be placed in the most advantageous position to protect the Atlantic for the democracies and to stop the spread of war to the Pacific."

This point was included, with fuller explanation as to its necessity, in the Committee's Confidential Statement of Policy issued early in November.

The value of such an understanding for both these purposes can readily be seen. In the Pacific it would make a Japanese attack on the Dutch East Indies or Singapore less likely. It would therefore serve to prevent the extension of the war into the Pacific and make it more likely that the United States can avoid involvement in the war. How far such an understanding should go is a question that only the Government can decide, but it appears evident that it might advantageously include agreement concerning what British naval forces should be based on Singapore and what American forces on Manila, and arrangements for use by both navies of each other's Pacific bases under certain contingencies.

These two policy statements did not advocate the use of convoys by the United States, but it was implied if other measures did not succeed in maintaining the life line to Britain. Nor did they specifically call for the repeal of the Neutrality Act; but the proposed "revision of our international policy," which "would include a repeal or modification of restrictive statutes which hamper this nation in its freedom of action when it would cooperate with nations defending themselves from attack by nations at war in violation of treaties with the United States," could refer to nothing else. According to Eichelberger, everyone present at this meeting knew that the phrase referred to the Neutrality Act.

Two days after this meeting White attended a dinner at the Town Hall Club in New York City where he, for the Committee To Defend America by Aiding the Allies, received the annual award of the National Association of Accredited Publicity Directors for "the most distinguished service in the whole field of public opinion formation." H. A. Bruno served as toastmaster. Brock Pemberton, New York producer and onetime *Gazette* reporter, and Chancellor Harry Woodburn Chase of New York University paid tributes to White. The latter delivered an impromptu speech, during the course of which he described how the Committee had held rallies, put people on the radio, and persuaded the public to write to Congress and the President. He also pointed out how he and other leading figures in the Committee frequently consulted the President, Cabinet members, and the staffs of the Army and Navy before stating the Committee's objectives. According to the *New York Times* the next day, White also said: "We put General Pershing on the air, but the really smart trick we pulled was that after Lindbergh made his speech we put his mother-in-law [Mrs. Dwight W. Morrow] on the air—and was that a face card? It was!"

Two days later the *New York Times* editorially took White to task for what they considered to be boasting about the achievements of the Committee. They quoted excerpts from his speech dealing with General Pershing's and Mrs. Morrow's radio speeches and the interviewing of the Army and Navy staffs, remarking that "Mr. White's remarks in this instance are unfortunate. They obviously exaggerate the role that the committee played in the destroyer-base transaction. They will give many the impression that the general staffs of the Army and Navy are cooperating with the White committee in its efforts to influence public opinion. And by his reference to the 'smart tricks' that the committee 'pulled' Mr. White may needlessly arouse suspicions and injure the future usefulness of his committee."

The day this editorial appeared, Arthur Hayes Sulzberger, publisher of the *Times*, wrote to White saying: "I hope you will feel that the editorial we ran this morning was as constructive as it was intended to be. Certainly it was conceived in admiration and friendliness." On this letter White encircled the word "constructive" and in the margin wrote the words "For a gut shot, yes!" He wrote two letters to the *New York Times*, one for publication and the other a private letter to

Sulzberger. In the former he objected to the editorial's tone and pointed out that his talk had been extemporaneous. He felt that the reporter present had misunderstood his reference to playing a trick by having Mrs. Morrow and General Pershing go on the air.

"What I was trying to say," he wrote, "was that by bringing these citizens to our cause we had taken a trick, not played a trick, and I used the word 'face card' to indicate my figurative intention." Furthermore, he added, "my speech was intended to play down the importance of the Committee and its Chairman. Three times I said we hadn't made a convert, that we were merely crystallizing existing public opinion and implementing it to influence the government. . . . . "

In his letter to Sulzberger, White answered that the editorial had irritated him a great deal, since he felt that it was quite contrary to the tone of his remarks. Sulzberger wrote a long letter in reply, and his explanation of the editorial was as follows:

"We have recently been very much disturbed by the emanations from 'Room 2940.' I understand that you are not a part of the particular group that is represented by that vague and unrevealing title but, as you are well aware, it represents some of your close associates. We have been talking for several days about our responsibility in connection with the releases which come from '2940.' They apparently originate with different and varied groups, but we knew that the common denominator was '2940' and, as I have said, we were considering what we were obliged to do in the matter just at the time when your remarks were made.

"It seemed to us, very frankly, that you had misspoken, and we were anxious to protect the thing in which both you and we were interested. If we were oversensitive it was for the reasons given. I am sorry that we failed to convey in the editorial our respect and admiration for you."

By "Room 2940" was meant the Century Club group, or the Francis P. Miller group, some of whom were members of the New York and Washington chapters of the Committee To Defend America by Aiding the Allies. So White replied to Sulzberger by reminding him that he had told the *Times* people that the Century Club group had nothing to do with the policy of the Committee. He added, however, "they do cause me headaches!" The release from the Century Club group that had apparently annoyed Sulzberger was one condemning Herbert Hoover's plan of feeding the people of the smaller European nations. By late November this group was concentrating its activities on fighting the Hoover plan.

From November to his resignation in January, 1941, White showed increasing irritation at the activities of the Century group. On December 3 he wired Eichelberger to make sure that when Henry Van Dusen spoke in Pittsburgh against Herbert Hoover's plan he would not be publicized as representing the Committee in any way. Then he wrote a two-page letter to Eichelberger in which he revealed his dislike of the Century Club group's association with the Committee and reaffirmed his lifelong principle of not being too far ahead of public opinion:

"As I wired you about the Van Dusen thing: I am worried all the time about that Century Club crowd. They are probably more nearly right than I am. They are young men and of course are impatient with my leadership; . . . . I realize that probably my leadership is crippled by my slow judgment, by my desire to keep fairly abreast of public sentiment and not to get out too far in front. That has been a life technique and I cannot readjust my years to a new technique. . . . . "

White was worried not only by the activities of the Century Club group and the failure of the English supply ships to reach England but also by the accusation of his opponents that his Committee stood for the repeal of the Johnson Act and the Neutrality Act and, most important, that it desired war. In his December editorials he frequently stated that we should not go to war, because a declaration of war would slow down aid to Britain. This was a war, he said, that would be won on the assembly line; it was the job of the United States to speed up that production line. To those who were worried about the repeal of the Johnson Act he pointed out that it was not necessary to repeal the law in order to extend governmental financial aid to Britain, since the Johnson Act prevented only private individuals from loaning money to nations in default on their war debt. He concluded his editorial of December 6 thus:

"So why bother with the repeal. So long as this Johnson act is a sacred cow and gives milk to popular prejudice, let 'her graze and wag her tail and brush her own flies.' No one is going to shoot her for the mere fun of hearing the gun bang. So rally round the Johnson act and enjoy yourself! And remember, the Good Book says so plainly: 'There's more ways of killing a cat than choking it to death on butter.' And the same goes for the sacred cow."

When White wrote to Alf Landon vigorously denying that he and the Committee To Defend America by Aiding the Allies wanted to repeal the Johnson Act or the Neutrality Act, Landon suggested that the Committee should issue a statement, because it was his impression that a good part of the press thought White wanted these acts repealed. In a postscript to his letter of December 2 Landon stated: "In view of your letter, and the contrary interpretation that has been put on the recent statements of your committee, I think it's about time that a frank, candid, definite pledge to the American people be issued."

White, back in the Middle West by December, was no longer as conscious of the gravity of the international situation as he had been when he was in the East. However, keeping England in the fight for the protection of the United States' security necessitated more drastic action than had been taken during the summer and early fall.

VIII

Short of War?

The care and worry associated with the chairmanship of the Committee were definitely weighing heavily upon William Allen White's seventy-two years during the weeks just before the new year of 1941. He poured out his troubles to his old friend, Thomas Lamont, who was in essential agreement with him on the policy of the Committee. First of all, he was annoyed with the activities of the Century Club group. According to White, Eichelberger was likely to be influenced by Herbert Bayard Swope, Ulric Bell, and Herbert Agar of this group, and after talking with them he wanted to issue statements on every question that arose.

White also was afraid that the work of this group, because of its "radical trend," might ruin his own Committee with the public. These worries were taking a great toll on him personally, he admitted. "And as care can kill a cat I am getting to the point where I can't sleep under it, and I have got to get out from under it . . . . my doctor tapped me on the shoulder the other day and told me, 'watch out or I'll take charge of you,' and if he does I am going to follow. It won't be overwork. It will be the care that kills the cat."

On December 16 White received a letter from Roger Greene, associate director of the national organization, urging that the policy adopted on November 26 be clarified. "Perhaps this would mean making up our own minds more definitely," wrote Greene, "as to just what some of our statements mean. . . . . We are criticized both for making broad statements which might involve us in warlike operations and for being too cautious. This may indicate a happy medium or it may mean that our appeal is not now as effective as it was earlier." White's reply was that the Committee at this point should be a little behind, rather than a little ahead of, public sentiment. Furthermore, the Committee should not make any concrete proposals until after the government had stated its formal position on increased aid to Britain.

By December the Committee was facing a difficult problem. Aid to England was increasingly necessary for the survival of that nation and for the security of the United States. On the other hand, England lacked the ships to transport and convoy this material safely to her ports. For American aid to be effective, the United States might have to convoy, which would necessitate repealing the provision of the Neutrality Act which banned American ships from the war zone. American public opinion on these moves seemed to vary according to geographical location. The East and West coasts were more willing to accept such steps than the Middle West.

White, reflecting his own section of the country, could not agree with many eastern members of his Committee on the next step to take. He realized that England alone was not capable of transporting the material across the Atlantic in the face of German submarines and airplanes. But for the United States to convoy this material, or to revise the neutrality law, was a step that might lead to war. This was a real dilemma. White did not feel that he could sanction steps that might lead the United States into war, yet he and his policy committee on November 26 had called for the repeal of all legislation hampering effective aid to Britain.

Back home in Emporia in December, he began to speculate on what should be done. To charge, as some have done, that those members of the Committee who favored the repeal of the neutrality law and convoys were warmongers merely clouded the issue facing the American people at this point. The issue was whether or not to take steps to make our aid to England effective rather than letting it be sunk on the high seas. Since the attack on Pearl Harbor, it seems clear that war was inevitable for the United States whenever the Axis decided that the time was ripe, but White was not yet quite ready to admit this.

Then on December 18 he received a letter from Frederic Coudert warning him that Roy Howard of the Scripps-Howard newspaper chain was going to unleash an attack on the Committee. For two days the Kansan debated the course that he should take, and on December 20 he wrote this personal letter to Roy Howard:

"Look now, Roy, you and I have been buddies more or less and I hope I have deserved the honor of your friendship these twenty years and more and why I am sending this is on account that a friend in Washington says you are preparing to strafe our outfit and particularly me because we are heading HB for war. All right only this:

"The only reason in God's world I am in this organization is to keep this country out of war. I don't go an inch further or faster than Wendell Willkie or the American Legion or the American Federation or the National Grange; nor an inch further or faster than you went this month in the Filipino magazine on the eastern question. I am abreast of you and no further and I haven't changed since we talked in Chicago last

July. . . . . The President is following his own way. But the Johnson Act should not be repealed and we are not for it.

"Still one more charge: It is not true even remotely that we favor repealing [the neutrality law] to carry contraband of war into the war zone. . . . . If I was making a motto for the Committee To Defend America by Aiding the Allies, it would be 'The Yanks Are Not Coming.' We could not equip them and feed them if they went. We have less than two hundred thousand ready and we need them worse at home on the assembly belt than we need them in Europe. War would defeat the end for which our Committee is organized to defend America by aiding Great Britain and would bring on a thirty year conflict. The Yanks are not going because if they went to war they would lose our case.

"Not one official utterance of our organization has anything remotely suggestive that we feel the only alternative for American defense through aid to Great Britain is war. Moreover I have sat in all executive councils, all policy making committees and I have never heard war seriously discussed in any official group of our organization at any time. I hope you know that I am not a liar and I hope you feel I am not a sucker and I trust you will believe what I am writing."

Of course, White's purpose in writing this letter was to head off Howard's proposed attack, which he knew would hurt the Committee. Howard asked White if he could publish this letter in his papers, and after a day's thought White gave his permission, provided that personal references be deleted and that the end be changed to read: "never heard war as an alternative objective seriously discussed by an official group of our organization at any time. America will go to war or stay out of war not because we make Hitler mad but only when, as and if Hitler thinks he can win the war. And so long as we arm behind the British fleet and England fights while we arm,

Hitler never will think he can win the war unless he starts war to slow down aid to Britain. Any organization that is for war is certainly playing Hitler's game."

White seems to have had a threefold purpose in mind when he authorized Roy Howard to publish this letter as an interview, which appeared in Scripps-Howard papers on December 23, 1940. One purpose was to answer the "leonine accusations of fanatic opponents"—the America First Committee, Verne Marshall's No Foreign Wars Committee, such men as Rush Holt. A second purpose seemed to be White's desire to serve notice on the Century Club group and the eastern wing of the Committee in general that the Committee To Defend America by Aiding the Allies should not move too fast for opinion in the Middle West. His last purpose was to make his own position on aid to Britain clear to the American public.

Although he wrote to Eichelberger on December 23 that Howard might be leading him into a trap, when he saw the spread given to the letter and the editorial that the Scripps-Howard Alliance wrote commending it, he wired G. B. Parker, editor-in-chief of the newspaper chain, "Swell editorial. Hope I can deserve it. If you know of anyone assuming to represent us challenging my statement to Howard let me know. Deeply grateful to you and Howard and your service for this chance to get the position of our committee straight before the country. Warm personal regards and all the Christmas fixin's."

The publication of this interview, however, immediately stirred up vigorous comment from the Century Club group, from members of the White Committee, and from the various individuals and groups in opposition to effective aid to Britain. General Robert E. Wood, Retired, national chairman of the

America First Committee, issued a statement on December 24 saying that White's views were in agreement with the America First Committee's position. Charles A. Lindbergh sent the following statement to the *New York World-Telegram* on December 24:

"Mr. White has rendered a great service to this country by clarifying his position, and the position of his committee. He has given us new hope for a united America at a time in our history when unity is essential. Many of us have felt in the past that Mr. White's committee was intentionally leading us to war. . . . .

"Mr. White has now clarified this situation. He tells us that the committee as a whole does not approve the interventionist views of some of its members. He offers us objectives upon which most Americans can unite. He asks us to stay out of war. He opposes convoying with our navy, the repeal of the Johnson act, the carrying of contraband into the war zone on American ships. He offers us as a slogan the motto 'The Yanks Are Not Coming,' and tells us that our intervention would lead to a 30-year conflict. In short, he offers us a basis of national unity that every American should welcome as a sign of growing strength among our people. . . . .

"The important thing is that we unite on the destiny of America; on the necessity of building strength at home and keeping out of war abroad. In this Mr. White has today given us an example of true leadership."

Verne Marshall, chairman of the No Foreign Wars Committee, however, refused to accept White's statement that the White Committee had no war aims. Marshall declared that he had heard his opponent assert in a speech before the Union League Club in November that "it is time for us to take sides in this war." Marshall had heard correctly, but he had interpreted the speech incorrectly; White had meant by taking

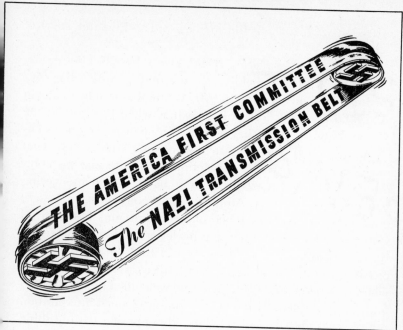

THE AMERICA FIRST COMMITTEE
The NAZI TRANSMISSION BELT

Friends of Democracy believes members of the America First Committee should re-examine the policies of the organization in the light of the fact that it is being used as a Nazi transmission belt. We believe they should consider the implications of these facts:

1. A large part of the audiences of many America First meetings are members of pro-Nazi organizations.

2. Nazi propaganda is distributed at many of these meetings.

3. Nazi organizations not only distribute, the literature of the America First Committee but recruit members and raise money for the committee.

4. The Nazi press in the United States has stamped the program of the America First Committee with its approval.

5. The propaganda ministries of the democracy-hating Nazi and Fascist governments endorse the policies of the committee.

In view of these facts, we believe the America First Committee should reorganize on a basis which does not lend itself to misuse as a Nazi transmission belt.

FRIENDS OF DEMOCRACY, INC.

L. M. Birkhead, National Director

National Headquarters:
Fidelity Building
Kansas City, Missouri

Eastern Regional Office:
103 Park Avenue
New York, N. Y.

The Friends of Democracy, Inc., felt strongly, as the covers of their brochure show sides that we merely should increase aid to England, short of war.

The *San Francisco People's World*, December 28, also refused to believe White. It baldly asserted that he was a liar. According to its interpretation, "Mr. White was simply giving an alibi, and one that doesn't hold water, when he wrote in the Scripps-Howard press that he is not in favor of America's entering the war. It is a new attempt to confuse the people, who have been convinced by the actions of White and his committee, that he was fronting for a band of war-mongering bankers, militarists and Administration politicians."

White received a number of telegrams and letters from Committee members protesting his letter to Howard. Herbert Bayard Swope wired on December 24 that the interview was causing great distress in the East, distress which increased when Lindbergh and General Wood welcomed him as an ally; and, Swope added, "I hate to see you dragooned into position not of opposing war but of seemingly opposing the big thing the Committee is seeking, all out aid to England." On the same day Henry Sloane Coffin let White know that he would resign if the chairman opposed steps that were essential to aiding England.

It seems clear that White leaned over backward in certain of his statements to Roy Howard. For instance, his assertion that "the only reason in God's world I am in this organization is to keep this country out of war," although true enough, was misinterpreted by some Committee members and supporters to mean that White was unwilling to fight German aggression under any circumstances. J. Lionberger Davis of St. Louis wrote him that we should keep out of war if possible, but if it became necessary we should be willing to fight. Later, on January 7, 1941, White wrote to Frederic R. Coudert, Sr., that by his statement that the Committee was organized to keep us out of war he had meant, of course, "only so long as that was a possible course." Obviously, from this letter he was not for peace at any price, nor was he an advocate of appeasement of Hitler. His statement to Howard, however, did not make this clear.

In the national headquarters of the Committee there are many letters and telegrams protesting White's statement. The protests came not only from the Atlantic seaboard but from all over the country. Anita McCormick Blaine of Chicago wired Eichelberger that White should be asked to resign; Lucille Allen Beck, executive secretary of the Colorado chapter, wired that there was a great upheaval in her committee; Chauncey Hamlin, chairman of the Buffalo chapter, wired Eichelberger that he would resign if the Committee backed up White; Mark Ethridge wired that members of the Louisville chapter were restive under White's statement; Kempton Ellis of the Los Angeles chapter wrote Eichelberger that he and some of his friends would resign if the Committee officially backed up White. These are only samples of the complaints that poured into the national office in New York City. They were written by people who were not members of the Century Club group but who feared that White had become an "appeaser."

The Executive Committee of the Committee To Defend America by Aiding the Allies became worried over the manner in which Lindbergh and Wood were trying to capitalize on White's interview; they knew from close association with White that he was not even remotely close to the position of these two men. They were also upset by the protests from Committee members about the interview. Some people disliked White's use of "The Yanks Are Not Coming," a slogan invented by the Communists when the war first broke out; others felt that White's statement that the Committee did not favor the repeal of the neutrality law was in conflict with the official policy statement of November 26.

The Executive Committee had called a meeting as soon as it saw the Howard interview in the *World-Telegram*. On December 24, Lewis Douglas, on behalf of the Executive Committee, telephoned White and followed the call with a telegram, suggesting that White issue a statement that his interview merely expressed his "profound hope that this country will remain at peace, a hope that is shared by the entire American people;" that it was a reflection of the position of the Committee, which prayed that the defeat of the Axis powers could be accomplished without this country's becoming engaged actively in the conflict; and that it was not a denial of the policy of the Committee that all aid to enable England to withstand the Axis attack must be given. To the Executive Committee this last point was extremely important. It was their feeling that White's statement to Howard was not in sympathy with the official policy adopted November 26, which read: "We favor through Congressional action a revision of our international policy. This would include a repeal or modification of restrictive statutes which hamper this nation in its freedom of action when it would cooperate with nations defending themselves from attack by nations at war in violation of treaties with the United States."

On Christmas Day Frederick McKee, representing the Executive Committee, flew to Emporia to persuade White to issue a statement which would clarify his stand and definitely demonstrate that White was not for peace at any price, as all the Committee members knew. White, however, refused to issue another statement. The following day, Clark Eichelberger, Lewis Douglas, Herbert Bayard Swope, Frank Boudreau, and Thomas Finletter wired White suggestions for an open letter to answer Lindbergh and Wood. Eichelberger added this comment to the suggestions: "In light of almost twenty years friendship and my loyalty to you please believe me when I say misunderstanding over your Howard interview having national repercussions and unless we can agree quickly on statement sent you our movement is threatened with disaster."

White took some suggestions from this letter and drew up a statement in his own style. The Executive Committee, however, did not feel that it was clear enough and asked him not to release it. To this request he acceded. In a telephone conversation with Eichelberger concerning the proposed letter to Lindbergh, White inquired why he had not been asked to sign a round-robin letter to President Roosevelt urging the President to do "everything that may be necessary to insure defeat of the Axis powers." Lewis Douglas and James B. Conant had prepared this round-robin letter, which was not sponsored by any organization. It pledged its complete approval of the President's plan, which he had outlined at a press conference on December 17, to lend armaments to Britain in order to "remove the dollar sign from American aid."

The Douglas-Conant letter was designed to strengthen President Roosevelt's hand in this proposal. Published on December 27 in the *New York Times*, it stated that "the material of war and the military and naval air strength we now have and the implements we can now produce are enough to make certain the defeat of the axis powers, so long as Britain is on her feet and fighting; but with Britain down, they are not enough and may not in the future be increased enough to hold the world at bay."

Eichelberger replied to White's question as to why he had not been asked to sign the letter by saying, "I didn't think you would want to sign it." But Mr. White did, and he added his name to the list of a hundred and seventy other prominent people who had signed it. This action mystified his Executive

Committee, in view of the fact that he had not publicly clarified his Howard interview. They considered the round-robin letter to have more warlike implications than the repeal of the neutrality law or the convoy issue.

Trouble in the ranks of the White Committee over the Howard interview came out into the open on December 27 when Major General John F. O'Ryan resigned because the policy enunciated by White was "pallid and ineffective." Two days later, Mayor Fiorello La Guardia released to the press a letter that he had written White. This letter, bearing the greeting "My dear and good friend," read in part:

"I read your statement saying what the Committee to Defend America by Aiding the Allies would not do. Strange, when the going was good for the Allies, you and others were strong in saying what you would do.

"Now the going is bad, you are doing a typical Laval.

"It occurred to me that the Committee had better divide. You could continue as chairman of the 'Committee to Defend America by Aiding the Allies with Words' and the rest of us would join a 'Committee to Defend America by Aiding the Allies with Deeds.' . . . . "

To add insult to injury, in White's view, the New York City chapter of the Committee made Mayor La Guardia its honorary chairman. On December 30 Herbert Bayard Swope publicly backed La Guardia's attitude toward White.

In spite of the public reaction to the Howard interview, which seemed to be dividing opinion within the Committee, the day before the La Guardia statement appeared White had reaffirmed his position on effective aid to England in a private wire to the President, who was to address the nation on the twenty-ninth about the foreign situation: "Don't let Bert Wheeler's crowd beat your ears down. And don't pull your punches on appeasers. Shoot the works. The way to keep out of war which is our common aim is not to flutter white feathers in an hour of danger. I am with you and our Committee will support a strong policy of every safe and legal aid to Great Britain. The country is with you."

The President in his speech warned the people that they faced an emergency comparable only to war. He pledged increasing aid to Britain and stated that the present efforts of the United States toward war production were not enough. "We must have more ships, more guns, more planes—more of everything. This can only be accomplished if we discard the notion of 'business as usual.' This job cannot be done merely by superimposing on the existing productive facilities the added requirements for defense. . . . . We must be the great arsenal of democracy." The President went on to observe that there were some individuals who were saying that the United States should be friendly with the Axis:

"They tell you that the Axis powers are going to win anyway; that all this bloodshed in the world could be saved; and that the United States might just as well throw its influence into the scale of a dictated peace, and get the best out of it that we can. They call it a 'negotiated peace.' Nonsense! Is it a negotiated peace if a gang of outlaws surrounds your community and on threat of extermination makes you pay tribute to save your own skins? Such a dictated peace would be no peace at all. . . . .

"If Great Britain goes down, the Axis powers will control the continents of Europe, Asia, Africa, Australia, and the high seas—and they will be in a position to bring enormous military and naval resources against this hemisphere. It is no exaggeration to say that all of us in the Americas would be living at the point of a gun—a gun loaded with explosive bullets, economic as well as military."

When the speech was over White wired the President: "You have rallied America with a magnificent call. No patriot can withhold his support. You have renewed our faith in democracy here in our country and have made America again the hope of the world. We proudly pledge you our full support." In the *Emporia Gazette* of December 30, 1940, he had the following comments to make on the speech:

"It was a great speech. It will give courage to free men fighting all over the earth and to free countries in the dungeons of Nazi captivity.

"There was something in the speech more than the mere promise to be the arsenal of democracy. It was also to be the great dynamic power house of the moral purpose of a democracy. We Americans take leadership in a world that is menaced by the counter-revolution of Fascism in its various forms —Naziism, Bolshevism—all one breed of hell cats that gnaw the heart out and take the self-respect and spirit out of the human body and make it a machine that is the servant of a ruthless state.

"Abraham Lincoln at Gettysburg did not more clearly and simply proclaim the cause men fought for eighty years ago than did President Roosevelt last night in his winged message that flew around the world. Americans have reason to be proud of the voice that spoke for them."

This editorial was a vigorous notice to those who thought that White had deserted the cause of aid to Britain. Nevertheless, he was adamant about the attempt of the Executive Committee to get him to make a statement definitely modifying his Howard interview.

To Henry Haskell of the *Kansas City Star* he wrote on December 31 that he had made the Howard interview to find out how many Committee members "were hellbent for war." He was now satisfied that some of the members of the New York

City chapter and other seaboard chapters like Baltimore and Washington fell into this category.

The situation, however, was not so simple as White visualized it in this letter to Haskell. The Executive Committee had received protests from Committee members all over the country, not just from the East. Undoubtedly some of these people favored war, but many truly felt that White's Howard statement as it read was not in agreement with the Committee's previous policy. The Executive Committee and the national Policy Committee finally on December 30 adopted a policy statement which reaffirmed that of November 26, and thus they went on record as being opposed to White's Howard interview.

When Eichelberger wired on December 26 that the Scripps-Howard article was still having unfortunate repercussions, White tendered his resignation as chairman of the Committee To Defend America by Aiding the Allies in these words:

"Appreciate full gravity of situation and am of course amazed that I am so far behind the procession but here I stand, can go no faster nor no further. And of course believing as I do I should not be leading an organization which has different aims and objectives from mine. I felt and still feel that we should deny the charges specifically and categorically made against us first that we were advocating or favoring repealing the neutrality law to send our ships into belligerent waters with contraband goods, second that we favored convoys and third that we favored the repeal of the Johnson Act and fourth that we had a concealed objective of war. This last is to me most important to deny. If war comes it should come after we have made manifest our profound belief that it is the last and perhaps most futile gesture. This being my belief I cannot play hypocrite to my convictions. So our problem now, our only problem, is to ease me out of the chairmanship with as little harm to the organization as possible. Next to our country I wish to conserve that organization. But I must not sacrifice my convictions. I am willing to go now. I am willing to hang on until we can make the transition to a younger man easily and naturally. But in all events it must be understood definitely and finally without question or discussion that I go. . . . . ''

Two days later he wrote to Lewis Douglas reaffirming his statement that he must resign. He pointed out that he had written the Howard letter in order to forestall an attack, and he had not consulted the executive or policy committees about it, "because I supposed and still think, I was inside of the intentions of the Committee as expressed by the policy of November 26." He added that he had received as many telegrams from Committee members in the Middle West supporting his stand as he had from New York City opposing his stand. However, even if only a minority of the Committee opposed him, he felt that his resignation was inevitable. He told Mr. Douglas that he would announce it at a dinner in January at which he was to receive the *Churchman* award for distinguished service to the United States during the year 1940. The resignation was settled, there was to be no turning back.

In spite of White's pending resignation Lewis Douglas sent him a telegram, on January 1, 1941, on behalf of the Executive Committee urging him to come to New York to quiet the rebellion in the Committee's ranks and to direct the campaign that would be necessary in the next three weeks to carry out the Committee's program of support for President Roosevelt's Lend-Lease proposal. The telegram was sent to make it clear that White, in the eyes of the others, had failed adequately to clarify the Howard interview, even by his resignation. White realized that this was an ultimatum—an ultimatum that he could not carry out. It would mean that he would have to be in New York for the balance of his chairmanship. Living in a New York City apartment in January was not conducive to good health at his age. Also, and more important, Mrs. White had been ordered to spend the winter on the desert because of her sinus infection, and he felt that he could not leave her alone in a strange hotel in the desert country.

All New Year's Day White was nervous, tired, and absentminded; he wandered about the house and ignored his guests —Mrs. W. L. White, her brother, Dr. Royle Klinkenberg, Frank Clough, managing editor of the *Gazette*, and Mrs. Clough. Dr. Klinkenberg was quite worried about his host's health. Finally Mr. White said to his guests, "I am going upstairs to lie down. Please don't go. I will be back." He started to go and then looked back and said, "These clothes feel tight on me. I shall take them off." When he reached the stairs he turned again and said, "I almost caved in. I almost caved in." For the old man such an admission was extremely unusual.

That day, after long meditation, White sent the following telegram to Hugh Moore, Lewis Douglas, and Clark Eichelberger:

"The urgency of events has created a new tempo in our work and hence the need for quick decisions and close consultations. This I cannot give unless I come to New York for the winter. Mrs. White and I must leave for Arizona next week. At least for a month in a critical period I shall be unable to give as much time to the Committee as I have been giving. The Committee needs a full time chairman. Obviously I can serve the committee best by asking the executive committee to accept my resignation. I reach this decision with regret yet I know it is wise. To every member of the executive committee I send my warm personal regards and the season's best wishes."

White also urged Eichelberger to announce the resignation

the next day, January 2. He likewise asked that the announcement that he would remain as honorary chairman be withheld until after the new chairman was appointed. Eichelberger carried out White's wish in regard to announcing the resignation that day, but he insisted that White permit the announcement that he would remain as honorary chairman to be made with it. This White assented to with the remark, "I said okay with that resentment that a man feels when he is thwarted by a friend."

In an editorial to the home folks on January 3, 1941, he wrote about his resignation:

"The job was too big a one for me, and after all, I have my own life to live, and again after all I wanted to celebrate my 73rd birthday in peace and devote the year or two or three that may be left to me to writing some books and helping with some chores around the house here in Emporia and Kansas. . . . . I had a definite sense that the war fever was rising and I didn't like it. All my life I have been devoted to peace, to the belief that war is futile and in this particular case to the conviction that if we could keep Great Britain fighting for our cause, this would never become our war. The President said it in his speech when he divided the functions of the World War and declared that we should be the arsenal. The arsenal with its assembly belt is just as important as the front line trench and I felt that the arsenal of democracy was the American job. . . . . "

Just before White's resignation was released to the press on January 2, Clark Eichelberger, William Emerson, representing the New England chapters, and John A. Morrison, Adlai E. Stevenson, and Clifton M. Utley, representing the Chicago chapter, talked to White in a conference telephone conversation. All of these people exept Eichelberger urged him to continue as chairman; but White's answer was that he was tired, that his wife was sick, and that he could not stand any more battering from the New York crowd.

The letters that White wrote in the weeks following his resignation showed clearly that he had been worried over the danger of approaching war and the identification of his Committee as a warmongering committee. He laid the blame for this war spirit at the door of the small Century Club group and stated that he had resigned so that a younger man, who could stay in New York to curb the Century Club "hotspurs," might be appointed. However, he seemingly chose to forget the difficulty caused among many non-Century Club people by his Howard interview.

As a matter of fact, White's resignation as chairman of the Committee To Defend America by Aiding the Allies probably would have come fairly soon even without the Howard interview and the events that followed it. As he said, the old man was exhausted, Mrs. White was sick, and he had mentioned to Eichelberger and others during his November visit to New York City that he would have to resign before long. It must also be remembered, in considering the causes of his resignation, that White had the middle westerner's antagonism toward New York City. Time and again in his letters he expressed irritation over this city's considering that it was the whole country, and the failure of the New York City committee people to realize that the temper of the people in the Middle West was different from that in the East. White always felt on the defensive about New York.

Not long after he had resigned he received a letter from Christopher Emmet of the New York City chapter explaining the actions of this group. Emmet said that they had interpreted the Howard letter to mean that White no longer felt it necessary to maintain the life-line to England. They were also irked that he had not consulted the Executive Committee before sending the Howard letter. Furthermore, he said that they had appointed Mayor La Guardia honorary chairman of their chapter only to prevent further resignations from the New York City chapter.

"I beg you not to let isolationist newspapers go on undoing all the splendid work you and your Committee have accomplished ever since last May," added Emmet. "To have you echo their charge of 'Warmonger' against important parts of your Committee is worth a million dollars spent on Nazi propaganda."

In his answer to this letter White reiterated his belief that the Committee should hold to a middle-of-the-road position: "I have felt that we should not prepare this country for war," he said. "I have felt that if we are as efficient in moving Congress and the President toward arming ourselves and Great Britain we can avoid war. When I said that the life-line between Great Britain and the United States should be maintained I meant it, but I did not mean by going to war. I meant by building, lending, and renting ships but not convoys and not sending contraband of war into belligerent waters. I never thought of it. I didn't suppose anyone else had, and I was amazed and surprised that there was any disagreement with that viewpoint." White would not change his position, even though his own son, in England, urged him to do so. He merely said that his son was entitled to his own opinion.

The venerated chairman's resignation from the Committee brought forth a varied reaction from the American public and press. Thomas Lamont, of the Morgan banking interests, who had been in agreement with White's policies as chairman of the Committee, wired him that he did not blame him for resigning, although he himself had hoped that because of White's outstanding service his action might be deferred. Douglas

Fairbanks, Jr., wired his regrets that White was resigning. Alexander and Mary Chatin of the Miami chapter; John A. Morrison and Adlai E. Stevenson, heads of the Chicago chapter; Thomas Finletter of the National Policy Committee; Frank L. Polk, an influential member of the Committee; and Huston Thompson of Washington, D. C., among many others, wrote or wired White expressing their gratitude for his work and their sorrow at his resignation.

Some letters came from opponents of the Committee To Defend America by Aiding the Allies. One dissenter in Evanston, Illinois, interpreted White's resignation to mean that he had changed his mind on the foreign situation. Senator Wheeler wrote praising White's resignation. White's reply, on January 8, showed that he was already overcoming his exhaustion and was regaining his sense of humor, now that his great responsibility was at an end. He wrote: "Thank you for your kind words. The older I get the curiouser life seems. When we pass over, you and I will get on a big pink cloud, swing our feet over the earth and spit on the hypocrites. . . . . "

Apparently under the illusion that White had broken with the Committee, General Robert Wood on January 7 wired him a public letter asking him to join the America First Committee. The answer came in the form of an editorial in the *Gazette* on January 9, saying that the editor would like to end the name-calling between the two committees but that he was irrevocably against the America First Committee because of its lack of desire to aid England.

The newspaper reaction to the resignation was as varied as were the personal ones White received. Such papers as the *Boston Herald*, the *Baltimore Sun*, and the *New York Times* praised White's work as chairman and agreed that he was entitled to a rest. The *New York Times* said in part on January 4:

"His friends know that his health has not been too good recently. After doing a magnificent job he has earned a vacation.

"No one who knows him doubts his fervent and courageous love for democracy. As much as any one man in the United States he helped win public support for the 'arsenal of democracy' policy which the President proclaimed last Sunday evening. His name and personality made the White Committee a going concern in its first difficult days. In carrying on, as it intends to do, the committee will still benefit by the prestige given it by William Allen White and by the trust and affection which he has inspired in millions of Americans.

"Like the rest of us he has no doubt been pulled two ways—toward doing everything possible to beat Hitler and toward doing nothing that will get us into war. In this conscientious facing of a difficult problem, as in his hatred of stupidity, tyranny and injustice, we would like to think that he is a representative American. We do know that this would be a poorer, more cynical, less generous country without Will White of Emporia."

The *Kansas City Times* had said, a day earlier, "No one could accuse 'Old Bill White' of being a warmonger or interventionist. . . . . Now Mr. White is retiring to give place to a younger man who can devote more attention to the work. Certainly he has done his indispensable share to the vast advantage of the nation and the world." Many other newspapers similarly praised White's work and concluded that he deserved nation-wide honor for the work that he had done.

The *Chicago Tribune*, however, on January 4 took advantage of the resignation to reaffirm its stand that White was merely a front, who finally had to resign because the wolves in the Committee "got him." The *Christian Century* for January 8 adopted much the same attitude, contending that "the eastern interventionist end of the William Allen White Committee to Defend America by Aiding the Allies" had taken "its honored chairman for a ride." The *Saturday Evening Post* of February 1 stated that the Committee had long stood for war but knew better than to name their objectives in the beginning and that a lot of innocent people had fallen for their strategy, until the Committee became openly warlike toward the end of December.

On January 6 White went from Emporia to Chicago to attend a regional conference of the middle western chapters of the Committee. Present at the meeting were Clark Eichelberger, John A. Morrison, Quincy Wright, Adlai E. Stevenson, and Clifton M. Utley, among others. The conference agreed that the new chairman should be (1) a middle westerner; (2) a Republican; (3) a man of national prestige; (4) beloved and admired throughout the country; (5) a person with direct access to government sources. The conference feared, however, that White would prove to be the only member with all these attributes.

White himself felt that the Committee would function a good deal better if it had a western office, either in Cleveland, Cincinnati, Detroit, or Chicago. The Committee should recognize that its success depended on the West and the Middle West. This had long been a point of dispute. John Morrison, director of the Chicago chapter and middle western coordinator, as early as September, 1940, had urged that the national headquarters be moved to Chicago because the opposition to aid to Britain was centered in Chicago around the *Chicago Tribune* and the America First Committee.

The conference agreed on this point, finally, and went on record as favoring that the middle western regional office at Chicago be made a national headquarters and its director be co-director with the head of the national office at New York. They also recommended that the Executive Committee should meet in New York, but that the Policy Committee should always meet at some point in the Middle West.

The obvious person for the chairmanship, White then suggested, was Wendell Willkie. He also felt that Charles P. Taft of Cincinnati had all the necessary qualities and that former Senator Gibson of Vermont filled the bill, except that he was not a middle westerner. In the afternoon the conference voted for its choice of the new chairman, stating its preference in the following order: Wendell L. Willkie, Ernest W. Gibson, Adlai E. Stevenson, Lewis W. Douglas, and Lloyd Stark of Missouri.

Upon his return to Emporia from this conference, on January 8, White sent a telegram to Hugh Moore of the national Executive Committee, suggesting that they make John Morrison (then director of the Chicago office) a co-director with Clark Eichelberger. He added that he hoped "in this connection you will give Mr. Eichelberger more and more authority. He is energetic, tactful, and has lots of common sense and will get you into no trouble. It seems to me that he has earned a promotion. . . . . " He followed this up with a letter to Hugh Moore about Committee affairs, setting forth his advice to the new chairman and voicing his reluctance to remain as honorary chairman.

Moore, however, insisted that White remain in that position saying that to refuse "would be a calamity to the cause to which I feel you have dedicated your life." Although the Executive Committee had felt that White should resign, they realized that it had been his name and prestige and guidance that had made the Committee a success.

When the choice of Ernest W. Gibson as the new Committee chairman was publicly announced, White wired his congratulations and offered his services in the following words: "I want to help you whenever I can. It is a great job and I know you will rise splendidly to it. The American people are behind our committee and I know they will give you the support that they have given me as chairman of our organization. Call on me when you think I can serve you."

It was on January 6, while White was in Chicago, that President Roosevelt delivered his annual message to Congress. The message was largely devoted to warning that isolation was impossible, and it called for a "swift and driving increase in our armaments" both for defense and for the use of the fighting "democracies" abroad. It declared that the United States would not be intimidated by the threats of the dictators and that the United States looked forward to a future day when the four freedoms—freedom to worship God, freedom of speech, freedom from fear, and freedom from want—would be the basic principles of society. After hearing this speech over the radio, White wrote an editorial praising it as a "New Magna Charta." His glowing terms are worth reproducing, as evidence of the great power of the speech.

The people of the United States, through their President, have given to the world a new magna charta of democracy. The President's message to the new congress will be a notable one long after the men who heard it are dead and the immediate cause that put wings on Mr. Roosevelt's words have been forgotten. Who knows the name of the barons who met King John on the Island of the Thames a thousand years ago? Who knows the basis of the dispute that brought forth the charter of democratic liberties that memorable day? But the charter lived. The hopes it raised, the faith it set up, the impulse it gave to human liberty through all the centuries have transformed the Magna Charta into the charter of freedom. In it were the seeds of human progress in the Western world.

So today this flaming message of President Roosevelt encircling the globe, will kindle the fire of faith in men, freemen and boundmen, over the whole round earth. His words were more than rhetoric. Backed by the might of a great nation his words become deeds. The nobility in its utterance transcends its language. For the man and the occasion made a drama that will lead the people of the earth to new freedom. It will give to aspiring men everywhere new hopes. Men and nations yet unborn will share the vision, the courage and the wisdom of this day. And the hour will mark the opening of a new era in the world.

If America had no other mission in the world than to send forth those glowing winged words that carried the new faith for a new world, our country would have justified all the sacrifices its founders have given, all the hope that they have consecrated with their blood and toil. It was a great day, a great occasion, a great man—all three united—that spoke to the world today.

Several weeks after this, toward the end of February, White went to New York City to receive the annual award given by the *Churchman*, an Episcopal weekly paper, to the person who in its opinion had rendered the most outstanding service to the country in the past year. The speakers at the dinner were Dr. Hu Shih, Mrs. J. Borden Harriman, Clarence Streit, Clark Eichelberger, and Wendell Willkie, all of whom were united in their tribute to White. Dr. Guy Emery Shipler, editor of the *Churchman*, presented him with a bronze plaque. The award came to White as a result of a poll of eight hundred religious and lay organizations, representing all creeds.

White's speech of acceptance was a ringing call for the United States to assume its duty in the world and was by no means limited to the question of aiding the Allies. "With such a crisis, in such a world, facing the people of America from Patagonia to Hudson's Bay," he said, "no one can guarantee peace. Only a fool would say that any course is sure to bring peace." Provided the English won, the United States and England had a great task to do. The less privileged nations of Europe must be given not only liberties but the sources of these liberties. "I mean explicitly this," he stated: "We must try to help the free democracies to set up a world society in which no nation can feel with any reason that it is denied those raw materials, those basic sources of national growth, whether they be harbors or metals or the right to trade freely upon the oceans of the world, those raw materials which are necessary to maintain a competent civilization of self-respecting citizens."

At first it might be necessary to police the gangster nations "until they see that good will on this earth pays better than the ruthless use of force to secure their just rights. You ask me: 'Why should we police the world?' And I tell you there is something hard and practical in duty. Cain's question is not enough. We are indeed and in truth our 'brother's keepers.' Would it not have been cheaper twenty years ago in cold dollars and cents to take our place in the League of Nations than to spend the billions we are spending today for defense? If we shirk our duty now we shall have to spend another national treasure twenty years from now when today's babies in Europe are old enough to fight. Until the evils that make them fight are abolished, we shall have the same old job to do over again and again. Or else pay the same price or more to live in a world that hates us for the loot within our borders."

White had not repudiated the objectives of his Committee. Now that he was no longer its leader, he seemingly felt free to go further in his internationalism than he had before. He never showed any confusion on the moral issues involved. It was only the legal barrier which he could not hurdle, and which he felt that the Middle West did not wish to tear down. The Middle West was behind the East Coast in realization of the actual situation, and White was not ahead of the Middle West.

IX

The Inevitable Occurs

AFTER WILLIAM ALLEN WHITE'S RESIGNATION AS CHAIRMAN, the Committee To Defend America by Aiding the Allies underwent a reorganization. White was to be honorary chairman and a member of the Executive Committee. Gibson, who was elected chairman to replace White, had just finished a term in the Senate during which, as a Republican, he had supported aid to the Allies. He held the position of chairman until May, 1941, when as an Army Reserve officer he was called into active service. When he relinquished the chairmanship in May, Clark Eichelberger assumed the position. Also in January, Lewis W. Douglas was elected chairman of the national board, and these men were made vice-chairmen of the Committee: Chester H. Rowell, Dr. William Emerson, Dr. Frank Kingdon, Dr. Frank Graham, Robert E. Sherwood, and Rev. Henry A. Atkinson.

The major work of the Committee during January and February, 1941, was to arouse public support for the President's proposal to "sell, transfer, lease, lend, exchange or otherwise dispose of" articles of defense to Great Britain. On January 10 the text of the bill implementing this move was introduced into Congress, with the curiously historic number of H.R. 1776. The Washington office of the Committee prepared a series of "information letters" (written by Livingston Hartley and Donald C. Blaisdell) for the local chapters, describing to them the necessity of passing bill H.R. 1776 and reporting the stand of various senators and members of the House. The January eighteenth letter, for instance, stated:

"The great majority of the American people have made it abundantly clear that they wholeheartedly support two policies. The first is the preservation of American security by aiding Britain and her allies to defeat Germany. The second is the preservation of American peace by avoiding involvement in the war.

"To attain both these objectives when Europe and Asia are convulsed by war will demand exceedingly skillful policy by the United States. To bring about Allied victory without involvement in the war is a problem in strategy, which requires that the President should have authority to regulate the flow of material aid to Britain as the changing situation and their needs and ours may necessitate. Such authority, so vital to the preservation of both our security and our peace, is provided in this Bill."

The America First Committee and other isolationist-minded groups and individuals opposed the Lend-Lease Bill because they felt that it would involve the United States in war and that it would make the President a dictator. The answer of the Committee To Defend America by Aiding the Allies was, first, that we would not have to fear war in the United States if Britain could defeat Hitler in Europe, and that Britain could do so if we gave her enough material aid; and, secondly, that the powers that were granted to President Roosevelt did not touch individual liberty or increase powers he already had to take action outside the borders of the United States which might lead to war. The bill included only powers to be exercised within the United States in the one field of regulating American production and distribution of war materials for our own forces and for those of nations whose defense was deemed vital to our defenses.

On January 31 the Washington office of the Committee sent a letter to local chapters and national committee members warning that undue delay by Congress on the Lend-Lease Bill might undermine the security of the United States and damage faith in democratic institutions. The national headquarters in New York, finding that the isolationist organizations were flooding congressmen's mail with letters opposed to the Lend-Lease Bill, urged all members to counteract this by writting letters which would demonstrate to Congress that a majority of the people favored the measure. To stimulate this letter-writing campaign, Eichelberger and Gibson spoke at five large middle western mass meetings, held at Minneapolis, St. Paul, Kansas City, St. Louis, and Chicago.

During the campaign for the Lend-Lease Bill, the Committee To Defend America by Aiding the Allies released a great quantity of pamphlet literature to explain to the public the necessity of passing the measure. The Chicago chapter, for instance, published a sixteen-page pamphlet entitled *The Atlantic Is Not 3,000 Miles Wide*, emphasizing the ease with which Germany could invade South America if Britain should be crushed. It also made a movie short entitled *It Can Happen Here*, which depicted the routes by which the Nazis could threaten the Americas, and distributed it to local theaters, churches, settlement houses, schools, business conventions, and social organizations.

The national headquarters released a handbill entitled "The Truth about the Lease-Lend Bill," which again answered the charge that the bill would make the President a dictator and urged all citizens to write to their senators and representatives demanding passage of the act. The Chicago committee alone mailed 100,000 letters and distributed 30,-000 handbills at factory gates calling for immediate action in favor of the measure. All over the country the various local chapters held rallies, distributed literature, and sponsored a flood of letters to congressmen.

The Committee To Defend America by Aiding the Allies was not the only source from which came support for the passage of President Roosevelt's measure. Harry L. Hopkins, who had just returned from England, reported that a supply of American munitions meant the difference between life and death to Britain. Wendell L. Willkie, the defeated Republican presidential candidate, made several speeches in favor of the bill. He, too, flew to England to study the actual situation and upon his return appeared before the Senate Foreign Relations Committee on February 11. He stressed the urgency of increased aid to Britain and advocated even greater quantities than the Administration had requested. The Republican party, however, did not wholeheartedly follow Willkie's leadership. Senator Robert A. Taft of Ohio rejected Willkie as the leader of their party when he gave his support to the President's bill. Herbert Hoover and Alf Landon also were opposed to the measure.

The bill finally passed the United States Senate on March 8 by 60 votes to 31, and the House of Representatives on March 11 by 317 votes to 71. That the public had been aroused to wholehearted support of the bill was demonstrated not only by the congressional vote but by the greatly increased popularity of its sponsor, the President. A Gallup Poll, taken shortly after the bill's adoption, showed that, whereas the President had been popular with 55 per cent on election day, he now had 72 per cent of the public with him. The Lend-

Lease Bill officially acknowledged that the United States supported one side in the war. It was clear now that the United States was embarked upon a course of nonbelligerency instead of sympathetic neutrality. The main purpose of the act was "to make the United States the arsenal of democracy." Under it our industrial might would squarely oppose the Axis powers. The United States was pledged, first, to strive to keep Great Britain from being defeated and then to enable Great Britain to take the offensive. It was plain that a majority of Americans felt that this was the wiser course to follow. They were realizing at last that if the Allies should fall, the United States would have little chance for peace, alone in a world surrounded by hostile dictatorships.

Six days after Congress passed the Lend-Lease Bill, the Committee To Defend America by Aiding the Allies issued a new statement of objectives. This called for the full mobilization of American economic life, regardless of the sacrifices that would be necessary on the part of business, labor, agriculture, and the consumer; the use by the American government of whatever means it found expedient to deliver the war materials to the Allies, including "(1) repair of Allied naval vessels in American waters; (2) supply to the Allies of all possible merchant tonnage; (3) transfer to the Allies of additional destroyers and other naval craft; (4) permission to the Allies to organize convoys in American ports; (5) convoy of ships with American naval vessels if need be."

Other objectives were congressional revision of legislation to permit Allied recruiting of Americans; the freezing of all foreign assets in the United States in order to check Nazi activities in the Western Hemisphere; a firm policy in the Pacific, including "(1) increase of American naval strength in the Far East; (2) increased aid to China; (3) extension of embargoes on war materials to Japan; (4) clear indication of our determination to prevent the conquest of Singapore and the Dutch Indies; (5) opening by the United States and Great Britain of Far Eastern naval bases to each other's fleets; and (6) a clear naval understanding between the two countries"; and, last, strenuous efforts to combat Nazi and totalitarian propaganda in the Americas, with care, however, to preserve civil liberties and the Good Neighbor Policy.

During the latter part of March, the Committee warned its members that the sinking of Allied shipping in the Atlantic had reached a dangerous point. To keep the Atlantic life-line open, the United States would have to provide more ships for the Allies or cut down losses by convoying supply ships with American warships. Envisaging the problem of convoys in the future, the national organization stated on March 28:

"If the time should come that the British lifeline should be seriously threatened and our war materials are piling up on the docks on this side of the Atlantic, then the question of convoys must be faced. . . . . It cannot be stated too often that the decision does not lie with us, when and if war shall be declared, for Hitler has abundantly shown by his past actions that he needs no provocation to wage war whenever he considers that his best interests will be served. Materials which go to the bottom of the ocean are no aid to the British, and are a great loss to us; better no aid at all than futile half-measures."

While the Committee To Defend America by Aiding the Allies was displaying concern over the sinking of Allied ships, Germany on March 25, 1941, announced that it was extending the zone of war operations to the borders of Greenland. This was a direct challenge to the security of the Western Hemisphere, and it seemed to presage a German attack on Greenland. America replied by occupying Greenland with American armed forces. The United States negotiated an agreement with the Danish minister in Washington which recognized the wisdom of this step. When the Danish government, under the domination of the Nazis, repudiated their minister's action, Secretary Hull stated that it was obvious that the government of Denmark acted under duress.

The occupation of Greenland was a defensive move, but it also was a step toward safeguarding the supply lines to Great Britain. The Committee To Defend America by Aiding the Allies hailed it as such but insisted that this was not enough. During the last week in April, Lewis W. Douglas and Ernest W. Gibson, speaking for the Committee, unequivocally urged that the United States convoy merchant ships to England. Douglas pointed out that if English shipping losses continued for long, England would be in a desperate position—"so desperate that we may be left alone, dangerously alone to face a hostile world ruled by force and dominated by the Axis powers whose ambitions, so they openly declare, are to recast the world, including ourselves, in their own evil image."

During March the Allies lost 437,730 tons of shipping. To aid the British in convoying their ships, President Roosevelt announced on April 9 the transfer of ten Coast Guard cutters to England. Two days later he withdrew the southern part of the Red Sea from the list of combat zones in order to permit American merchant ships to carry supplies to Egypt through the Suez Canal. This step was taken in order to counteract Axis moves in the Mediterranean-Balkan region. German planes, operating from Italian bases, were continuously attacking British convoys sailing through the Mediterranean Sea. On April 6 German forces invaded Yugoslavia and Greece. Although British troops were sent to aid Greece, she had to surrender in a little over two weeks. Meanwhile, late in March, German and Italian forces had attacked the British in Libya, and General Wavell had been forced to retire to the Egyptian frontier.

Then on June 22, 1941, without warning, Germany attacked Russia. During the preceding January, Sumner Welles had warned the Russian ambassador that Germany had marked Russia for an attack in the following June. Welles, the day after the German invasion, announced:

"If any further proof could conceivably be required of the purpose and projects of the present leaders of Germany for world domination, it is now furnished by Hitler's treacherous attack upon Soviet Russia. We see once more, beyond peradventure of doubt, with what intent the present Government of Germany negotiates 'nonaggression pacts.' " Pointing out that "Hitler's armies are today the chief dangers of the Americas," Welles asserted that "any defense against Hitlerism, any rallying of the forces opposing Hitlerism, from whatever source these forces may spring, will hasten the eventual downfall of the present German leaders, and will therefore redound to the benefit of our own defense and security."

The Committee To Defend America by Aiding the Allies approved of Welles's statement and called the attack upon Russia part of the Battle of Britain and the Battle of America. The United States, they said, should now extend all possible aid to Russia and should conclude an agreement with China, the Dutch East Indies, Britain in the Far East, and Russia to immobilize Japan as an active Axis partner. Sentiment within the United States favoring American aid to Russia grew so strong that on August 2 the acting secretary of state informed the Russian ambassador, M. Constantin Oumansky, that the United States had decided to extend economic assistance to strengthen the Soviet Union in its struggle against aggression.

A number of individuals in this country, however, were opposed to any aid to Russia. Senator Taft held that "a victory for Communism would be far more dangerous to the United States than a victory for Fascism." Senator Wheeler proposed that the United States "just let Joe Stalin and the other dictators fight it out." Congressman Stephen A. Day, one of the favorites of the America First Committee, speaking in Pittsburgh on July 18, told his audience:

"In my last broadcast [June 16, 1941] I warned against the treasonable scheme of Union Now with Britain, devised to make the United States a colonial dominion of the British Empire, to fight and pay for Britain's wars and to forever surrender American citizenship for the mongrel slavery in which American men and women of today would be on a level with the hordes of India and the tribesmen of Africa. I could not believe that in less than two weeks these same Americans would be virtually threatened with the surrender of the American citizenship to follow under the bloody flag of communism and to proclaim the leadership of Stalin, blood-soaked with the murder of over 2,000,000 innocent people in what was formerly Russia."

Such isolationists as these completely misjudged the mood of America. As Walter Lippmann observed, America and Russia were "separated by an ideological gulf and joined by the bridge of national interest." Although the American people disliked communism, they nevertheless realized that a German defeat of Russia would increase the Nazi threat to American security. When isolationist congressmen tried to exclude Russia from Lend-Lease aid in the fall, they found that they were able to muster few votes.

While bloody fighting was taking place in Russia, less spectacular but very important events were taking place along the Atlantic supply lines. German sinkings of Allied shipping in the Battle of the Atlantic were reaching appalling totals. By late June the Committee To Defend America by Aiding the Allies realized that war could not be avoided by the United States, since it seemed that only complete and active participation on the part of the United States could defeat the Axis. The Committee, speaking through Clark Eichelberger, stated that the Battle of the Atlantic must be won immediately and that the United States must win it. All members of the Committee were urged to rally enthusiastic support for American naval participation in the Battle of the Atlantic. On July 3 the Committee published advertisements in the *New York Times* and the *New York Herald Tribune* urging the President to use the Navy to clear the Atlantic of German submarines and to deliver the goods to England. On July 28 it launched a "Battle of the Atlantic Week," during which petitions to the President were circulated.

When the news that American forces had landed in Iceland was released on July 7, the Committee was enthusiastic in its support of the step. President Roosevelt's orders to the American Navy were that they should take all necessary steps "to insure the safety of communications in the approaches between Iceland and the United States." The United States by this move assumed responsibility for keeping the Atlantic lane clear as far as Iceland. American security would have been endangered had Hitler been able to occupy this outpost. Shortly after Germany had invaded Denmark in 1940, British and Canadian troops had occupied Iceland, but these forces were now needed elsewhere. The United States carried out its occupation of the island, therefore, as a measure of self-defense.

The German attack on Russia had also seriously affected the situation in the Far East. If Germany should defeat Russia, Japan would be in an extremely advantageous position. Great Britain and the United States would have to con-

OKAY, MR. PRESIDENT, GO AHEAD "CLEAR THE ATLANTIC"

THE AMERICAN PEOPLE know we are "at war" with Hitler. They know the difference between an undeclared war and a declared war.

Hitler has made a *fatal mistake.*

He has *misjudged* the American people and the American mind.

We may seem to fumble and bumble. We talk when we should be acting and argue when we should be agreeing. We *appear* hopelessly divided. So Hitler has assumed "America is easy; America can be taken when the time comes" *BUT*

YOU ARE WRONG, MR. HITLER. You have been looking at the rainews of America, but you haven't seen the mind or the heart. The truth is . . the American people know they are "at war" with you! Don't think the man in the street here doesn't understand what your propaganda experts think is so clever—the convenient subterfuge of an "undeclared war"

Sure, there are quite a few people right here repeating Hitler's words—playing his game conciously or unconciously. We think it would be foolish, because undemocratic, to silence these people, but we know it would be doubly foolish, because fatal, to follow them.

* * *

Write or wire the President, your Senator, your Representative, that you think it vital to America to "CLEAR THE ATLANTIC." Or tear out the coupon and send in.

But the Majority of Us Have Made Up Our Minds!

People know that President Roosevelt's policy is to keep Hitler guessing. They feel he can beat Hitler at his own game and they are for it.

But they are not guessing what they themselves are going to do.

They have heard the Secretary of the Navy say, "Now is the time to strike" He should know.

They have heard the President say, "The goods we make must be delivered to England. This should be done; this will be done; this must be done"

The American people say, "Okay Mr President, go ahead. Convoy.—Deliver the goods" Americans have always thought that American ships, American goods, American lives should be protected wherever we send them. They still do.

Fifty-five per cent of the people (a larger percentage of the votes than President Roosevelt received in the last election) say that the time has come in our convoys. They know that this means the use of our naval air force as well as naval ships—that it may mean shooting—*and they are for it.* To win the Battle of the Atlantic now may save many American lives later.

It goes against the American grain to be second-best in *anything,* and obviously we can't afford to be second-best in war.

So let us, purely in our own interest, see England has a *better chance* than we have given her to date of finishing the job we want done,— *licking Hitler.* In addition to convoying, let us send every army and navy plane the President can "comb out of our forces" and the maximum product of our airplane factories.

Let us man these planes with American pilots, —Americans who have volunteered. Remove the obstacles to British recruiting here.

Let us occupy bases in the Atlantic and Pacific necessary for the defense of America.

America's Greatest Weapon

The time has come for *all* the people to support the majority of the people in that which they are determined to do and in that which they have made up their minds must be done—*wipe out Hitler. America's greatest weapon is a united and determined America.*

Hitler makes up his mind and then *ACTS* with *SPEED.* Once we are united on what should be done, no one can best us at that game.

Back up the Secretary of the Navy's proposal to use the navy and air forces to *clear the Atlantic* of the German menace.

Join us in urging the President to

CLEAR THE ATLANTIC!

COMMITTEE TO DEFEND AMERICA

BY AIDING THE ALLIES • BY DEFEATING THE AXIS POWERS • BY DEVELOPING MEANS FOR PERMANENT PEACE

8 WEST 40TH STREET, NEW YORK, N. Y.

	Vice Chairmen	
Ernest W. Gibson, Jr. *National Chairman*	Henry A. Atkinson	Frank P. Graham	Hugh Moore *Chairman, Executive Committee*
Leslie W. Dunphe *Chairman, National Board*	Barry Bingham	Mrs. J. Borden Harriman	Ellsworth Bunker *Chairman, Finance Committee*
	William Emerson	Frank Kingdon	Frederick K. McKee *Treasurer*
Clark M. Eichelberger *National Director and Acting Chairman*	Douglas Fairbanks, Jr.	Chester H. Lowell	
	Robert E. Sherwood	Roger S. Greene *Associate Director*

INVITATION

COMMITTEE TO DEFEND AMERICA
8 West 40th Street, New York City

1. Enclosed is my contribution of $_____ to help arouse America to the urgency of clearing the Atlantic.

2. Please send me information on the Chapter in my community or information on how to organize a Chapter □

Name _____
(Please print so that we can address matter sent to the other side)

Address _____
(Please print so that we can address matter sent to the other side)
(Please make checks payable to Frederick G. Hoffen, Treasurer)

Courtesy of the "New York Herald Tribune"

This advertisement urging American convoys appeared not very long before Pearl Harbor.

centrate their military strength in the Atlantic to meet a triumphant Hitler. This would leave Japan free to establish her "New Order" all over the Far East. During the summer of 1941, while Germany and Russia were locked in deadly combat, a war of nerves was carried on between Japan and the United States. On July 23, reports came from the Vichy French government that it had permitted Japan to land troops in French Indo-China to "co-operate" with Vichy in the defense of that colony. Two days later, President Roosevelt countered by freezing all Japanese assets in the United States. The British Empire and the Dutch East Indies took similar steps, and the result was a practical cessation of trade with Japan. The obvious purpose of this economic warfare was to deter Japan from militarily joining the Axis.

As revealed in a release on July 27, the attitude of the Committee To Defend America by Aiding the Allies in this threatening situation was:

"Our policy statements have always made the point that America was confronted with one war, waged by the Axis powers upon civilization, and that the battles in the various parts of the world were parts of that war. We have always urged embargoes upon Japan, increasing aid to China and a blunt warning to Japan that we would not tolerate occupation of Singapore and the Dutch East Indies.

"We feel now, as we have always felt, that the most crucial battle is the Battle of the Atlantic. . . . .

"But, we feel that we can win the Battle of the Atlantic and, at the same time, take a strong position in assisting China and opposing Japan in the Far East such as our Government is now doing."

The events which were making war more and more inevitable for the United States every week led to ever closer collaboration with Great Britain. On August 14 it was announced to the world that President Roosevelt and Prime Minister Churchill had just met in the Atlantic Ocean. The two men signed a joint declaration—the Atlantic Charter—which was not a plan of action to defeat Hitler but the announcement of a peace program to be adopted "after the final destruction of the Nazi tyranny." The Charter recognized that future world peace depended upon international collaboration; the right of all peoples to choose the form of government under which they would live; equal rights to trade and equal access to raw materials by all nations; and the freedom of the seas.

The Committee, speaking through Eichelberger, wholeheartedly pledged its approval of the agreement but was disappointed that a plan of action against Hitler had not been made. Eichelberger said: "We must point out with all possible vigor that the United States will have a right to participate in the building of the future world peace if it will make its full contribution to the defeat of the aggressors. Consequently our participation in the conflict should be speeded up."

During the fall of 1941 the American Navy was finally forced into a shooting war. Units of the fleet patroling the sea lane to Iceland had orders to defend themselves if attacked. On September 4 it was announced that the American destroyer "Greer" had been fired on by a German submarine. At a press conference and over the radio on September 11, President Roosevelt advised the country that the American Navy had now been given instructions to shoot at the enemy on sight. By this time Hitler had built up a case against himself even in the eyes of many isolationists. The "Robin Moor" had been sunk in the middle Atlantic on May 21; the American-owned "Sessa" had been torpedoed on August 17; the "Greer" had been attacked on September 4; the "Steel Seafarer" had been sunk in the Red Sea on September 7; the "Montana" was sunk on September 11.

On September 23 President Roosevelt told his press conference that the continued sinking of American ships required the revision of the Neutrality Act to permit our ships to be armed for their own defense. Although Congress had abandoned the freedom of the seas as an American doctrine at the time of the passage of the Neutrality Act (1935), it had become apparent in the past few months that freedom of the seas was essential to American security. The Lend-Lease Bill had not advocated the freedom of the seas; in March, 1941, at the time that this act was passed, it was hoped that if the United States transferred equipment to the Allies, the Allies would be able to carry it safely to their own shores. Events in subsequent months demonstrated that they were unable to do this. To defeat Hitler it was becoming necessary for the United States to deliver Lend-Lease material to the ports of the Allies. The Neutrality Act, however, prohibited American ships from entering belligerent ports and from sailing through combat zones.

In a message to Congress on October 9, the President recommended the repeal of those sections of the Neutrality Act which prohibited the arming of merchant ships and which forbade American ships from entering belligerent ports and sailing through combat zones. The President pointed out that "in the Neutrality Act there are various crippling provisions. The repeal or modification of these provisions will not leave the United States any less neutral than we are today, but it will make it possible for us to defend the Americas far more successfully and to give aid far more effectively against the tremendous forces now marching towards the conquest of the world. . . . . "

The Committee To Defend America by Aiding the Allies

called upon all its members to flood Congress with telegrams and letters approving the repeal of these provisions of the Neutrality Act. Eichelberger, just back from a visit to England, made a tour of the country to stimulate enthusiasm for the repeal, and the Committee put a number of prominent people on the radio. In a Committee release on October 18 Eichelberger said:

"After three weeks in Great Britain I am convinced that while the British Isles cannot be invaded, Britain cannot win the war, by which I mean the destruction of Hitlerism, without the military participation of the United States. . . . . First of all I mean that the American people must make it clear to the world that they are in the war and intend to stay in it until Hitlerism is eliminated from the face of the earth. The United States has been in the war for some time, but that fact has not yet been made clear to the world. Once the United States clearly indicates that it is in the war and means to see it through, the British, the people in exile, the Russians, the Chinese and even the Germans themselves will know that there can be but one outcome to the present conflict."

The revision of the Neutrality Act was speeded up by the announcement on October 17 that the destroyer "Kearny" had been struck by a torpedo. A few days later the nation learned that eleven sailors had been killed aboard the "Kearny." On October 27 the President acknowledged that the United States, as far as the Navy was concerned, was in a shooting war, because she had been attacked by Germany. The President said: "We have wished to avoid shooting. But the shooting has started. And history has recorded who fired the first shot. . . . . Hitler has often protested that his plans for conquest do not extend across the Atlantic Ocean. His submarines and raiders prove otherwise. So does the entire design of his new world order. . . . ."

The isolationists in and out of Congress during October and November talked as if the United States could chose peace or war, when in reality events had reduced her choice to submission or resistance to aggression. If the United States were to resist, resistance had to be made effective, unhampered by restrictions in the Neutrality Act. The Committee To Defend America by Aiding the Allies observed that "the isolationist argument has centered on the thesis that the choice before the Senate is the issue of peace or war. This argument is not new; it was constantly repeated during the battle over the Lease-Lend Bill. For some reason that has not been explained publicly, those isolationists who have characterized the carrying-out of the destroyer deal and the adoption of the Lease-Lend Bill by America as 'acts of war' do not apply that term to the sinking of American ships and the torpedoing of an American destroyer by Germany." As an example, they cited Senator C. Wayland Brooks of Illinois, who about this time made a speech entitled "This Is Not Our War."

On October 30 the sinking of the destroyer "Reuben James" gave increased weight to the arguments in favor of revision of the Neutrality Act. When the act had been passed in 1935, it had been designed to prevent the sinking of American ships, since it was held that this might lead the United States into war. The act, however, had even failed to prevent the sinking of ships which were traveling waters far away from combat zones—witness the sinking of the "Robin Moor." Events of that sort should have made it plain that the United States had no opportunity to choose between peace and war. And, in spite of the propaganda efforts of the isolationist congressmen and the America First Committee, the majority of the people realized in the fall of 1941 that the only choice for the United States was between war and submission to the Axis powers.

On November 7 the United States Senate by a vote of 50 to 37 repealed those sections of the Neutrality Act which prevented the arming of merchant ships and which forbade American ships from entering belligerent ports and sailing through combat zones. Six days later the House of Representatives concurred in the Senate's action by a vote of 212 to 194. With this repeal, which finally repudiated the shortsighted policy adopted in 1935, the United States returned to its traditional foreign-policy concept of freedom of the sea. The close vote in the House of Representatives, however, demonstrated that many congressmen had not adjusted their thinking to meet the situation of an inevitable war. The two major parties in the House voted as follows: Democrats, 187 for, 53 against; Republicans, 22 for, 137 against. In spite of the farsighted leadership of men like Wendell Willkie and William Allen White, the Republican party was still at this late date either dominated by isolationism or obstructionist opposition to whatever the President favored.

Within a few short weeks of this vote, the United States was attacked at Pearl Harbor by the Japanese. Since 1939 American foreign policy had undergone significant transitions. Strict neutrality had been abandoned in order to give aid short of war to those countries whose resistance to aggression was helping to defend the security of the United States; when the "Reuben James" was sunk, the idea that America could be the arsenal while others did the fighting had to be abandoned—after this America became a limited belligerent by conducting operations along the Atlantic life-line; all-out war came only with direct all-out attack on the United States by Japan.

The Japanese had devoted themselves to feverish preparations for war during the fall of 1941. General Tojo, who became head of the Japanese cabinet in October, dispatched

Saburo Kurusu to Washington with the minimum demands of the Japanese empire. These demands were that Japan be given full access to the resources of the Netherlands East Indies, that trade relations with the United States be restored, and that the United States stop all aid to China. Secretary Hull countered by demanding that the Japanese withdraw their forces from China and Indo-China and pledge the territorial integrity of China. Meanwhile, Japanese forces poured into Indo-China for the coming assault on southeastern Asia. In a final attempt to avert war President Roosevelt sent a personal appeal to Emperor Hirohito. On December 7 Japan replied by bombing Pearl Harbor.

During 1941, while the Committee To Defend America by Aiding the Allies was carrying on its efforts to arouse the American people to an awareness of the menace of a totalitarian victory, a new internationalist organization—the Fight for Freedom Committee—had been formed. It was publicly launched on April 19, 1941. This committee sprang from the nucleus of the Francis P. Miller group. It was organized at this time because its members felt that the Committee To Defend America by Aiding the Allies was equivocating and failing to lead public opinion as it had in the past. The officers of the Fight for Freedom Committee were Senator Carter Glass, honorary chairman; the Right Rev. Henry W. Hobson, chairman; Francis P. Miller, vice-chairman; Mrs. Calvin Coolidge, vice-chairman; Ulric Bell, chairman of the Executive Committee; Wayne Johnson, treasurer; and F. H. Peter Cusick, executive secretary.

The official attitude of this group was that the United States was already "at war" and "regardless of what we do, Hitler will attack us when he feels it to his advantage. . . . . But we are still largely blind to the fact that there is no lasting choice between war and peace. We still think in terms of keeping out of a war in which we are already engaged in every sense except armed combat. We have too long left the main burden of winning a victory to other people. Thus we are in the unmoral and craven position of asking others to make the supreme sacrifice for this victory which we recognize as essential to us." The Fight for Freedom Committee was pledged to war against the Axis, against Hitler's New Order which was based on the oppression of man. The Committee also pledged itself against domestic injustice. To carry out its purpose of a "Fight for Freedom" the Committee propounded the following program:

We must not only meet force with force wherever we can effectively bring our physical power to bear, but we must meet the enemy upon his own chosen battleground, the battleground of mind and spirit.

We must not merely defend today's democracy against the murderous attempt of foreign tyrants to destroy it, but we must make democracy tomorrow far stronger than it is today.

We cannot do this with mere words. We can do it by action.

As a united people we must arise not only to bear arms against the enemy without, but to develop here at home a way of life so just, a brotherhood of man so real, as to give the lie to those who say that democracy is dead—destroyed by the machine age—who say that we must accept the way of the machine and discard the way of free human beings.

We can win this supreme test of democracy at home even as we fight the foreign enemy abroad. We can win on both fronts, if we remember in every waking moment of our lives that we are one people, and that we have one common purpose. Whether we are white or black—Catholic, Protestant or Jew—rich or poor—from the North or South or East or West—we are one. If we waste our strength in internal dissension, we shall surely be conquered, as other nations were conquered who were unable to achieve internal solidarity. But if we stand united, if we consider only our common purpose, we shall conquer, and we shall live as free men in a world released at last from the scourge of slavery.

We must be militantly on guard to protect the right of free workers to organize and bargain collectively; we must protect this right against infringement by government or private enterprise. We must protect the nation as a whole against irresponsible or selfish interests of whatever nature. This is not a matter of legislation but of aroused public opinion.

We must jealously guard our Bill of Rights and militantly oppose all forms of racial or religious discrimination—wherever and in whatever guise they may crop up under the strain of the times and the stimulus of Nazi propaganda.

The chairman of this Committee, the Right Rev. Henry W. Hobson, Episcopal bishop of southern Ohio, had been wounded while serving as an artillery officer in the first World War. In a militant sermon delivered December 1, 1940, he had pointed out that no one hated war more than he did but that there were "evils worse than wars." He added that "there are values in life which are of such supreme importance for man's whole well-being that they are worth not just sympathy, not just material backing, not just moral indignation which spends itself in lofty words—but worth dying for. As a Christian I cannot find these values in any program which would substitute a spirit of patriotic isolationism and selfish appeasement for the truth that as children of God we, 'members one of another,' have a world-wide responsibility for the well-being and the rights of man."

Shortly after the establishment of the national Fight For Freedom Committee in New York City, local chapters in other cities were set up. In Chicago, Courtenay Barber, Jr., and Albert Parry, formerly of the Chicago chapter of the Committee To Defend America by Aiding the Allies, opened headquarters. The Chicago branch of the Committee was officially launched on July 2 when an advertisement was placed in the Chicago newspapers. The work of this chapter consisted of distributing literature, placing news stories in the papers about the crisis facing America, holding rallies, and fighting the America First Committee and its powerful supporter, the *Chicago Tribune*. The Chicago Fight for Freedom Committee felt that Colonel Robert McCormick and his paper were real enemies of democracy and as such should be actively opposed.

On July 29 the Chicago chapter of the Fight for Freedom

Committee held a large rally at Orchestra Hall on the theme, "What's Wrong with the *Chicago Tribune?*" The principal speaker, Edmond Taylor, former foreign correspondent of the *Tribune*, lashed at the methods used by this newspaper; and the rally went on record as advocating the establishment of a new morning newspaper which would "truthfully reflect the sentiments and adequately represent the people of this great community." In the following weeks, the Committee circulated petitions advocating the starting of a new paper, collecting some fifty thousand signatures. This committee seems to have helped prepare the way for the founding of the *Chicago Sun* in December, 1941, by Marshall Field and Silliman Evans. The Chicago branch of Fight for Freedom was a "poor man's" committee. It received few gifts of over $100, in startling contrast to the amounts received by the America First Committee.

The Fight for Freedom Committee, in the months before Pearl Harbor, put such prominent people as Alexander Woollcott on the radio, sent Herbert Agar on a speaking tour of the nation, held rallies, distributed literature, and stimulated a letter-writing campaign to congressmen to make sure that Congress would not hear only the cries of the America First Committee and other vocal isolationists. The Fight for Freedom Committee envisaged the United States playing the role in world politics that its industrial and naval strength ordinarily would have dictated. Both this committee and the Committee To Defend America by Aiding the Allies operated on the premise that it was of supreme importance to prevent the three Axis powers from triumphing over the democracies and thereby destroying the balance of power.

The individuals who composed the Fight for Freedom Committee believed that the United States should have declared war long before Pearl Harbor, and some of them had signed a public statement calling for such a step as early as June, 1940. The members of the Committee To Defend America by Aiding the Allies understood the importance of the balance of power, too; but most of them, at least up to the summer of 1941, held firmly to the position that aid to the Allies would relieve the United States of the necessity of actual armed conflict.

William Allen White represented the typical view of the latter group. He realized that the Committee's policy of advancing its objectives from time to time left it open to the charge of edging the country closer and closer to war according to a premeditated plan. But as long as Hitler and the Axis did not stand still with their onslaught on the British Empire and Russia, the Committee, which believed in defending the United States by aiding the opponents of aggression, could not stand still. He (and with him the majority of the Committee members) was perfectly sincere in his desire that the United States should avoid war if this course were possible, and his simple and invariable answer to the charges of opponents was that the opponents overlooked the necessity of altering the Committee's program to fit the rapidly changing events of a dynamic situation.

It seems clear that the steps that the United States took from September, 1939, to December, 1941, to place itself unequivocally on the side of the opponents of the Axis had little to do with the involvement of the United States in a military war. The United States was in much the same position during these years as it had been at the time of the first World War. What happened depended rather upon what Germany and her allies did than upon what the United States did. Once war broke out, no nation could isolate itself from the effects of that war. The best hope for peace in the United States, prior to 1939, had been through co-operation with other states to prevent armed conflict. International co-operation, however, broke down when Germany plunged Europe into war in September, 1939; and it was inevitable that that conflict in time would engulf the whole world. Arousing America to an awareness of the danger of an Axis victory and fighting to send aid to those countries which were actually in a shooting war with the Axis, while America launched her own defense program, were the major contributions of the internationalist committees between 1939 and 1941. When war did come, the United States because of their activities was better prepared to wage a military war, and she did not have to enter the field of battle against the Axis all alone.

Perhaps it was fortunate that Pearl Harbor came and forced upon the vast majority of Americans an awareness that when brute force is loose in the world, it is our business to stop it. Aid short of war was not enough. Realization came that any country which prized its comforts and pleasures more than its freedom would lose its freedom and eventually its comforts and pleasures as well. Those leaders who upheld the isolationist position from 1939 to the time of Pearl Harbor did a great disservice to the United States by morally disarming that segment of our people which accepted their leadership. Their statements, declaring, for instance, that an Axis-dominated Europe and Asia would make no difference to the United States, overlooked one very important thing—our people's own interest in the democratic way of life.

That interest, which had made America the hope of the world during the preceding one hundred and fifty years, could not be allowed to die. It cannot be allowed to die now.

X

The Battle of the Future

THE FIGHT IS NOT OVER—EITHER ON THE BATTLEFIELDS OF Europe and Asia or in the press and council chambers of the United States. We still have the war to win; and when we have done that, we shall have the peace to win. There are still those who hold to the isolationist viewpoint, who are spending the days of this war preparing to lead us back into their exaggerated form of nationalism just as soon as the war is won. They must not have the factors of 1919 on their side—partisan politics, war-weariness, lack of understanding of what should be done to make a world which can keep the peace. It is up to the people of America to defeat them—the battle at home is just as important for the future as that abroad.

United Nations leaders have already taken several steps in the right direction. When President Roosevelt and Prime Minister Churchill drew up the Atlantic Charter in August, 1941, they set forth a series of minimum proposals which they considered would lead to a better world. They called for the right of all peoples to choose the form of government under which they would live; for equal access to raw materials for all nations; for international collaboration in the economic field.

They asked for the establishment, after the destruction of Nazi tyranny, of a peace under which people could live in freedom from fear and want and the abandonment of the use of force in international affairs. The Atlantic Charter also indicated that a "permanent system of general security" should be established.

The establishment of the United Nations organization, composed of those countries which were opposing the Axis, was a step toward international collaboration. By the time the United States had entered the war, events had demonstrated to most thinking Americans that in this highly industrialized world it was impossible for any nation to isolate itself from the ebb and flow of world affairs. If the United States wanted peace in the postwar world, co-operation with peace-loving nations to maintain that peace would have to be pursued. Prominent leaders were warning America that she must continue not only in war but in peace to think in world terms. Prime Minister Churchill very bluntly told the Congress of the United States on December 26, 1941, that this war need not have happened had the peace-loving nations worked together during the previous twenty years. Wendell L. Willkie, after covering thirty-one thousand miles in less than fifty days, emphatically declared that "there are no distant points in the world any longer. . . . . Our thinking in the future must be worldwide."

At the same time that the governments of the United Nations were discussing postwar problems, countless private American citizens in groups or individually were also thinking in terms of the world after the war. After the Japanese attack on Pearl Harbor, both the Fight for Freedom Committee and the Committee To Defend America by Aiding the Allies formally disbanded. These organizations, however, knew that their work was not done—is not yet done. They did not forget that, after fighting and winning wars, there are still the problems of winning the peace. They were sure that isolationists would again raise their voices in an attempt to dissuade the American people from assuming their world responsibilities. The Committee To Defend America by Aiding the Allies, therefore, joined with the Council for Democracy to launch a new organization—Citizens for Victory: To Win the War, To Win the Peace. The Fight for Freedom Committee aided in the launching of Freedom House. The directors of Freedom House declared on January 22, 1942, that "freedom, like peace, has become indivisible. Our many inventions have made a world in which the enslavement of one may lead to the enslavement of all. America is in danger today because, when she was safe, she did not help protect the safety and freedom of others. . . . . "

War necessities have steadily brought about closer and closer collaboration among the United Nations. The foreign ministers of the United States, Great Britain, and Russia, as well as the Chinese ambassador to Moscow, meeting in October, 1943, considered the problems of closer co-operation in the war and the peace. In a significant declaration the conferees emphasized "the necessity of establishing at the earliest practicable date a general international organization, based on the principle of the sovereign equality of all peace-loving States, and open to membership by all such States, large and small, for the maintenance of international peace and security." The success of this meeting was an important step toward the hope of a peaceful world.

Probably there is little doubt that the specter of the United States Senate—a Senate which had defeated in the generation following the first World War the means of American co-operation with other powers—hovered over the deliberations of the foreign ministers during these conferences. Even before the conferences in Moscow, the House of Representatives had passed the Fulbright Resolution calling for the creation of "appropriate international machinery with power adequate to establish and maintain a just and lasting peace." The Senate, too, had before it a resolution sponsored by Senators Ball, Burton, Hatch, and Hill which unequivocally called for the United States to join an international organization of nations. However, when the results of the Moscow conferences were released, Senator Connally drew up a rather weak resolution approving in general the pledge of international cooperation. Senators Pepper, Ball, Burton, Hatch, and Hill amended the Connally Resolution to include a phrase from the Moscow agreement. This amended resolution, which passed the Senate on November 5, 1943, by a vote of 85 to 5, read:

Resolved, That the war against all our enemies be waged until complete victory is achieved.

That the United States cooperate with its comrades-in-arms in securing a just and honorable peace.

That the United States, acting through its constitutional processes, join with free and sovereign nations in the establishment and maintenance of international authority with power to prevent aggression and to preserve the peace of the world.

That the Senate recognizes the necessity of there being established at the earliest practicable date a general international organization based on the principle of the sovereign equality of all peace-loving states, and open to membership by all such states, large and small, for the maintenance of international peace and security.

That, pursuant to the Constitution of the United States, any treaty made to effect the purposes of this resolution, on behalf of the government of the United States with any other nation or any association of nations, shall be made only by and with the advice and consent of the Senate of the United States, provided two-thirds of the senators present concur.

In spite of their favorable vote, certain senators, betraying their isolationist leaning, immediately stated that they considered their vote to be "meaningless" and that they were not bound by it. Had they forgotten and ignored the fact that a war had been brought on by a similar ostrich isolationism in the twenties and thirties? These utterances raised disquieting fears that the Senate would repeat its role of 1919. Openly and to the public, it seemed, as was the case in 1919, that the vast majority of their group were for an international association of nations, but through parliamentary strategy the question might be so manipulated as to lead again to the defeat of America's participation in the maintenance of peace once the war was won.

In order to avert such a repetition of tragedy, Senator Joseph H. Ball suggested that the executive branch of the government keep in close contact with the legislative side of our government. He urged the inclusion of members of Congress on the American delegations to international conferences. Senator Ball ably pointed out that Congress can get all the facts necessary to a sound judgment "only if some of its members participate in the conferences at which the commitments are made."

The people of the United States, of course, may not find themselves entirely satisfied with all the solutions that are worked out by such international conferences as have been held or may be held. But this time we cannot afford to sulk, disagreeing over picayune details, and then pick up our marbles and try to withdraw from the world. Senator Ball realized these dangers when he suggested that the Senate might be more willing to ratify a treaty with some unavoidable imperfections in it if some of its own members were on the peace delegation. It is significant, furthermore, that William Allen White had recommended that a powerful citizen's committee be functioning to rally public sentiment for support of an international association of nations and to prevent such a momentous issue from degenerating into a

"LAST TO LEAVE THE ARK"

ISOLATIONISM

1919

U.S. SENATE

INTERNATIONAL COLLABORATION

FRED O. SEIBEL

Seibel in The Richmond Times-Dispatch

A 1943 View of the Senate

partisan fight between the President and the opposition party in the Senate.

While the great majority of Americans now seem convinced of the need for an international organization of nations with the power to enforce its commitments, many of the same voices that told America that "it is not our war" in the days before Pearl Harbor are still doing their best to take America along the road of isolationism once the war is over. In fact, many of these same voices have done and are doing their best to create disunity and opposition to the war effort itself. They will be some of the same voices which after the war will try to lead America along the lonely nationalist road to false security.

Ellis O. Jones, head of the National Copperheads, told a Los Angeles audience on December 11, 1941, that he "would rather be in this war on the side of Germany than on the side of the British!" Court Asher, publisher of *X-Ray* (Muncie, Indiana), stated in January, 1942, "Pearl Harbor sank more than battle wagons; it sank the hopes of Jewry in this country." On March 12, 1942, E. J. Garner, publisher of *Publicity* (Wichita, Kansas), told his readers, "With your loyal support and distribution to right-thinking Americans the Mongolian Jew-Controlled Roosevelt Dictatorship will be smashed."

Father Coughlin's *Social Justice* for weeks after Pearl Harbor charged that Roosevelt and "the Jews" got the United States into the war. Elizabeth Dilling, author of *The Red Network* (1931), which listed as Communists, among others, William Allen White, Chief Justice Charles Evans Hughes, Mayor La Guardia, and Mrs. Roosevelt, in her *Patriotic Research Bureau Newsletter* for Christmas, 1941, charged:

"We have belligerently and persistently aided the Communist-backed Chiang Kai-shek regime of China with millions, insisted on the Burma road remaining open to menace Japan with war supplies to be used against them. We have lavished Soviet Russia with war materials; refused to make any concessions.

"For persistent aggressive meddling and threatening in lands where we do not belong, we have no peer. This policy has now evoked the long-desired-and-worked-for war."

Because of its seditious content *Social Justice* was barred from the mails on April 14, 1942. Pelley's the *Galilean*, Asher's *X-Ray*, and Garner's *Publicity* were soon after similarly suppressed. Laura Ingalls, George Sylvester Viereck, and Ralph Townsend found themselves in jail. On July 23, 1942, the Department of Justice indicted twenty-seven men and one woman on charges of conspiracy to provoke disloyalty and revolt in the armed forces. Among those indicted were Elizabeth Dilling, Gerald B. Winrod, Prescott Dennett, William Dudley Pelley, and E. J. Garner. This indictment did not stop Mrs. Dilling. Her *Patriotic Research Bureau Newsletter* for August 7, 1943, opened with the following paragraph: "Will we have another phoney Willkie-F.D.R. 'election' in 1944? Will we be given another 'choice' between the stooges of International Socialist–Communist Collectivist Judaistic world government? This query now haunts Americans who permit themselves to think."

In 1943 Rev. Gerald L. K. Smith of Detroit (who once had been a close associate of Huey Long, the late "Kingfish" of Louisiana) launched a new America First party. In the spring of 1942 Smith had started the publication of his magazine monthly, *The Cross and the Flag*. He told a reporter, "Make no mistake about it. America First is a nationalist party—the nationalist party. I am the only man who had the guts to go out and organize the America Firsters after Pearl Harbor. . . . . All we want now is a seat at the council table, a voice in determining the Republican presidential candidate. Barring a miracle, we are not going to run a third party ticket in 1944. Of course, if the realists in either party would give us a Wheeler or a Nye there would be no America First Party. . . . . " Furthermore, he observed that "the form of isolationism in 1947 will make the 1920 variety look like an international conspiracy."

After Pearl Harbor powerful newspapers, as well as the Smiths, the Dillings, the Father Coughlins, also did their best to cast suspicion on America's allies and undermine the faith and the confidence of the people in the war effort. William Randolph Hearst's *New York Journal-American* on March 30, 1942, asserted: "Of course Russia is not a full partner of the United Nations. She is a semi-partner of the Axis." The *Chicago Tribune*, July 7, 1942, charged that "our totalitarian government now lacks only the abolition of the representative assembly." This was the same paper which on October 27, 1941, less than six weeks before the Japanese attack on Pearl Harbor, had said: "What vital interest of the U.S. can Japan threaten? She cannot attack us. That is a military impossibility. Even our base at Hawaii is beyond the effective striking power of her fleet." The *Chicago Sun*, on May 18, 1943, reported a Tokyo radio in an English-language broadcast as declaring that McCormick, publisher of the *Chicago Tribune*, was "conducting a one-man crusade for the defense of true Americanism and for the salvation of the United States from the hands of the radical internationalists led by Mr. Roosevelt." On May 15, 1944, under the headline "TRIBUNE CARTOON SHOWERED ON ANZIO YANKS," The *Chicago Sun* also told the story of how the Germans were attempting to sow distrust of our Allies among our troops by distributing to them one of the *Tribune's* pictorial attacks on Russia.

Certain congressmen still refused to apprehend the meaning

of world events over the preceding decade. Senator Robert A. Taft told a Chicago audience on August 6, 1943: "We are not engaged in any crusade for democracy, or for the Four Freedoms, or for the preservation of the British Empire." Representative Clare E. Hoffman on August 12, 1943, proposed to end the war and collaborate with the Axis because "you can't collaborate with people after you have killed them and slaughtered them. . . . . War pursued to the bitter end is a bitter tragedy, and the sooner we can stop it the better." Senator Robert R. Reynolds, chairman of the Senate Military Affairs Committee, wrote in his publication, the *National Record*, July, 1943: "I was an isolationist, and I am a thousand times more isolationist today than I was before we became engaged in this war. But that is my privilege. However, I prefer to be referred to as an American Firster, or a Nationalist."

Some congressmen preferred to try to stir up resentment over rationing and other necessary wartime restrictions. Representative Harold Knutson of Minnesota on March 23, 1942, publicly asked: "Will Americans graciously bow down to all the totalitarian decrees which will restrict their sugar, their motor cars, their oil, their apparel, their way of life and their pocketbooks, simply to satisfy the ambitions of those who understand victory to be the complete overthrow of their enemies?" Senator Brooks of Illinois charged on February 11, 1944, that the Roosevelt Administration "under the guise of winning the war" was trying to regulate completely the lives of all Americans.

When Wendell L. Willkie withdrew from the race for the Republican presidential nomination, in April, 1944, the joy of the "iso-nationalists" knew no bounds. William J. Grace's Republican National Revivalist Committee of Chicago said that Willkie's name was "a brand of political canned goods of the lowest and most disgusting grade. The canned goods is a stew of internationalism. It is campaign oratory, alienism, psychopathic hallucinations of grandeur and crazy world pacification ideas." At the same time the *Chicago Tribune* gloated, for Willkie had denounced it in his campaign for primary delegates in Wisconsin. When Willkie ran a poor fourth in the Wisconsin primary election, the *Tribune* (April 6, 1944) declared that "the people of Wisconsin have spoken. As citizens they are for America and an American newspaper. .... Our long, bitter fight to save this country is heading toward a triumphant conclusion."

The *Tribune* overlooked not only the fact that it had denounced Governor Dewey, the man who ran first, as "Anti-American" for advocating an Anglo-American military alliance the preceding September, but also that the No. 2 man in the race—Lieutenant Commander Stassen—was an avowed internationalist. It went on to say that the Wisconsin primary was a vindication of "America First" principles and a repudiation of "internationalism and un-Americanism."

In the "One World" of the present, only the constant strife of war and turmoil faces a nation that refuses to work with other nations for the common good. The American people who are suffering from the plague of war must see clearly by the grave lessons of many years that their stubborn isolationist sleep brought neglect of their responsibilities to other nations. A failure to co-operate with the nations of the world in the years to come will imperil both the present generation and the generations to come. A wide, world-embracing view, with all its responsibilities, is theirs to adopt. This is America's self-interest. It is not only *her* self-interest, but the interest of all peoples and all nations. Not only current events but also our own traditional principles demand this wider outlook.

Notes

The following notes, arranged by chapter, are not meant to serve as a bibliography; for the complete background of the text see the Selected Bibliography which follows the notes. These notes, likewise, list only published source material. All the letters to and from William Allen White mentioned in the text, as well as his unpublished article, "A Democratic Adventure," are in the possession of Mrs. White, in Emporia, Kansas. The various Committee statements that are quoted can be found in the Committee's archives mentioned in the Bibliography.

CHAPTER I

PAGE

3. The quotation from Carl Becker is from *How New Will the Better World Be?* (New York: Alfred A. Knopf, 1944), p. 120.

6–10. For the statement from Lodge's daughter and further material on the Senate's defeat of the League see Walter Johnson, "Let Us Not Repeat 1919," *Facts*, June, 1943, and "Senatorial Strategy, 1919–20: Will It Be Repeated?" *Antioch Review*, winter, 1943; and D. F. Fleming, *The United States and the League of Nations, 1918–1920* (New York: G. P. Putnam's Sons, 1932).

14. In his *American Neutrality* (New Haven: Yale University Press, 1935), pp. 56–78, Seymour points out that German unrestricted submarine warfare was intended to do more than stop the export of munitions from the United States. After studying the German documents, he concludes that it was designed to strike at the general economic capacity of Britain to continue the war. The memorials of the German Admiralty staff which analyzed the results of the submarine campaign dealt not with the interruption of England's importation of munitions but with the effect the sinkings would have on English economic life, particularly the shortage of food and the rise in prices. Seymour adds that "the historian must thus conclude that the unrestricted submarine campaign resulted from much wider and more complicated conditions than the American export of ammunition. The German

documents by no means bear out Senator Clark's impression that there is 'no evidence whatever' to show we would have entered the war except for that export. The submarine campaign, according to those who planned it, was designed to sever all the arteries of British economic life. . . . . An American embargo upon munitions in the narrow sense would have had very slight deterrent effect upon the German naval leaders. Even an absolute embargo upon all American exports to the Allies, including foodstuffs, would not have touched the main points raised in the Admiralty Staff decisions."

16. For a discussion of Wilson's attitudes see Harley Notter, *The Origins of the Foreign Policy of Woodrow Wilson* (Baltimore: Johns Hopkins University Press, 1937).

16. The Seymour quotation is from *op. cit.*, pp. 3–5.

18. Lewis Einstein's article was "The United States and Anglo-German Rivalry," *Living Age*, CCLXXVI, 323–32. This article first appeared in the *National Review* (London), LX (1913), 736–50. See William C. Askew and J. Fred Rippy, "The United States and Europe's Strife, 1908–1913," *Journal of Politics*, IV (February, 1942), 68–79, for the background of Einstein's article.

18. The Lansing quotation is from John Foster Dulles and Robert W. Dulles, *War Memoirs of Robert Lansing* (New York: Bobbs-Merrill Co., 1935), p. 21. Used by special permission of the publishers.

19. The findings of the public opinion polls are summarized by Francis Sill Wickware in "What We Think about Foreign Affairs," *Harper's Magazine*, CLXXIX (September, 1939), 397–406. The polls mentioned in the rest of this chapter can be found in this article.

21. Henry L. Stimson's words are found in his article, "The Illusion of Neutrality," *Forum*, November, 1935, pp. 261–65.

21. The Seymour quotation is from *op. cit.*, pp. 177–78.

26. For his own description of these Far Eastern events see Henry L. Stimson, *The Far Eastern Crisis* (New York: Harper & Bros., 1936).

28. Allan Nevins in *America in World Affairs* (New York: Oxford University Press, 1942), pp. 110–11, points out the following moral to be drawn from this Japanese story: "The United States had an important stake, commercial, political, and sentimental, in the preservation of Chinese integrity and the Open Door. But it was unwilling to fight a costly war for the maintenance of its Far Eastern interests. Under these circumstances, its one hope of preserving them against a powerful and aggressive Japan lay in joining the League . . . . or at the very least, in clear, constant and cordial cooperation with the League. . . . . Partly because of American abstention from the League in its formative years, partly because of the selfishness and blundering of Great Britain and other member-powers, the forces which might have guaranteed world order had become divided and impotent. The stubborn isolationists in America, and the equally stubborn conserva-

tive appeasers in Britain and France, had played each other's game—and the game of the aggressor powers as well. The full grimness of the result was to become evident in December, 1941."

29. As an example of the internationalist position see, e.g., Seymour, *op. cit.*, pp. 179–80. Seymour stated: "For our own ultimate salvation, we must stand ready to cooperate vigorously with the States whose welfare, like our own, depends upon peace. We must support every measure calculated to stamp out the immediate threat of war whenever it appears."

30. The story of the meeting between Roosevelt, Hull, and the senators is from Joseph Alsop and Robert Kintner, *American White Paper* (New York: Simon & Schuster, 1940), pp. 44–46.

CHAPTER II

32. Mr. Fenwick's comments are found in Fenwick to White, November 16, 1939.

34. Apropos of President Roosevelt's remark about White's support: Hanging on the wall of White's study was an autographed picture of Roosevelt in a seersucker suit. It was inscribed "To William Allen White—from his old friend who is *for* him all 48 months." The letter appended to the picture read in part, "Dear Bill:—Here is the seersucker picture, duly inscribed by the sucker to the seer!" (March 4, 1938.)

34. White's explanation of his party stand is found in White to Neil C. Brooks, May 28, 1940.

35. In the *New Republic* (Vol. XCVI [September 21, 1938]) White wrote an article entitled "Moscow and Emporia." In it he pointed out that he had joined any society looking "towards a cultural alliance with Russia, or a group to promote the recognition of Russia" (p. 177). George H. Cless, Jr., wrote a viciously unfair article entitled "The William Allen White Reign of Terror," *Scribner's Commentator*, Vol. IX (December, 1940), in which he pointed to this statement by White and concluded that it was just another example of "William Allen White speaking, the patron saint of those who want to defend America by giving it away" (p. 42).

35. For White's advocacy of Latin-American rights see the *Emporia Gazette*, January 23 and February 13, 1918; June 14, 1921; February 13 and 16, 1928; January 5, October 23, and November 3, 1933. In 1930 White served on President Hoover's commission to investigate the withdrawal of United States Marines from Haiti, and he advocated the withdrawal and a good-neighbor attitude for the future.

39. In the *Emporia Gazette*, September 7, 1939, White wrote his answer to people who criticized President Roosevelt for changing his mind on the embargo. He asked why not "change your mind. The only man who doesn't change his mind is the man who uses scrambled eggs for brains and hasn't a mind to change."

45. Knox's, White's, and Landon's views on foreign relations in wartime are from Knox to White, September 25, 1939; White to Knox, September 28,

1939; Landon to White, October 3 and November 2, 1939; and White to Landon, November 13, 1939.

51–52. For a complete list of contributors to the Committee see "Financial Statement, Non-partisan Committee for Peace through Revision of the Neutrality Law, January 3, 1940" (in White manuscripts or office of the Union for Concerted Peace Efforts, 8 West Fortieth Street, New York, New York).

52. The Committee's expenses were as follows: salaries and social security taxes, $986.16; printing, $1,225.58; telephone and telegraph, $1,827.08; recordings, $1,045.46; travel and field expense, $682.95; publicity and mat story, $235.00; press clippings, $29.00; technical services, $800.00; appeal mailings and postage, $915.00; general postage, $220.41; special mailings, $69.34; rent for Washington, D.C., office, $35.00; shipping and errands, $37.00; office supplies and miscellaneous, $86.20.

CHAPTER III

60. White finally answered Sherwood's letter on December 27, 1939. Two days later Sherwood wrote back: "Your letter is the best I have ever received. I believed that, in this hour of tragic bewilderment, I could hear from you the voice of essential wisdom, and I have heard it." Mr. and Mrs. White had a deep personal interest in the war by this time, since their son, W. L. White, was in Europe, reporting the war and broadcasting for the Columbia Broadcasting System. On Christmas Day, W. L. White broadcast from the Finnish-Russian front a memorable talk entitled "The Last Christmas Tree." Robert Sherwood was deeply moved by the broadcast and inspired to write *There Shall Be No Night*—a play which won the Pulitzer Prize as the best of 1940.

63. White's feelings about England are revealed in "The Story of a Democratic Adventure," an unpublished manuscript. In this article, written during December, 1940, White stated that many of the people in the Committee To Defend America by Aiding the Allies "had no great love for the British ruling classes. . . . . We have not relented in our general theory that George III was a stupid old fuddy-duddy with instincts of a tyrant and a brain corroded and cheesy with the arrogance and ignorance which go with the exercise of tyranny. Yet I think I am safe in saying that our whole group felt as it was assembling, and feels now, that if Great Britain were inhabited by a group of red Indians under the command of Sitting Bull, Crazy Horse and Geronimo, so long as Great Britain had command of the British fleet, we should try to arm her and keep that fleet afloat."

70. Including those mentioned in the text, the members of the committee on May 20, 1940, were: Henry L. Stimson; Nicholas Murray Butler; Frank Knox; Governor Herbert Lehman of New York; Robert Watt, international representative of the American Federation of Labor; Freda Kirchwey, editor of the *Nation;* George E. Vincent, president of the Community Chests and Councils, New York City; Harry Woodburn Chase, chancellor of New York University; James W. Gerard, former minister to Germany;

Sidney B. Hall, superintendent of public instruction, Richmond, Virginia; Roswell G. Ham, president of Mount Holyoke College; Stephen Keeler, Episcopal bishop, Minneapolis; Frank L. Polk, former assistant secretary of state under Wilson; Grover C. Hall, editor of the *Montgomery* (Alabama) *Advertiser;* Episcopal Bishop Henry W. Hobson, Cincinnati; Alexander Mann, Episcopal bishop, Pittsburgh; James Truslow Adams, historian; Robert E. Sherwood, dramatist; Philip Marshall Brown, Washington, D.C.; John Temple Graves II, Birmingham, Alabama; William Yandell Elliott, Harvard University; Rev. John W. Frazier, Mobile, Alabama; Samuel R. Guard, editor of the *Breeders' Gazette;* Judge Oscar Leser, Baltimore; James M. Maxon, Episcopal bishop of Tennessee; Gene Tunney; Theodore Marburg, Baltimore; Miriam Hopkins, Hollywood; William L. Clayton, cotton broker, Houston, Texas; Mrs. Emmons (Anita McCormick) Blaine, Chicago; Harry Best, University of Kentucky; Evans Clark, president of the Twentieth Century Fund; Frederic Coudert, Sr., New York lawyer; Rev. Samuel A. Elliot, Arlington Street Church, Boston; William P. Ladd, dean of Berkeley Divinity School, Yale University; William J. Schiefferlin; Dr. James T. Shotwell, Columbia University; Charles A. Webb, the *Times*, Asheville, North Carolina; Allen D. Albert, past president of the Rotary International, Paris, Illinois; Lindsey Rogers, Columbia University; Rollen Benedict, Sioux Falls, South Dakota; Clifton M. Utley, Chicago Council on Foreign Relations; Mary E. Woolley, former president of Mount Holyoke College; and Dr. Quincy Wright, University of Chicago.

CHAPTER IV

74. In July, 1940, the local chapters of the Committee were distributed among the states as follows: Alabama, 4; Arizona, 3; Arkansas, 4; California, 14; Colorado, 3; Connecticut, 11; Delaware, 3; Florida, 7; Georgia, 4; Idaho, 2; Illinois, 6; Indiana, 6; Iowa, 13; Kansas, 9; Kentucky, 3; Louisiana, 2; Maine, 2; Maryland, 1; Massachusetts, 6; Michigan, 7; Minnesota, 2; Mississippi, 2; Missouri, 5; Montana, 1; Nebraska, 3; Nevada, 1; New Hampshire, 3; New Jersey, 31; New Mexico, 1; New York, 47; North Carolina, 22; Ohio, 8; Oklahoma, 3; Oregon, 3; Pennsylvania, 12; Rhode Island, 3; South Carolina, 7; South Dakota, 6; Tennessee, 4; Texas, 7; Utah, 1; Vermont, 4; Virginia, 6; Washington, 5; West Virginia, 4; Wisconsin, 5; and Wyoming, 1.

77. Donations to the national organization on June 18, 1940, can be taken as representative of that month:

Charles N. Swittig, Topeka, Kansas	$ 1.00
E. D. Knuchell, Los Angeles, California	1.00
L. C. Gorton, Springdale, Arkansas	1.00
Frances A. Thompson, Butte, Montana	10.00
B. L. McCullough, Seattle, Washington	1.00
J. L. Haw, Caledonia, Missouri	5.00
Ruth Dodge, St. Louis, Missouri	3.75
Thomas L. Greer, Barrington, Illinois	100.00
K. M. Clayberger, New York City	2.00

Effie Beckman Barrowe, New York City . . . . $ 50.00
Kenneth E. Stuart, Niagara Falls, New York 5.00
Morris A. Ring, New York City 1.00
S. C. Lamport, New York City 100.00
Martin Verb, San Diego, California 5.00
Ballard & Brockett, San Diego, California 5.00
Frank Greenwald, New York City 100.00
James L. Thomson, Hartford, Connecticut 50.00
Adelaide L. Thomson, Hartford, Connecticut 50.00
Abborn, Lexington, Kentucky 5.00
Henry J. Wolff, New York City 50.00
Eileen M. Keech, New York City 10.00
Mary B. Robinson, Weehawken, New Jersey 2.00
Emily Schwab, New York City 25.00
Margaret E. Layton, Georgetown, Delaware 5.00
Francis Spitze, New York City 5.00
Riley S. Marx, New York City 2.00
Sam K. Maybaum, New York City 2.00
A. Artega, New York City 1.00
Murray Anson, New York City 1.00

Total $598.75

94. Members of the Policy Committee were: Mrs. Emmons Blaine, philanthropist, Chicago; Dr. Frank G. Boudreau, president of the League of Na-
tions Association, New York City; Dr. Esther Brunauer, American Association of University Women, Washington, D.C.; Dr. James Bryant Conant,
president of Harvard University, Cambridge, Massachusetts; Frederic R.
Coudert, lawyer, New York City; Lewis Douglas, president of the Mutual
Life Insurance Company of New York; Thomas K. Finletter, lawyer, New
York City; Dr. Frank P. Graham, president of the University of North
Carolina, Chapel Hill, North Carolina; Dr. Frank Kingdon, president of
Newark University, Newark, New Jersey; Miss Freda Kirchwey, editor of
the *Nation*, New York City; Mayor Fiorello H. La Guardia, New York
City; Thomas W. Lamont, banker, New York City; Dr. Arthur Lovejoy,
Johns Hopkins University, Baltimore, Maryland; Frederick C. McKee,
businessman, Pittsburgh, Pennsylvania; Herbert Bayard Swope, journalist,
New York City; Dr. Robert A. Millikan, California Institute of Technol-
ogy, Pasadena, California; Hugh Moore, businessman, Easton, Pennsyl-
vania; Bishop G. Ashton Oldham, Albany, New York; James Patton, presi-
dent of the Farmer's Union, Denver, Colorado; Monsignor John A. Ryan,
Washington, D.C.; Dr. Charles Seymour, president of Yale University,
New Haven, Connecticut; Robert Emmet Sherwood, playwright, New
York City; James T. Shotwell, professor at Columbia University, New
York City; Huston Thompson, lawyer, Washington, D.C.; Dr. Henry P.
Van Dusen, Union Theological Seminary, New York City; Robert J.
Watt, American Federation of Labor, Washington, D.C.; W. W. Way-
mack, *Des Moines Register*, Des Moines, Iowa; and Dr. Quincy Wright, pro-
fessor at the University of Chicago, Chicago, Illinois.

110. The background of the Committee's legal position on the destroyer issue is found in Wright to Eichelberger, July 24, 1940; "Third Report of Subcommittee on Changes of Neutrality Law, November 19, 1940"; national Committee files; and Quincy Wright, "Present Status of Neutrality," *American Journal of International Law*, XXXIV (October, 1940), 391–415.

115. The thirty signers of the Miller petition were: Herbert Agar, editor of the *Louisville Courier-Journal;* Burke Baker, Houston, Texas; John L. Balderston, Beverly Hills, California, playwright and onetime London correspondent of the old *New York World;* Stringfellow Barr, president of St. John's College, Annapolis, Maryland; J. Douglas Brown, professor of economics at Princeton University; Richard F. Cleveland, Baltimore lawyer and son of President Cleveland; James F. Curtis, New York lawyer and assistant secretary of the Treasury, 1909–13; Edwin F. Gay, Pasadena, California, economist and former dean of the Graduate School of Business Administration at Harvard University; Edward T. Gushee, St. Louis, executive vice-president of the Union Electric Company of Missouri; Marion H. Hedges, Washington, research director and author; William H. Hessler, Cincinnati, writer on political economy; Calvin Hoover, Durham, North Carolina, economist, author, and editor; Leroy Hodges, Richmond, Virginia, economist and author; Edwin P. Hubble, San Marino, California, astronomer; Frank Kent, Baltimore, columnist of the *Baltimore Sun;* Edward R. Lewis, Chicago, historian and sociologist; George W. Martin, New York City; L. Randolph Mason, New York lawyer; Stacy May, New York, economist and social worker; Francis P. Miller, Fairfax, Virginia; Helen Hill Miller, wife of Francis P. Miller and secretary of the National Policy Committee of Washington, D.C.; Walter Millis, editorial writer of the *New York Herald Tribune*, author of *Road to War;* George Fort Milton, Chattanooga, Tennessee, newspaper publisher and historian; Lewis Mumford, Amenia, New York, writer; Winfield W. Riefler, Princeton, economist; Whitney J. Shepardson of New York, treasurer and director of the Council on Foreign Relations; Admiral William H. Standley, Retired, New York; William Waller, Nashville, Tennessee; George Watts Hill, Durham, North Carolina, banker and leader in the organization of co-operative marketing and farm organizations; Episcopal Bishop Henry W. Hobson, Cincinnati, who was a major in the last war (*New York Times*, June 10, 1940).

115. Lewis Douglas' dinner guests were: Herbert Agar; W. L. Clayton, Houston, Texas, cotton merchant; Henry Sloane Coffin, president of Union Theological Seminary; Lewis W. Douglas, president of the Mutual Life Insurance Company; Henry W. Hobson; Ernest M. Hopkins, president of Dartmouth College; Henry R. Luce, editor of *Time* and *Life;* Francis P. Miller; Whitney H. Shepardson; Rear Admiral Standley; and Henry P. Van Dusen, dean of Union Theological Seminary. Of this group, Agar, Clayton, Coffin, Douglas, Hobson, and Van Dusen were members of the White Committee.

This group's conclusions were as follows:

"1. That those threats to the American way of life and to the interests of the United States in Europe, Latin America and the Far East—against which threats the huge new defense program of this country is directed—all stem, in the last analysis, from the power of Nazi Germany.

"2. That the survival of the British Commonwealth of Nations (or a substantial part of it), free of German control, is an important factor in the preservation of the American way of life.

"3. That the survival of the British fleet (or a substantial part of it), free of German control, is a factor of critical importance in the defense of the United States and its interests.

"4. That the period within which the United States can act to protect her interests in these respects is a matter, not of years, but possibly of only a few weeks more.

"5. That the United States *should* act.

"6. That our action should be open and not furtive.

"7. That the following program should be undertaken.

"*a*) That the United States send its own ships to England, under its own convoys if need be, to evacuate British children.

"*b*) That food be transported to England in United States ships, under their own convoys if need be.

"*c*) That the extension of credit to Great Britain for any purpose be legalized.

"*d*) That the exportation of munitions of all kinds to Great Britain be expedited.

"*e*) That planes and ships of our Navy join in the protection of the British Isles and the British fleet.

"*f*) That, in consideration of these acts, undertaken or authorized by the Government of the United States, the British Government give their guarantee that, should the British Isles be invaded and occupied, they would not surrender the surviving part of their fleet to Germany, but base it on American ports and ports of the still free members of the Commonwealth.

"8. The above general program could be best brought about by negotiating a treaty with the British Government, which treaty would be subject to a ratification by the United States Senate."

116. Ernest Martin Hopkins in commenting on the Century Club group to the writer, January 21, 1942, wrote: "I don't know of anything which has ever seemed more amusing to me than the legend which grew up in some portions of the East here that the Century Club Group was a secret organization of conspirators meeting in private. All during the summer two years ago the telegrams announcing the meetings and announcing what would be the subjects of discussion were sent to me at Bar Harbor and telephoned over to our summer place at Southwest. A number of my friends spoke to me inquiring about the meetings on the basis of hearing the messages telephoned to me. Neither I nor, I think, any other member of the Committee concealed where we were going or what we were going to do, and, as a matter of fact, generally four or five of us would gather for cocktails in some

public place, talk over where we were going and what we were going to do, and then assemble without the slightest attempt at secrecy. Groups of two or three at a time would wander into the Century Club greeting friends and acquaintances whom they happened to meet and upon inquiry from anyone explaining with whom they were dining and for what purpose. Almost invariably the summer evenings were hot and no one took any trouble to close doors or windows of the dining room in which we were meeting and discussions went on perfectly freely while waiters came and went. There was about as much secrecy attendant upon the meeting as would pertain to an undergraduate mass meeting. In fact I went so far as to carry back accounts of the meetings each week to my friends on Mt. Desert Island."

116. Present at the Century Club on July 25 were: Robert S. Allen, Washington columnist; Joseph Alsop, Washington columnist; Ulric Bell, Washington correspondent of the *Louisville Courier-Journal;* Barry Bingham, publisher of the *Louisville Courier-Journal;* Ward Cheney; Henry Sloane Coffin; Clark M. Eichelberger; Harold K. Guinzburg, head of the Viking Press of New York; George Watts Hill, banker of Durham, North Carolina; Henry W. Hobson; Ernest M. Hopkins; Francis P. Miller; Geoffrey Parsons, chief editorial writer of the *New York Herald Tribune;* Frank L. Polk, New York lawyer and former undersecretary of state; Whitney H. Shepardson; Robert E. Sherwood; Admiral Standley; and Dr. Henry P. Van Dusen. Of this group of eighteen, ten were members of the White Committee. These were: Allen, Bingham, Cheney, Coffin, Eichelberger, Hobson, Hopkins, Polk, Sherwood, and Van Dusen. The full text of their resolutions can be found in the *St. Louis Post-Dispatch*, September 22, 1940, p. 3C.

CHAPTER VI

124. White's article, "Wendell Willkie," appeared in the *New Republic*, CII (June 17, 1940), 818–19. The editors of the *New Republic in* this issue differed with White and wrote: "William Allen White, that generous-hearted soul, seems to conclude in his article on Wendell Willkie in this week's New Republic that Mr. Willkie, besides being a slick article, is also a sincere liberal. But White has found it within his heart in the past to be tolerant of such Republican candidates as Harding, Coolidge and Hoover. We like him for his generosity, but we can't help being a little meaner about Mr. Willkie's record. We are inclined to lay more emphasis on the slickness, less on the sincerity."

128. According to Wendell Willkie, the most important contribution that William Allen White made to him was his encouragement to stand for aid to Britain in his speech accepting the nomination, all through the campaign, and afterward (Willkie to the writer, May 13, 1941).

134. For further background on the Triple Alliance see Forrest Davis and Ernest K. Lindley, *How War Came* (New York: Simon & Schuster, 1942).

140. For some of the activities of Congressman Fish see Michael Sayers and Albert E. Kahn, *Sabotage: The Secret War against America* (New York: Harper & Bros., 1942); and John R. Carlson, *Undercover* (New York: E. P. Dutton & Co., 1943).

CHAPTER VII

153. For Senator Holt's comments on the contributors to the Sherwood advertisement see the *New York Times*, June 16, 1940; the *San Francisco Leader*, July 27, 1940. Holt wrote a manuscript in 1941 entitled *Who's Who among the War Mongers*, for Flanders Hall, Inc., a Nazi propaganda agency. George Sylvester Viereck, later jailed for his Nazi activities in the United States, made some changes in the *Holt* manuscript. For some reason it was never published.

161. The material on Viereck and Dennett is from Michael Sayers and Albert E. Kahn, *Sabotage: The Secret War against America* (New York: Harper & Bros., 1942), pp. 187–91.

163. The following sources contain further material on the isolationist committees: Sayers and Kahn, *op. cit.*; John R. Carlson, *Undercover* (New York: E. P. Dutton & Co., 1943); M. Burns Staley, "America First Committee," unpublished M.A. thesis, Emory University Library; William C. Rogers, "Isolationist Propaganda and Isolationist Committees," unpublished Ph.D. thesis, University of Chicago Libraries.

166. White wrote a letter to Guy Stevens on December 21, 1940, about the attacks by Marshall: "He has no grudge against me and he isn't jealous of me. He is just one of those patriots who thinks he has to hate everyone else to love his country. God made him that way or the devil twisted him that way—I don't know. But it makes him most unhappy."

167. White's quoted statement is found in White to Hartley, November 2, 1940. A few days later, on November 6, White again wrote Hartley in these terms: "I suppose I am over-skittish. I am always reading whatever is written from our national office no matter to whom it is addressed, no matter in what confidence it is sent, as it might be read at an Investigation Committee of Congress. And I don't think that, at this time, so long as the British have plenty of credit, we should even discuss the repeal of the Johnson Act."

170. White's statement about the Hoover plan was repeated by Eichelberger in an interview with the writer on September 6, 1941. White told the writer, in an interview on November 13, 1941, that "I did not consider it wise to incur the hostility of an ex-President to our Committee." White had been quite close to Hoover during the preceding twelve years, and he did not want to destroy this relationship because of his Committee's opposition to the food plan.

170. White's description of his visit in Washington was given in an interview with the writer on February 28, 1941.

175. White to the *New York Times*, December 6, 1940. The *Daily Worker*, November 30, 1940, editorially made a great deal of the *New York Times*'s criticism of White. It charged that he was a front for Wall Street warmongers and a cynical old wirepuller, who was using the propaganda techniques of the last war to involve the United States again.

CHAPTER VIII

CHAPTER IX

Martin, Freda Kirchwey, Henry B. Cabot, Rev. C. J. Callan, Walter Millis, Lewis Mumford, Max Eastman, Dr. William Allen Neilson, Jack Altman, Dorothy Overlock, Dr. Conyers Read, Robert Spivack, Helen Gahagan, Rex Stout, Kenneth Thomson, James P. Warburg, Ralph Block, Dr. Frank P. Graham, Mrs. Robert E. Sherwood, Maxwell Anderson, Waldo Frank, Colonel William J. Donovan, Dr. Harry D. Gideonse, Dr. Christian Gauss, Humphrey Cobb, Rear Admiral Yarnell (Retired), Van Wyck Brooks, Kurt Weill, Frank Grillo.

224–25. The principles and purposes of the Fight for Freedom Committee are quoted from the *New York Times*, April 20, 1941.

225. Bishop Hobson's words are quoted from *The Lie of Isolationism*, distributed during 1941 in pamphlet form by the Fight for Freedom Committee and the Committee To Defend America by Aiding the Allies.

226. The records of the Fight for Freedom Committee are in the possession of Courtenay Barber, Jr., 29 South La Salle Street, Chicago.

Selected Bibliography

UNPUBLISHED SOURCE MATERIAL

Records of the Chicago Fight for Freedom Committee, in the possession of Courtenay Barber, Jr., 29 South La Salle Street, Chicago, Illinois.

Records of the Chicago and Mid-western Regional Office, Committee To Defend America by Aiding the Allies, formerly at 38 South Dearborn Street, Chicago, Illinois, now at the International Relations Center, 84 East Randolph Street, Chicago.

Records of the National Committee To Defend America by Aiding the Allies, 8 West Fortieth Street, New York, New York.

Records of the Non-partisan Committee for Peace through Revision of the Neutrality Law, 8 West Fortieth Street, New York, New York.

WHITE, WILLIAM ALLEN. Manuscripts. Emporia, Kansas.

———. "The Story of a Democratic Adventure." Unpublished manuscript. White wrote this article in December, 1940, just before he resigned. It was intended for the *Saturday Evening Post*, but his resignation made him decide against sending it to the magazine.

PUBLISHED SOURCE MATERIAL

The items listed in this section were published material that went to national Committee members and local chapters. Copies can be found either at the national offices or the local chapters.

Information Letters of the Washington Committee To Defend America by Aiding the Allies.

Policy Statements of the Fight for Freedom Committee.

Policy Statements of the National Committee To Defend America by Aiding the Allies.

Progress Bulletins of the National Committee To Defend America by Aiding the Allies.

Publicity Releases of the National Committee To Defend America by Aiding the Allies.

Congressional Record, 1939–44.

NEWSPAPER SOURCES

Chicago Daily News, September 1, 1939—December, 1941.

Chicago Tribune, September 1, 1939—June, 1944.

Emporia Gazette, June, 1895—December, 1941.

Kansas City Star, September 1, 1939—December, 1941.

Kansas City Times, September 1, 1939—December, 1941.

New York Herald Tribune, September 1, 1939—December, 1941.

New York Times, September 1, 1939—June, 1944.

St. Louis Post-Dispatch, September 1, 1939—June, 1944.

ARTICLES ON THE COMMITTEE TO DEFEND AMERICA BY AIDING THE ALLIES

CLESS, GEORGE H., JR. "The William Allen White Reign of Terror," *Scribner's Commentator*, IX (December, 1940), 38–43.

"Driving the Propaganda Engine," *Christian Century*, LVII (November 6, 1940), 1367–69.

ROSS, CHARLES G. "Inside Story of 'Propaganda Engine' to Send U.S. Army and Navy Equipment to Britain," *St. Louis Post-Dispatch*, September 22, 1940.

"Story of a Tide," *Time Magazine*, XXXVI (August 19, 1940), 12–15.

MAGAZINE SOURCES

Censored, May, 1940—December, 1941.

In Fact, May, 1940—December, 1941.

Scribner's Commentator, May, 1940—December, 1941.

Social Justice, May, 1940—April, 1942.

Christian Century, May, 1940—December, 1941.

Nation, May, 1940—December, 1941.

New Republic, May, 1940—December, 1941.

Saturday Evening Post, May, 1940—December, 1941.

GENERAL BOOKS AND ARTICLES

ALSOP, JOSEPH, and KINTNER, ROBERT. *American White Paper*. New York: Simon & Schuster, 1940.

ASKEW, WILLIAM C., and RIPPY, J. FRED. "The United States and Europe's Strife, 1908–1913," *Journal of Politics*, IV (February, 1942), 68–79.

BAILEY, THOMAS A. *A Diplomatic History of the American People*. New York: F. S. Crofts & Co., 1940.

BAKER, RAY STANNARD, and DODD, WILLIAM E. (eds.). *The Public Papers of Woodrow Wilson*. 6 vols. New York: Harper & Bros. 1925–27.

BECKER, CARL L. *How New Will the Better World Be?* New York: Alfred A. Knopf, 1944.

BENDINER, ROBERT. *The Riddle of the State Department*. New York: Farrar & Rinehart, 1942.

CARLSON, JOHN ROY. *Undercover*. New York: E. P. Dutton & Co., 1943.

The Conference of Brussels. Department of State Publications, No. 1232, "Conference Series," No. 37. Washington: Government Printing Office, 1938.

DAVIS, FORREST. *The Atlantic System: The Story of Anglo-American Control of the Seas*. New York: Reynal & Hitchcock, 1941.

DAVIS, FORREST, and LINDLEY, ERNEST K. *How War Came: An American White Paper; from the Fall of France to Pearl Harbor*. New York: Simon & Schuster, 1942.

DULLES, ALLEN W., and ARMSTRONG, HAMILTON FISH. *Can We Be Neutral?* New York: Harper & Bros., 1936.

DULLES, JOHN F. and ROBERT W. (eds.). *War Memoirs of Robert Lansing*. New York: Bobbs-Merrill Co., 1935.

EINSTEIN, LEWIS. "The United States and Anglo-German Rivalry," *Living Age*, CCLXXVI, 323–32.

FENWICK, CHARLES G. *American Neutrality: Trial and Failure*. New York: New York University Press, 1940.

FLEMING, DENNA FRANK. *The United States and the League, 1918–1920*. New York: G. P. Putnam's Sons, 1932.

———. *The United States and World Organization, 1920–1933*. New York: Columbia University Press, 1938.

GRISWOLD, A. WHITNEY. *The Far Eastern Policy of the United States*. New York: Harcourt, Brace & Co., 1938.

JONES, S. SHEPARD, and MYERS, DENYS P. *Documents on American Foreign Relations*. Vol. I: *1938–39;* Vol. II: *1939–1940;* Vol. III: *1940–1941*. Boston: World Peace Foundation, 1940–42.

MASLAND, JOHN W. "The 'Peace' Groups Join Battle," *Public Opinion Quarterly*, Vol. IV (1940).

MILLIS, WALTER. *The Faith of an American*. New York: Oxford University Press, 1941.

———. *Road to War: 1914–1917*. Boston: Houghton Mifflin Co., 1935.

———. *Why Europe Fights*. New York: W. Morrow & Co., 1940.

NEVINS, ALLAN. *America in World Affairs*. New York: Oxford University Press, 1942.

NOTTER, HARLEY. *The Origins of the Foreign Policy of Woodrow Wilson*. Baltimore: Johns Hopkins University Press, 1937.

Peace and War: United States Foreign Policy, 1931–1941. Washington: Government Printing Office, 1942.

QUIGLEY, HAROLD S. *Far Eastern War, 1937–1941*. Boston: World Peace Foundation, 1942.

RIEGEL, O. W. "The Pattern of the Unneutral Diplomat: Robert Lansing and the World War," *Southern Review*, summer, 1936, pp. 1–14.

RIPPY, J. FRED. *America and the Strife of Europe*. Chicago: University of Chicago Press, 1938.

ROGERS, WILLIAM C. "Isolationist Propaganda and Isolationist Committees." Unpublished Ph.D. Thesis in the University of Chicago Libraries.

SAYERS, MICHAEL, and KAHN, ALBERT E. *Sabotage: The Secret War against America*. New York: Harper & Bros., 1942.

SEYMOUR, CHARLES. *American Neutrality, 1914–1917*. New Haven: Yale University Press, 1935.

———. *The Intimate Papers of Colonel House*. 2 vols. New York: Houghton Mifflin Co., 1926.

SHEPARDSON, WHITNEY H. and SCROGGS, WILLIAM O. *The United States in World Affairs*. New York: Harper & Bros. Annual volumes for 1938, 1939, 1940.

SMITH, DENYS. *America and the Axis War*. New York: Macmillan Co., 1942.

STANLEY, M. BURNS. "America First Committee." Unpublished M.A. Thesis, Emory University Library.

STETTINIUS, E. R., JR. *Lend-Lease: Weapon for Victory*. New York: Macmillan Co., 1944.

STIMSON, HENRY L. "The Illusion of Neutrality," *Forum*, November, 1935, pp. 261–65.

———. *The Far Eastern Crisis*. New York: Harper & Bros. 1936.

UNITED STATES DEPARTMENT OF STATE. *Papers Relating to the Foreign Relations of the United States*, Suppl.: *The World War: 1916*. Washington: Government Printing Office, 1928.

WICKWARE, FRANCIS SILL. "What We Think about Foreign Affairs," *Harper's Magazine*, CLXXIX (September, 1939), 397–406.

SELECTED BOOKS AND ARTICLES BY WILLIAM ALLEN WHITE

The Martial Adventures of Henry and Me. New York: Macmillan Co., 1918.

"Through American Eyes," *New Europe*, XI (June 19, 1919), 223–27.

"The Peace and President Wilson," *Saturday Evening Post*, CXCII (August 16, 1919), 15 ff.

"First Shot in a New Battle," *Collier's*, LXIV (November 22, 1919), 5 ff.

"What Happened to Prinkipo," *Metropolitan Magazine*, December, 1919, pp. 1 ff.

"Will They Fool Us Twice?" *Collier's*, LXVIII (October 15, 1921), 5 ff.

"How To Stay Out of War," *Forum and Century*, XCVII (February, 1937), 91.

"Moscow and Emporia," *New Republic*, XCVI (September 21, 1938), 177-80; XCVII (December 7, 1938), 132–33.

Defense for America. Edited with an Introduction by WILLIAM ALLEN WHITE. New York: Macmillan Co., 1940.

"Is Our Way of Life Doomed?" *New York Times Magazine*, September 8, 1940, pp. 3 ff.

"Thoughts after the Election," *Yale Review*, XX (winter, 1941), 217–27.

Index